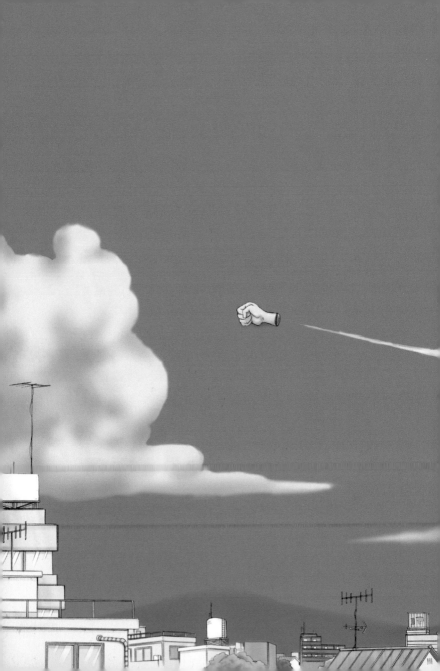

contents

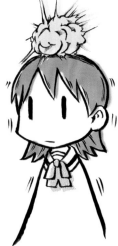

Explosion

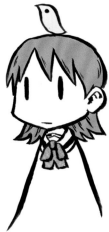

Bird on my head

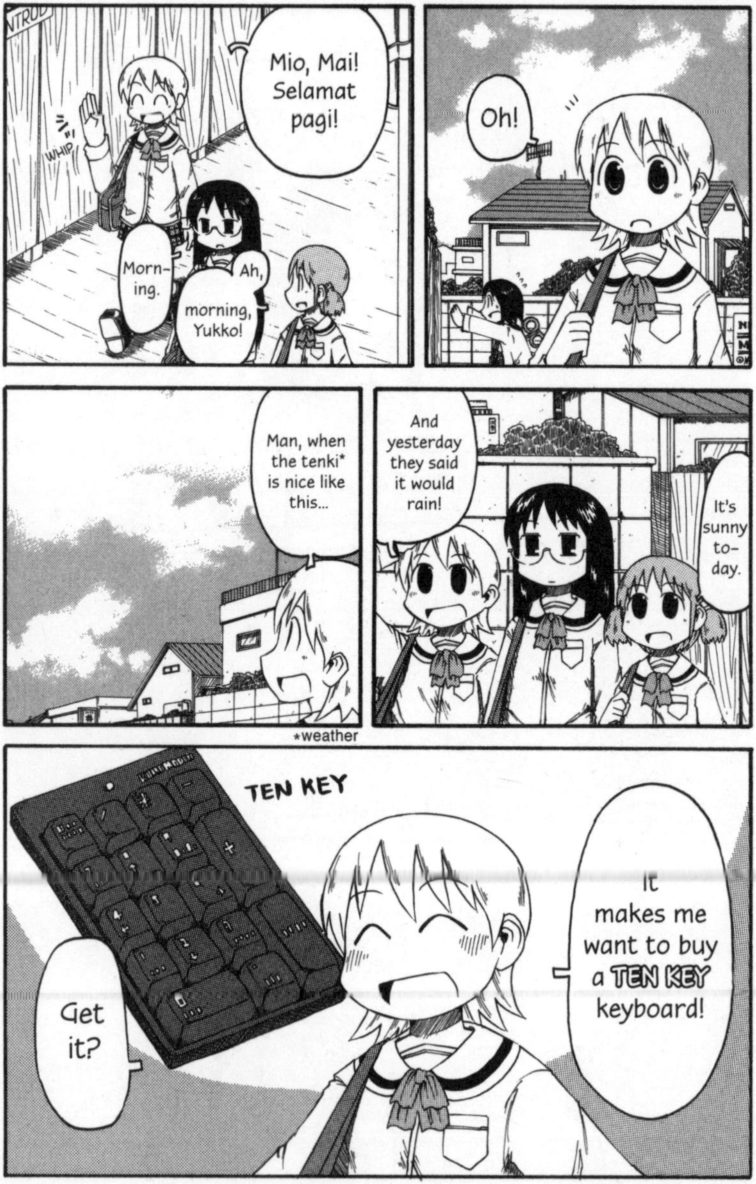
Oh!
Mio, Mai! Selamat pagi!
WHIP
Ah, morning, Yukko!
Morn-ing.
It's sunny to-day.
And yesterday they said it would rain!
Man, when the tenki* is nice like this...
It makes me want to buy a TEN KEY keyboard!
TEN KEY
Get it?

*weather

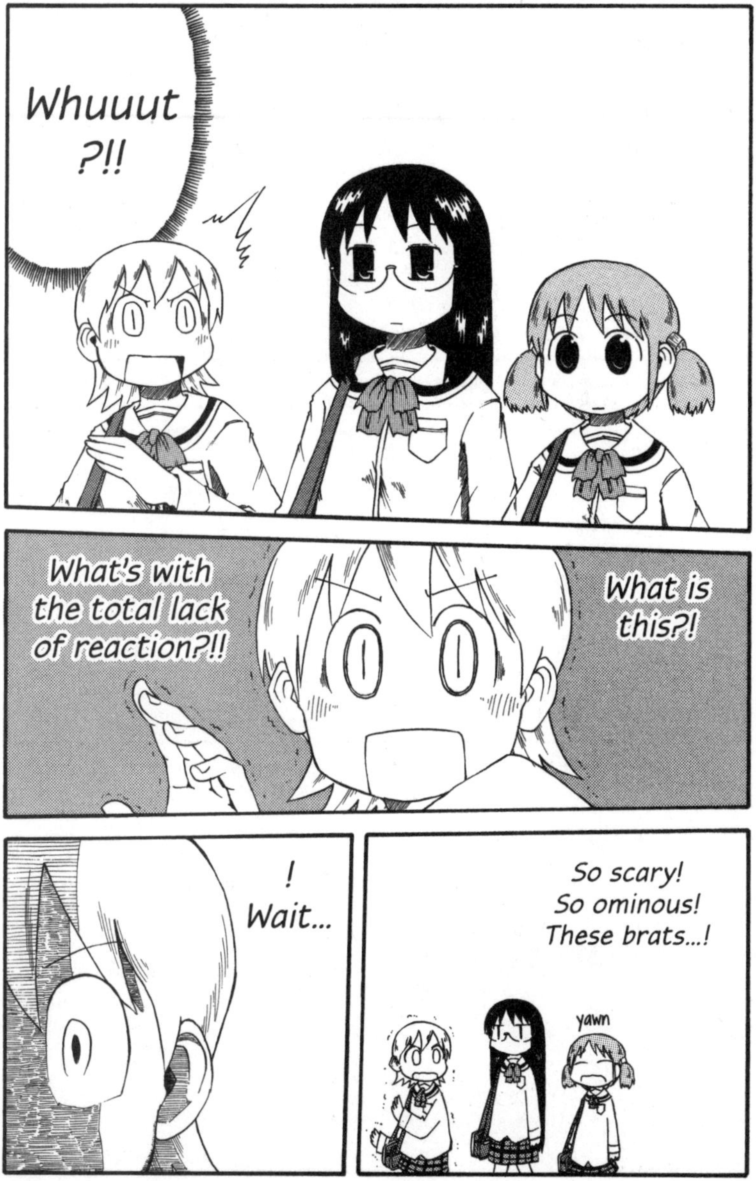
Whuuut ?!!
What is this?!
What's with the total lack of reaction?!!
So scary! So ominous! These brats...!
yawn
! Wait...

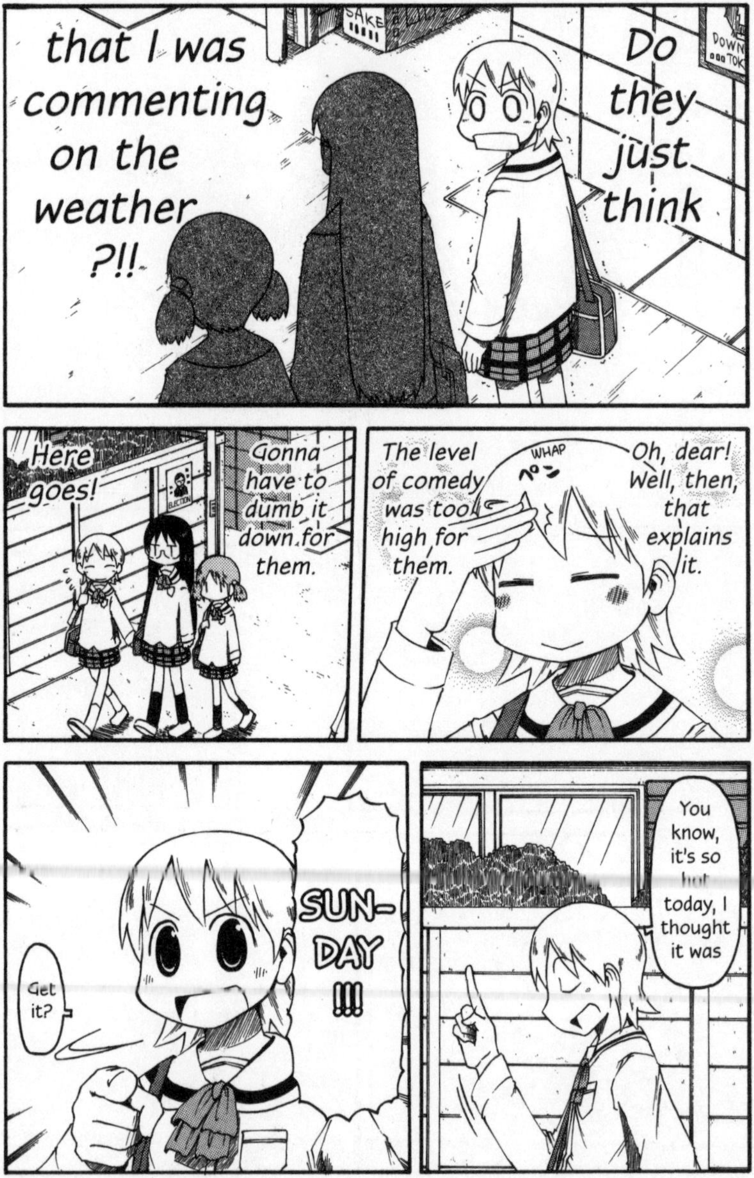
SAKE
Do they just think
that I was commenting on the weather ?!!
Oh, dear! Well, then, that explains it.
WHAP
The level of comedy was too high for them.
Gonna have to dumb it down for them.
Here goes!
ELECTION
You know, it's so hot today, I thought it was
SUN-DAY !!!
Get it?

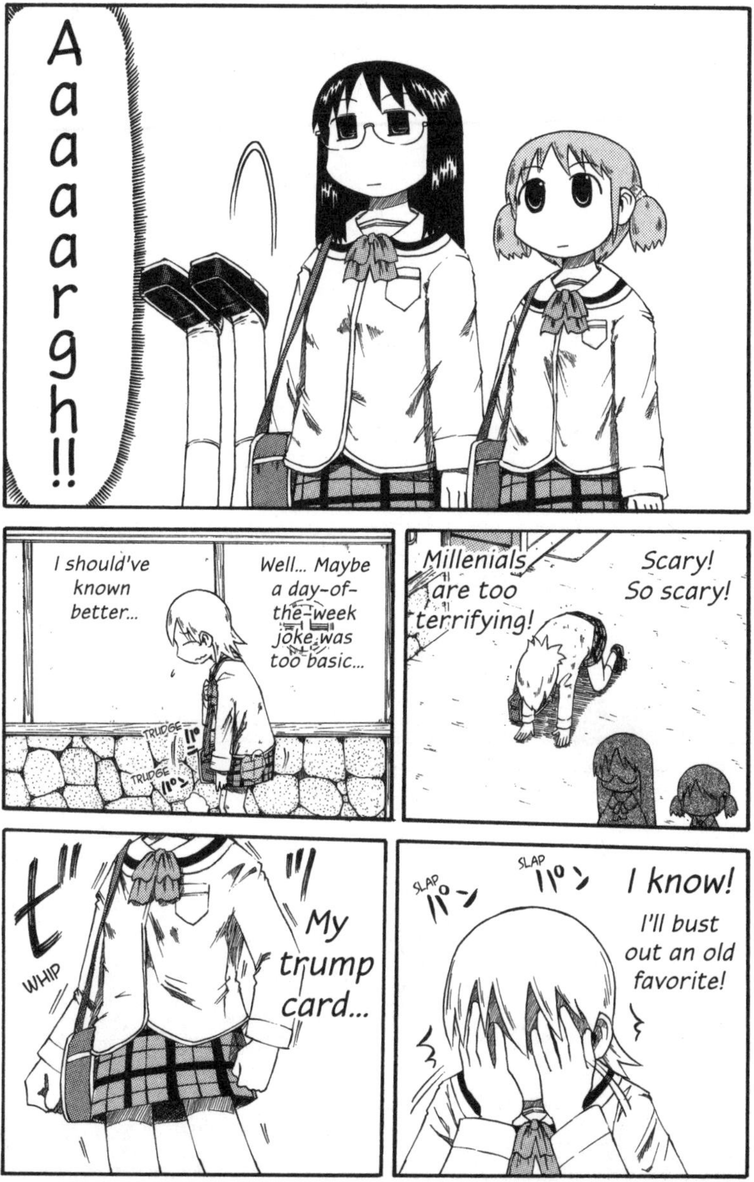
Aaaaargh!!
Scary! So scary!
Millenials are too terrifying!
Well... Maybe a day-of-the-week joke was too basic...
I should've known better...
TRUDGE
TRUDGE
SLAP
SLAP
I know!
I'll bust out an old favorite!
My trump card...
WHIP

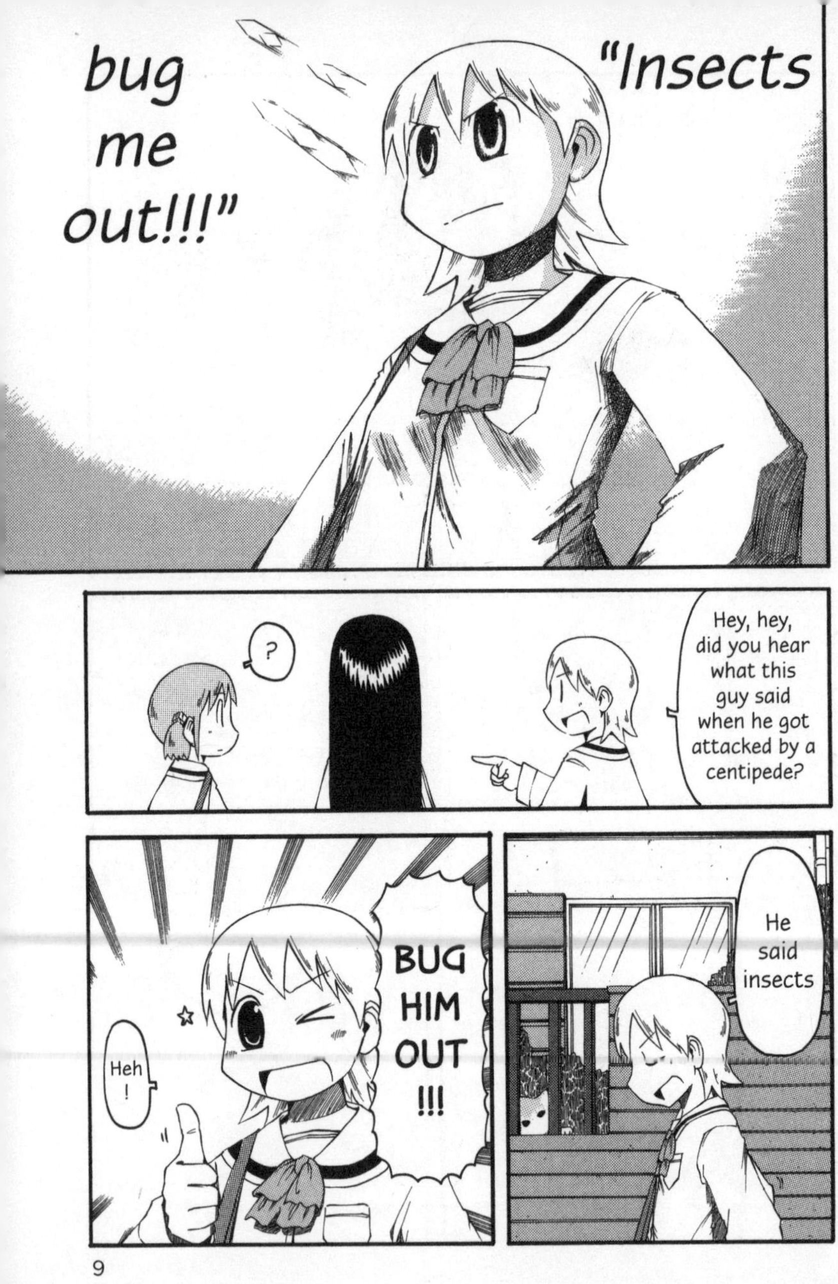
"Insects
bug me out!!!"
Hey, hey, did you hear what this guy said when he got attacked by a centipede?
?
He said insects
BUG HIM OUT !!!
Heh!

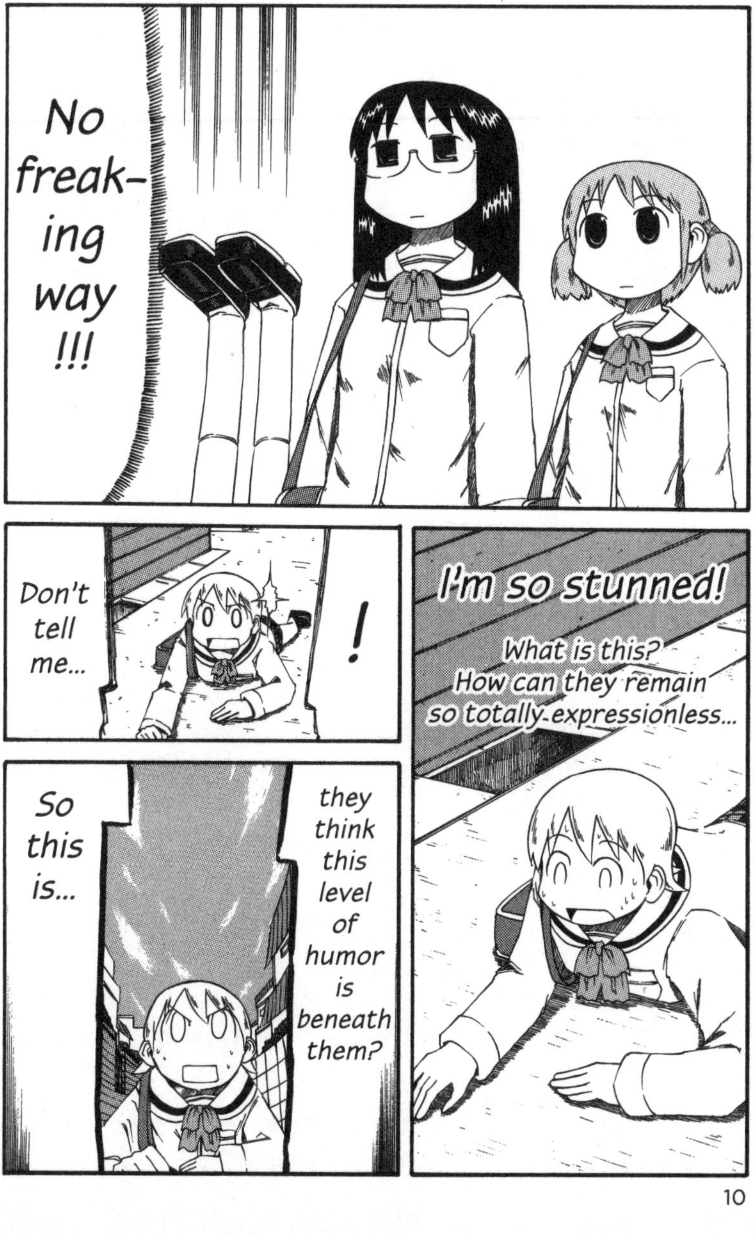
No freaking-ing way!!!
I'm so stunned!
What is this? How can they remain so totally expressionless...
Don't tell me...
!
So this is...
they think this level of humor is beneath them?

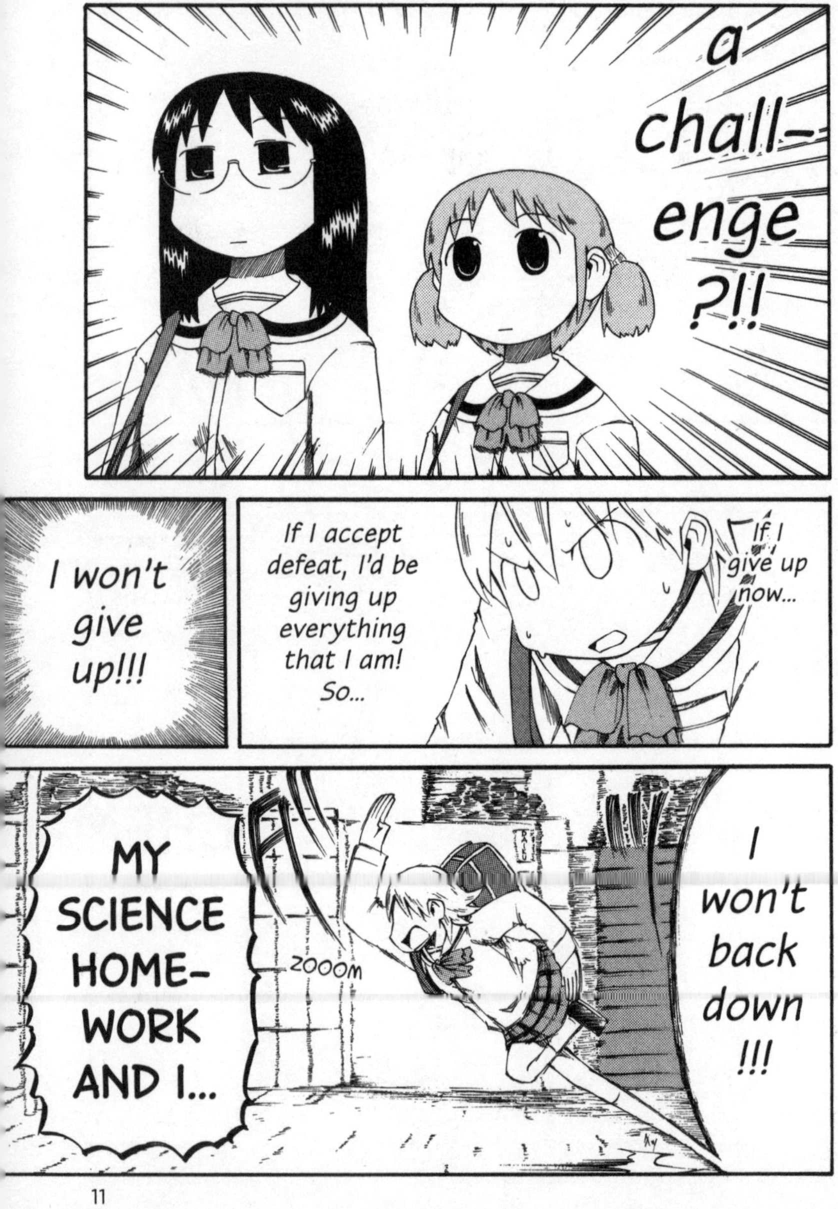
a chall-enge?!!
If I give up now...
If I accept defeat, I'd be giving up everything that I am! So...
I won't give up!!!
I won't back down!!!
ZOOOM
MY SCIENCE HOME-WORK AND I...

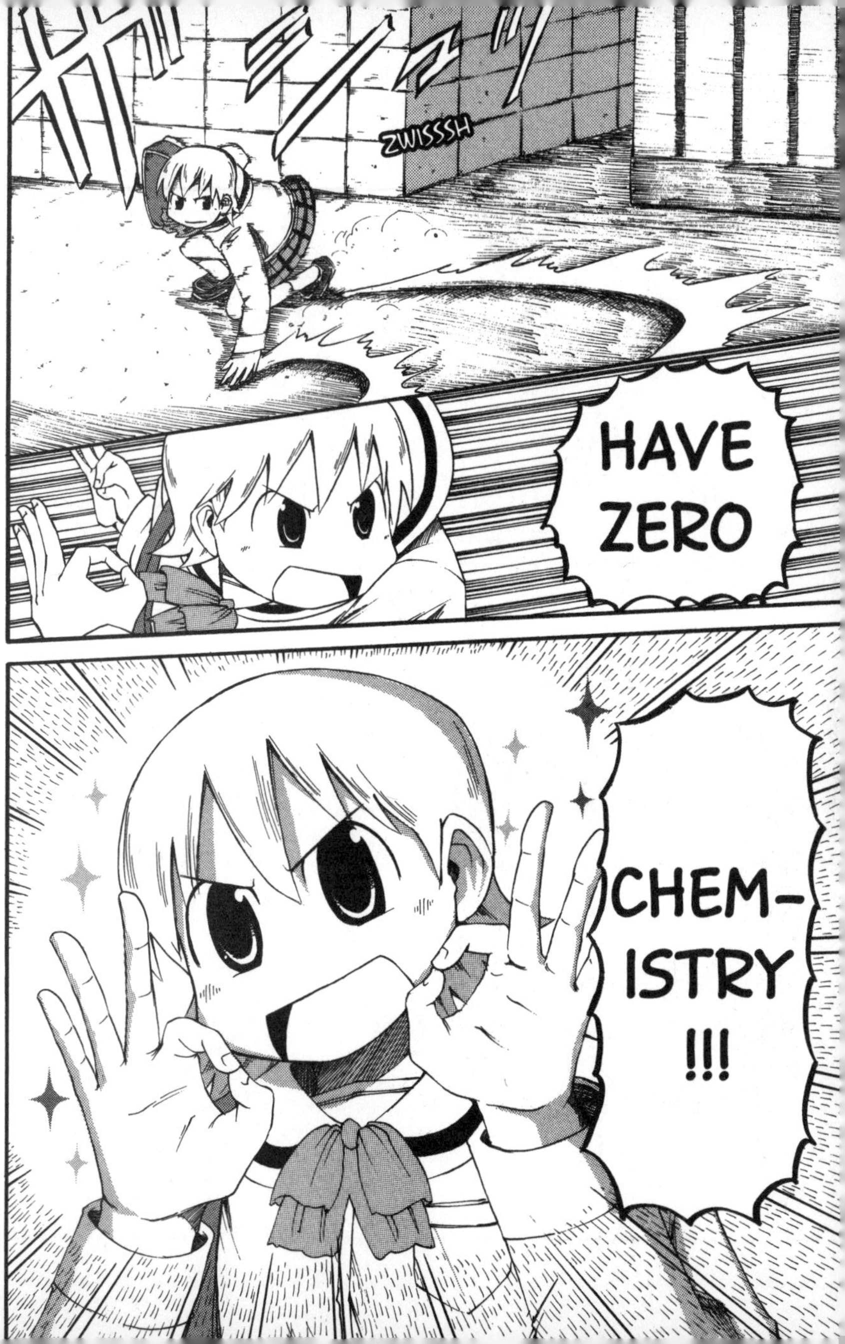
ZWISSSH
HAVE ZERO
CHEM-
ISTRY
!!!

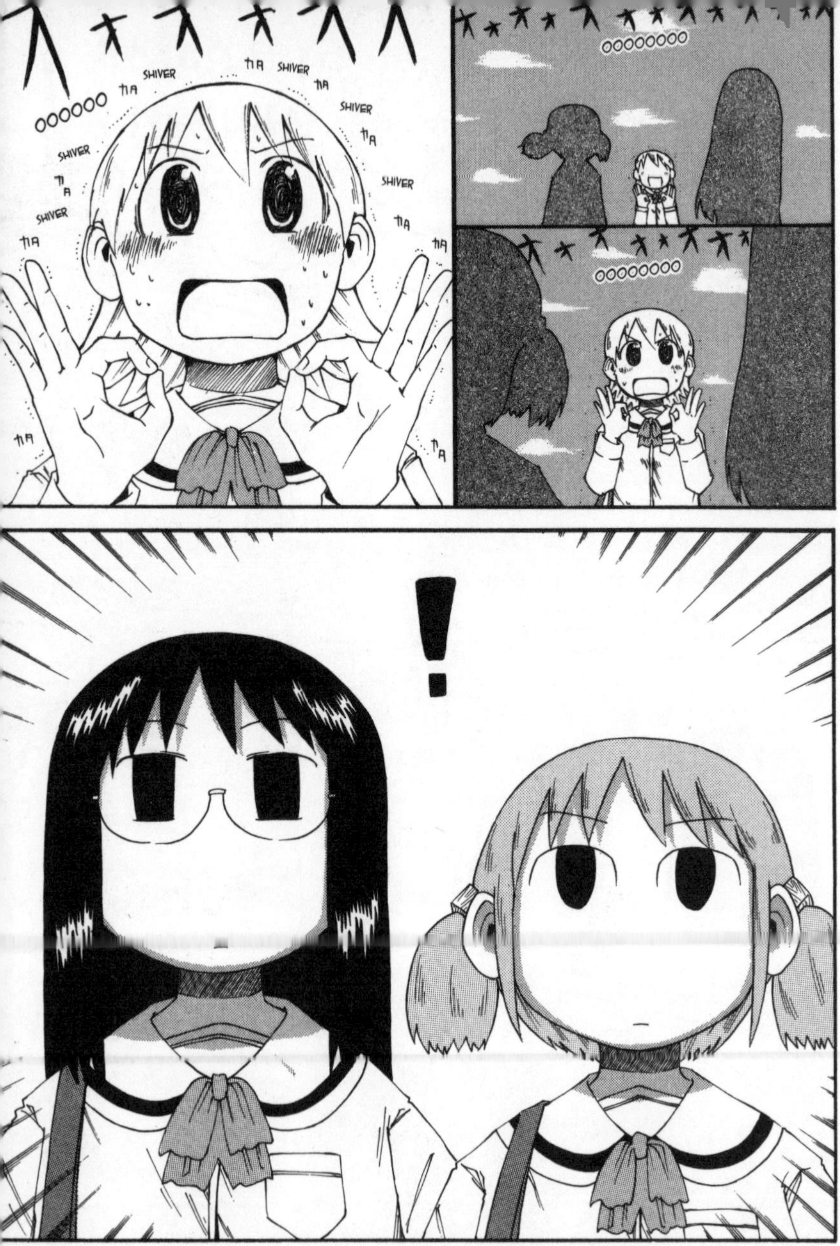
OOOOOOOO
OOOOOOOOO
OOOOOO
SHIVER
SHIVER
SHIVER
SHIVER
SHIVER
SHIVER
!

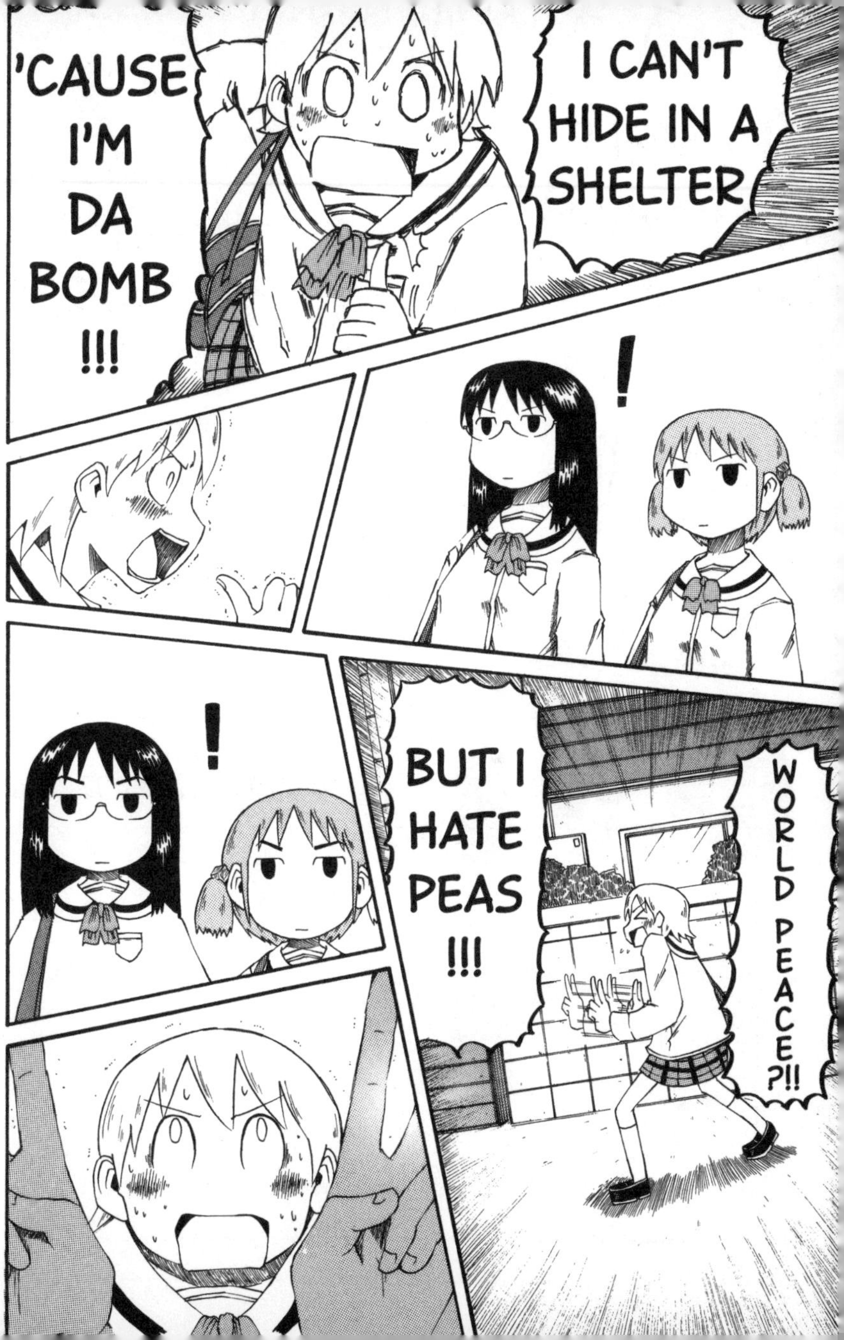

I CAN'T HIDE IN A SHELTER
'CAUSE I'M DA BOMB !!!
!
WORLD PEACE?!!
BUT I HATE PEAS !!!
!

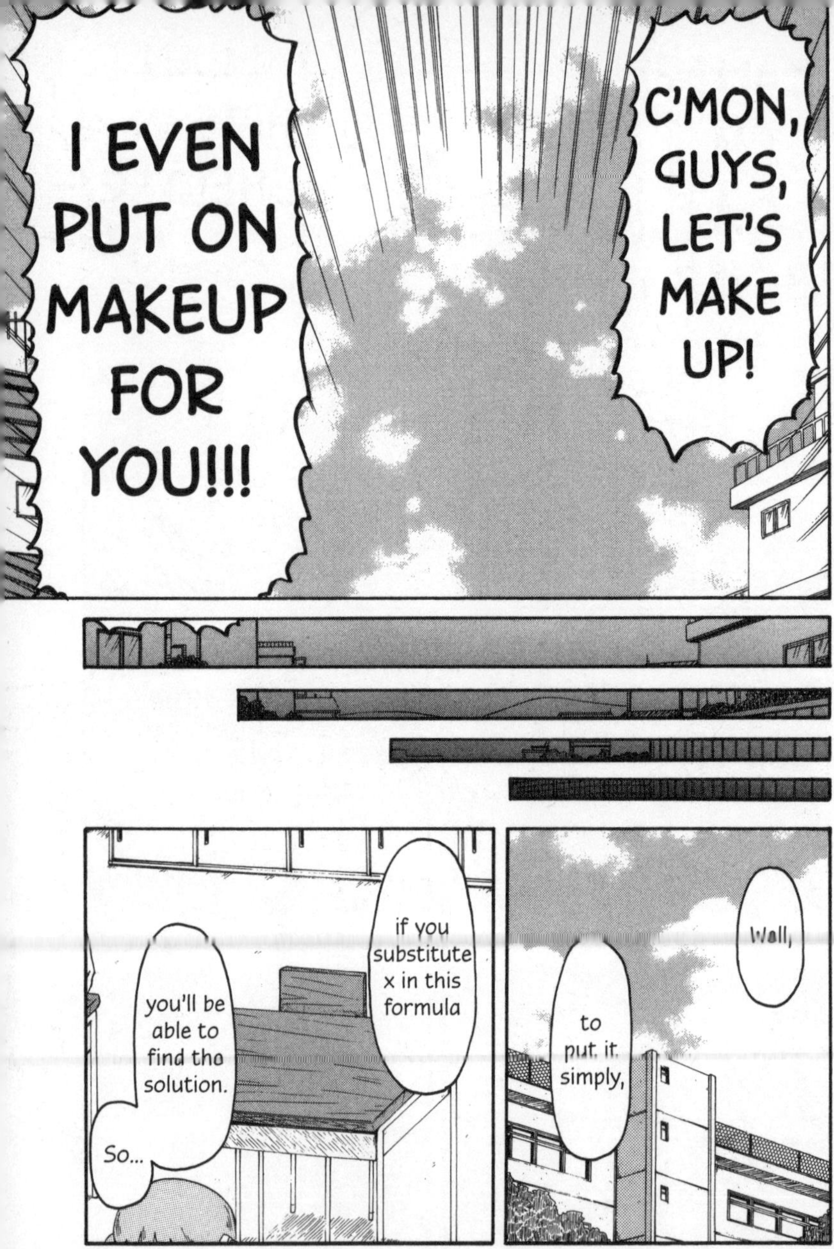
C'MON, GUYS, LET'S MAKE UP!
I EVEN PUT ON MAKEUP FOR YOU!!!
Well,
to put it simply,
if you substitute x in this formula
you'll be able to find the solution.
So...

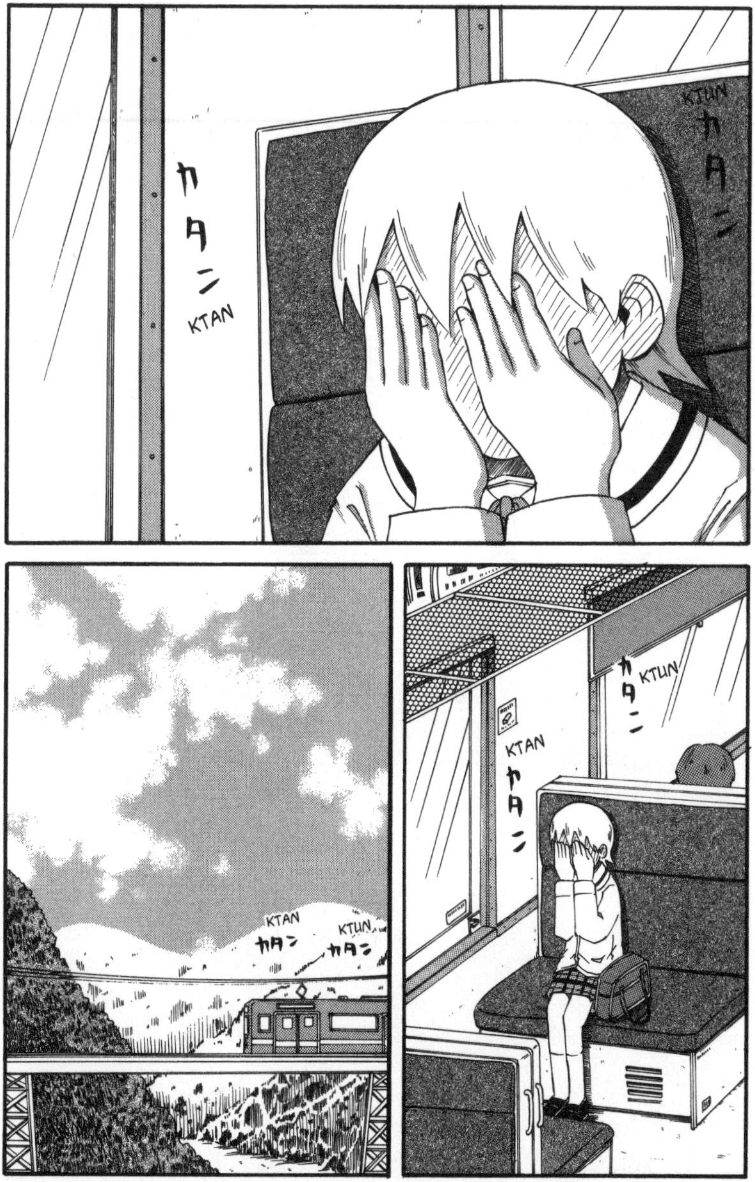
KTUN
カタン
カタン
KTAN
カタン
KTUN
KTAN
カタン
KTUN
カタン
KTAN
カタン

chapter 19: end

chapter 20

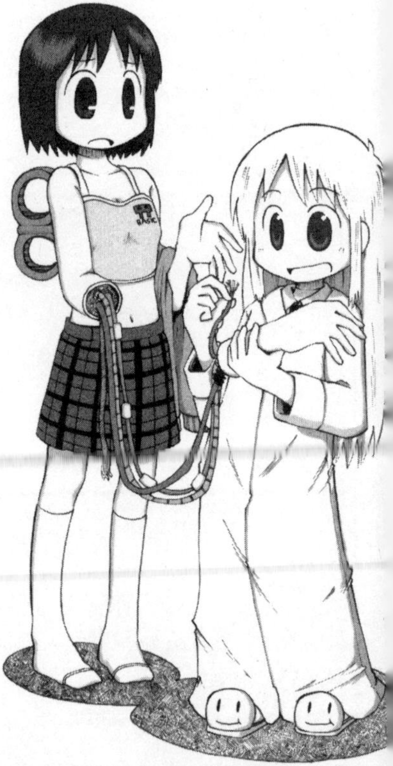

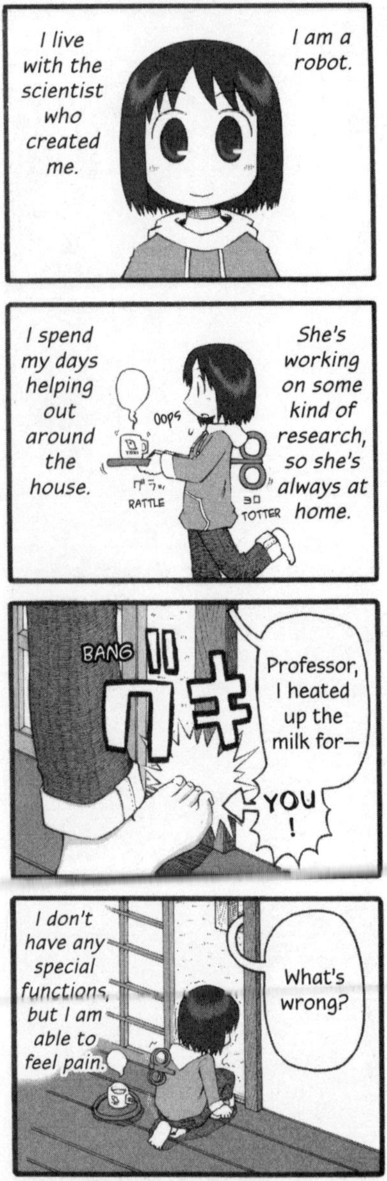
I am a robot.
I live with the scientist who created me.
She's working on some kind of research, so she's always at home.
I spend my days helping out around the house.
OOPS
TOTTER
RATTLE
Professor, I heated up the milk for—
BANG
YOU!
What's wrong?
I don't have any special functions, but I am able to feel pain.

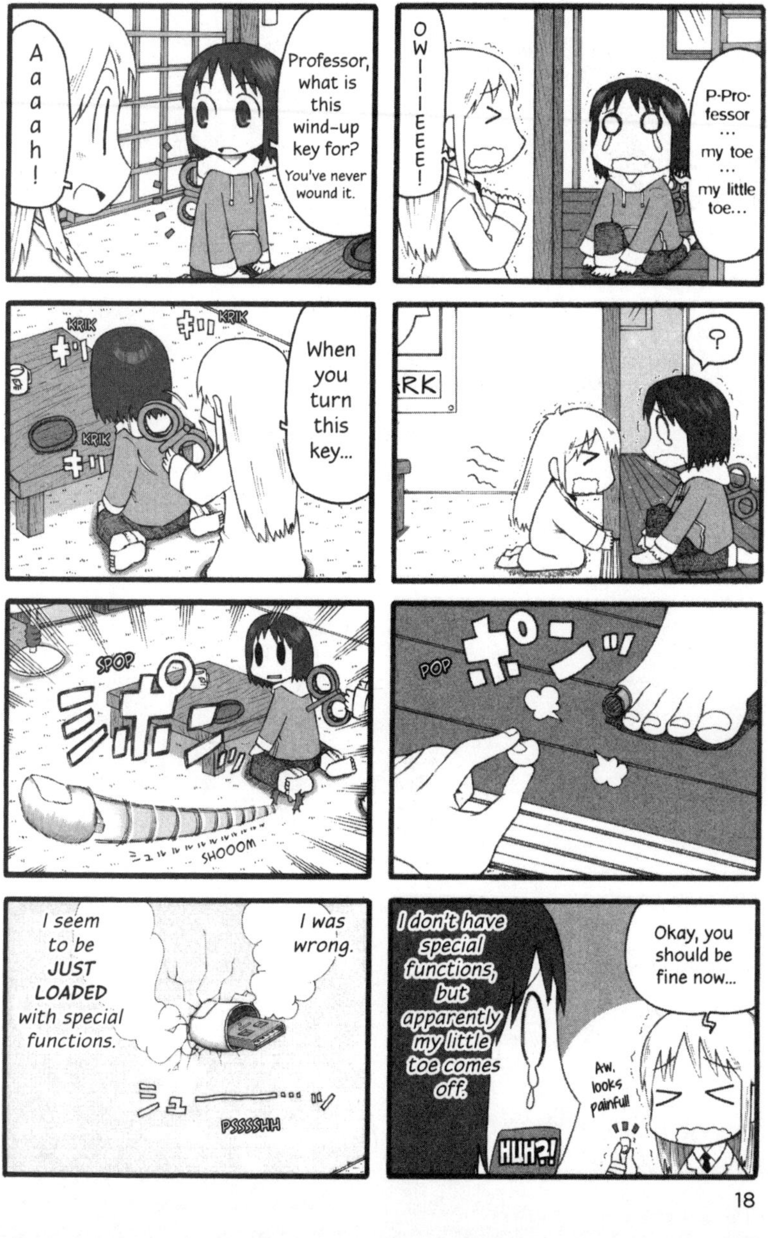
P-Pro-fessor … my toe … my little toe…
OWIIIEEE!
Professor, what is this wind-up key for?
You've never wound it.
Aaaah!
?
RK
When you turn this key...
KRIK
KRIK
KRIK
POP
SPOP
SHOOOM
Okay, you should be fine now...
I don't have special functions, but apparently my little toe comes off.
Aw, looks painful!
HUH?!
I was wrong.
I seem to be JUST LOADED with special functions.
PSSSSHH

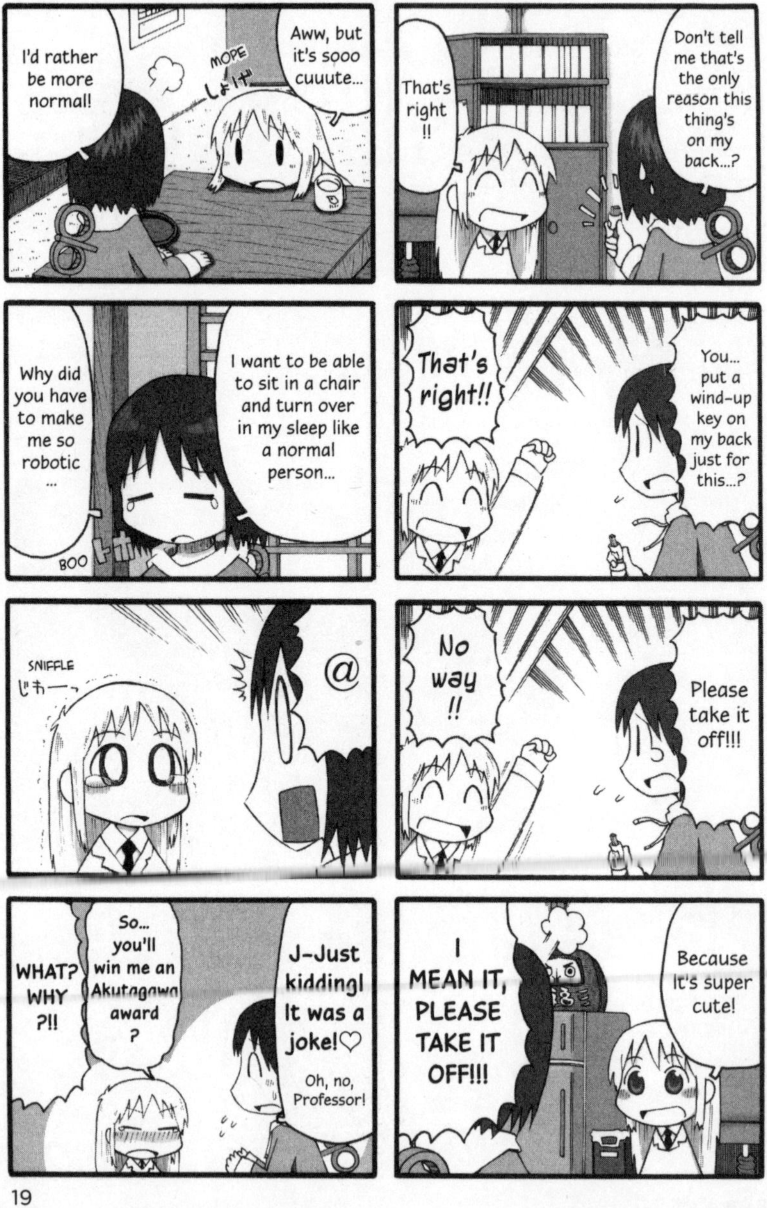
Don't tell me that's the only reason this thing's on my back...?
That's right !!
Aww, but it's sooo cuuute...
MOPE
しょげ
I'd rather be more normal!
You... put a wind-up key on my back just for this...?
That's right!!
I want to be able to sit in a chair and turn over in my sleep like a normal person...
Why did you have to make me so robotic ...
BOO
トホ
Please take it off!!!
No way !!
@
SNIFFLE
じわー
Because it's super cute!
I MEAN IT, PLEASE TAKE IT OFF!!!
J-Just kidding! It was a joke!♡
Oh, no, Professor!
So... you'll win me an Akutagawa award ?
WHAT? WHY ?!!

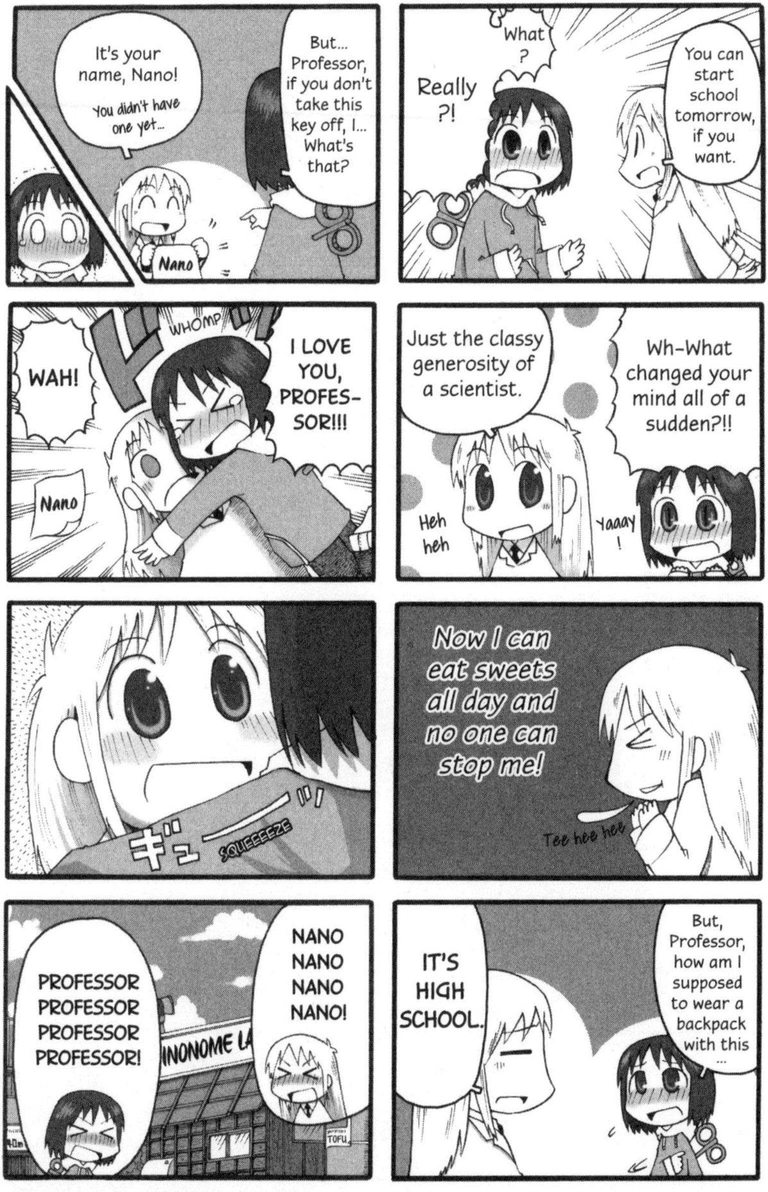
You can start school tomorrow, if you want.
What ?
Really ?!
But... Professor, if you don't take this key off, I... What's that?
It's your name, Nano!
You didn't have one yet...
Nano
Wh-What changed your mind all of a sudden?!!
Just the classy generosity of a scientist.
Yaaay !
Heh heh
I LOVE YOU, PROFES-SOR!!!
WHOMP
WAH!
Nano
Now I can eat sweets all day and no one can stop me!
Tee hee hee
SQUEEEEZE
But, Professor, how am I supposed to wear a backpack with this ...
IT'S HIGH SCHOOL.
NANO NANO NANO NANO!
PROFESSOR PROFESSOR PROFESSOR PROFESSOR!
INONOME LA
TOFU

chapter 20: end

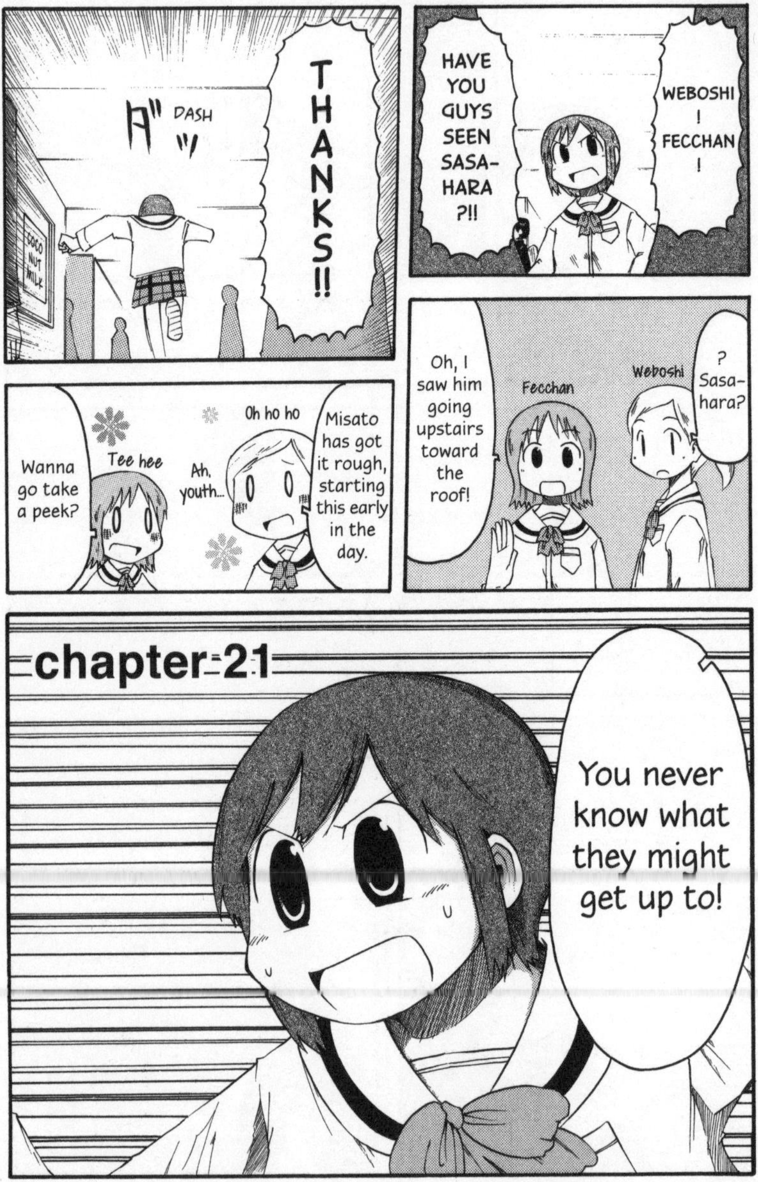
WEBOSHI! FECCHAN!
HAVE YOU GUYS SEEN SASA-HARA?!!
? Sasa-hara?
Weboshi
Fecchan
Oh, I saw him going upstairs toward the roof!
THANKS!!
ダッ
DASH
Misato has got it rough, starting this early in the day.
Oh ho ho
Ah, youth...
Tee hee
Wanna go take a peek?
COCO NUT MILK
chapter 21
You never know what they might get up to!

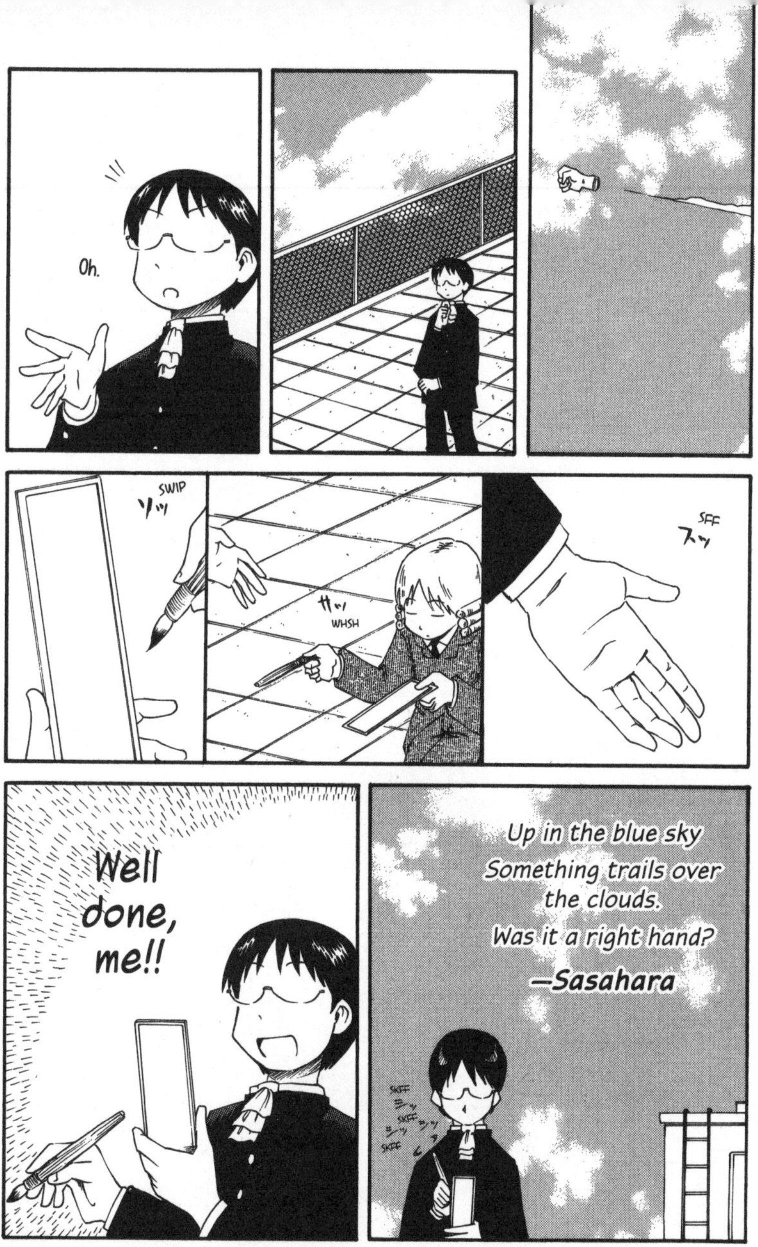
Oh.
SFF
スッ
WHSH
SWIP
Up in the blue sky
Something trails over
the clouds.
Was it a right hand?
—Sasahara
SKFF
SKFF
SKFF
Well done, me!!

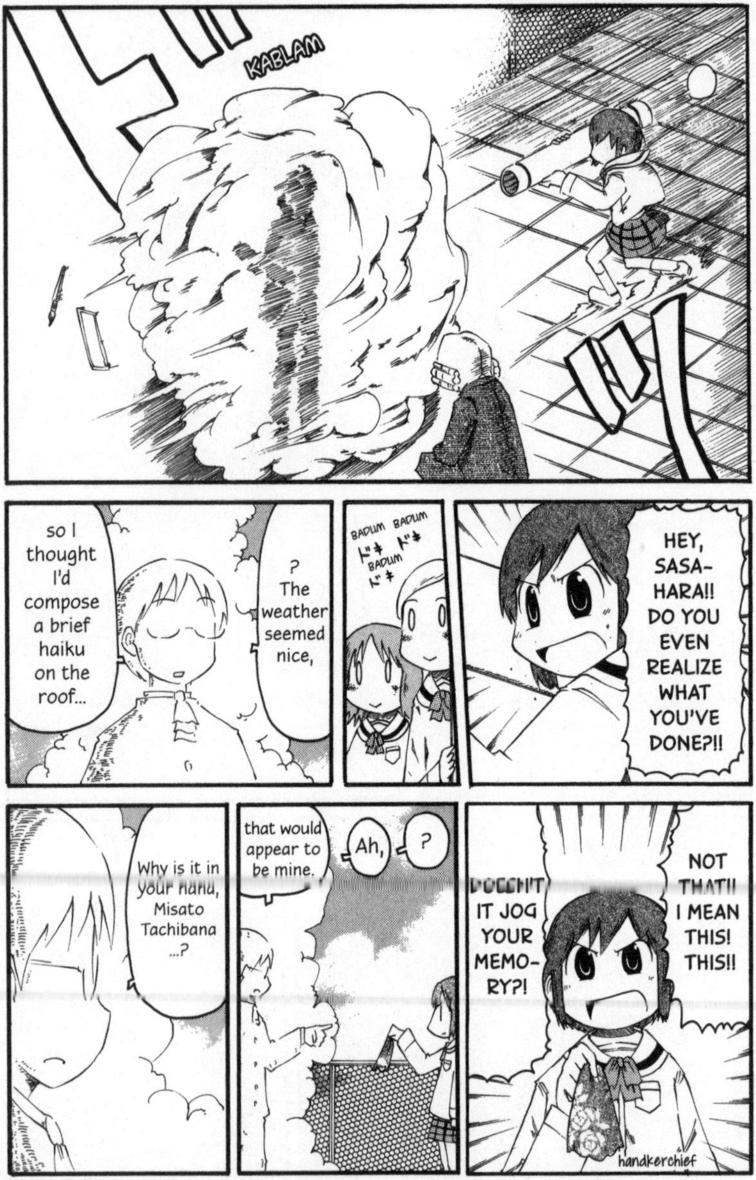

KABLAM
HEY, SASA-HARA!! DO YOU EVEN REALIZE WHAT YOU'VE DONE?!!
BADUM ドキ BADUM ドキ BADUM ドキ
? The weather seemed nice,
so I thought I'd compose a brief haiku on the roof...
NOT THAT!! I MEAN THIS! THIS!!
DOESN'T IT JOG YOUR MEMO-RY?!
handkerchief
?
Ah,
that would appear to be mine.
Why is it in your hand, Misato Tachibana ...?

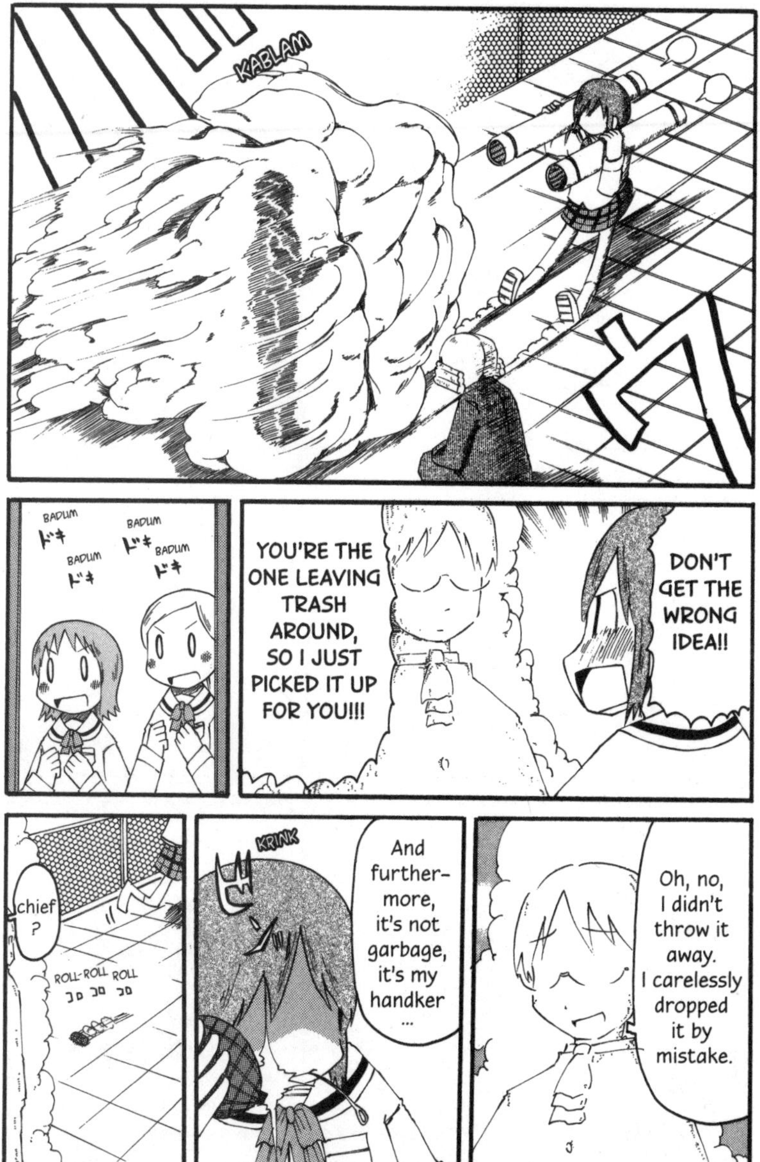
KABLAM
DON'T GET THE WRONG IDEA!!
YOU'RE THE ONE LEAVING TRASH AROUND, SO I JUST PICKED IT UP FOR YOU!!!
BADUM ドキ
BADUM ドキ
BADUM ドキ
BADUM ドキ
Oh, no, I didn't throw it away. I carelessly dropped it by mistake.
And further-more, it's not garbage, it's my handker ...
KRINK
chief ?
ROLL-ROLL ROLL
コロ コロ コロ

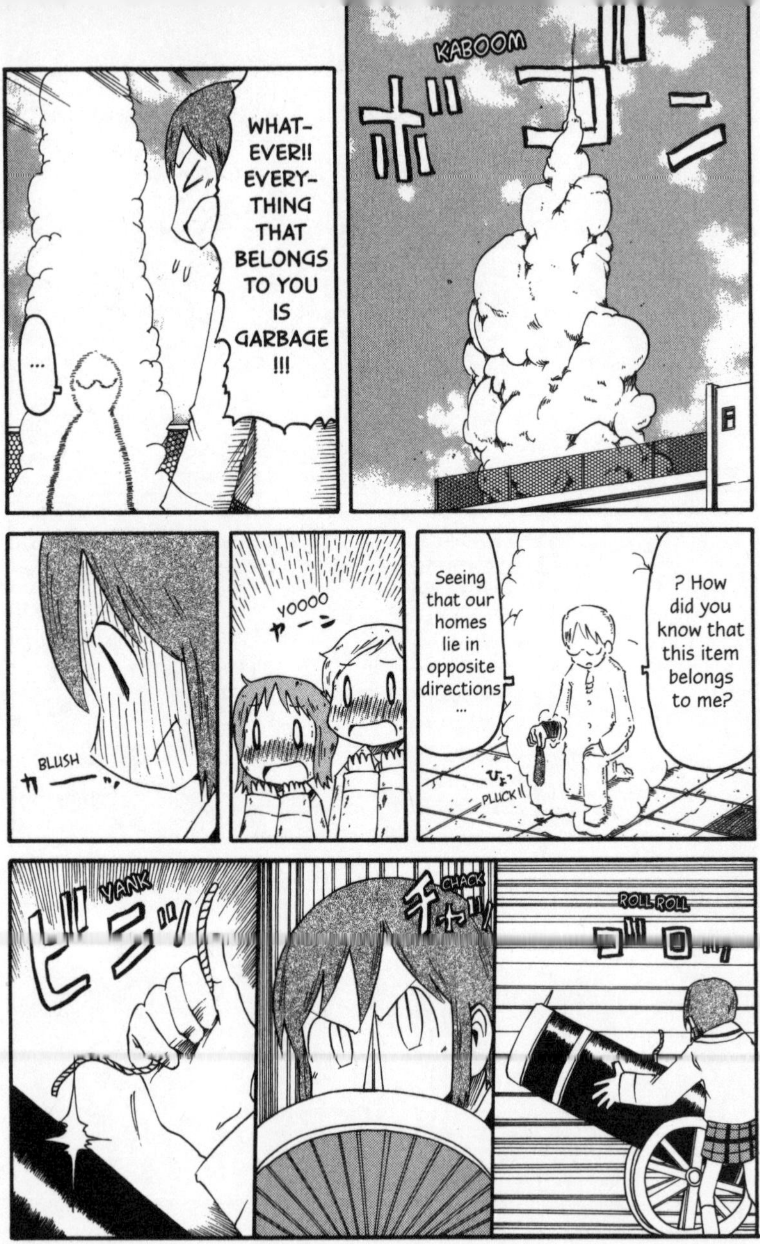
KABOOM
WHAT-EVER!! EVERY-THING THAT BELONGS TO YOU IS GARBAGE !!!
...
? How did you know that this item belongs to me?
Seeing that our homes lie in opposite directions ...
PLUCK
YOOOO
BLUSH
ROLL ROLL
CHACK
YANK

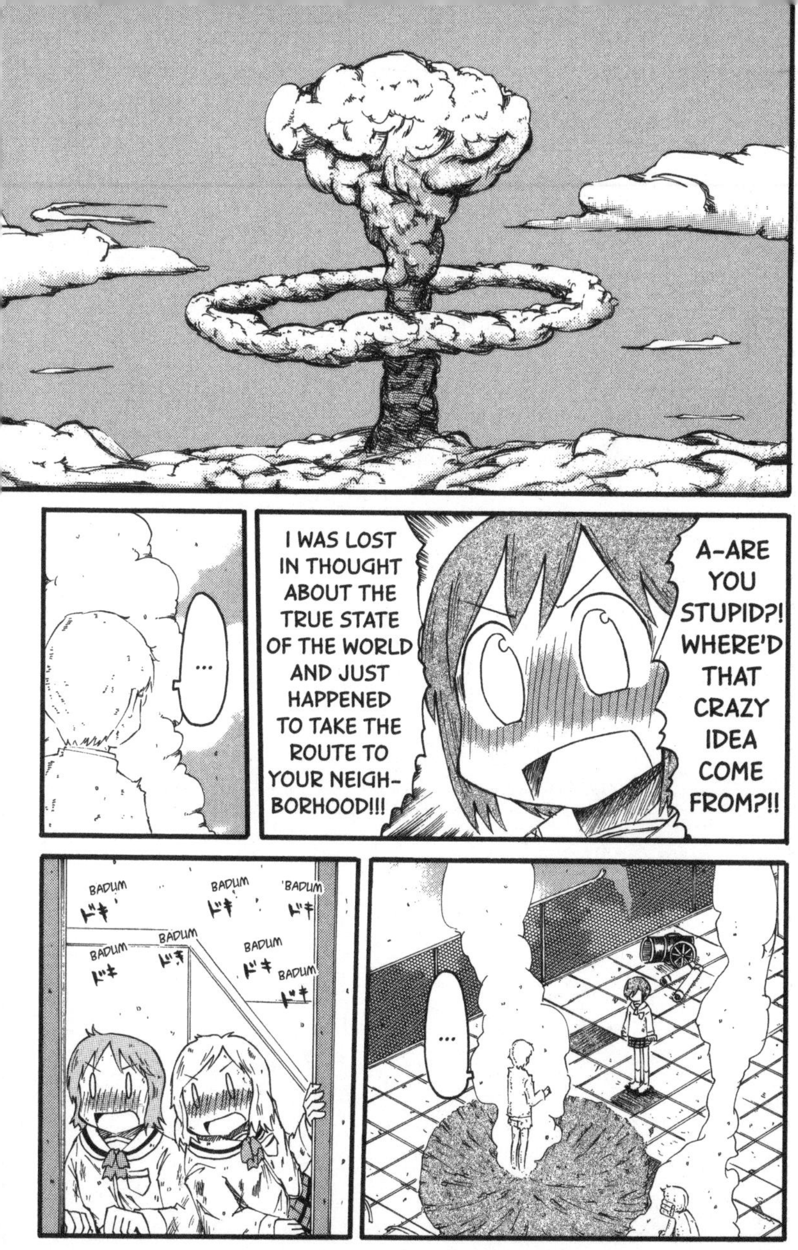
A-ARE YOU STUPID?! WHERE'D THAT CRAZY IDEA COME FROM?!!
I WAS LOST IN THOUGHT ABOUT THE TRUE STATE OF THE WORLD AND JUST HAPPENED TO TAKE THE ROUTE TO YOUR NEIGH-BORHOOD!!!
...
...
BADUM ドキ
BADUM ドキ
BADUM ドキ
BADUM ドキ
BADUM ドキ
BADUM ドキ
BADUM ドキ
BADUM ドキ

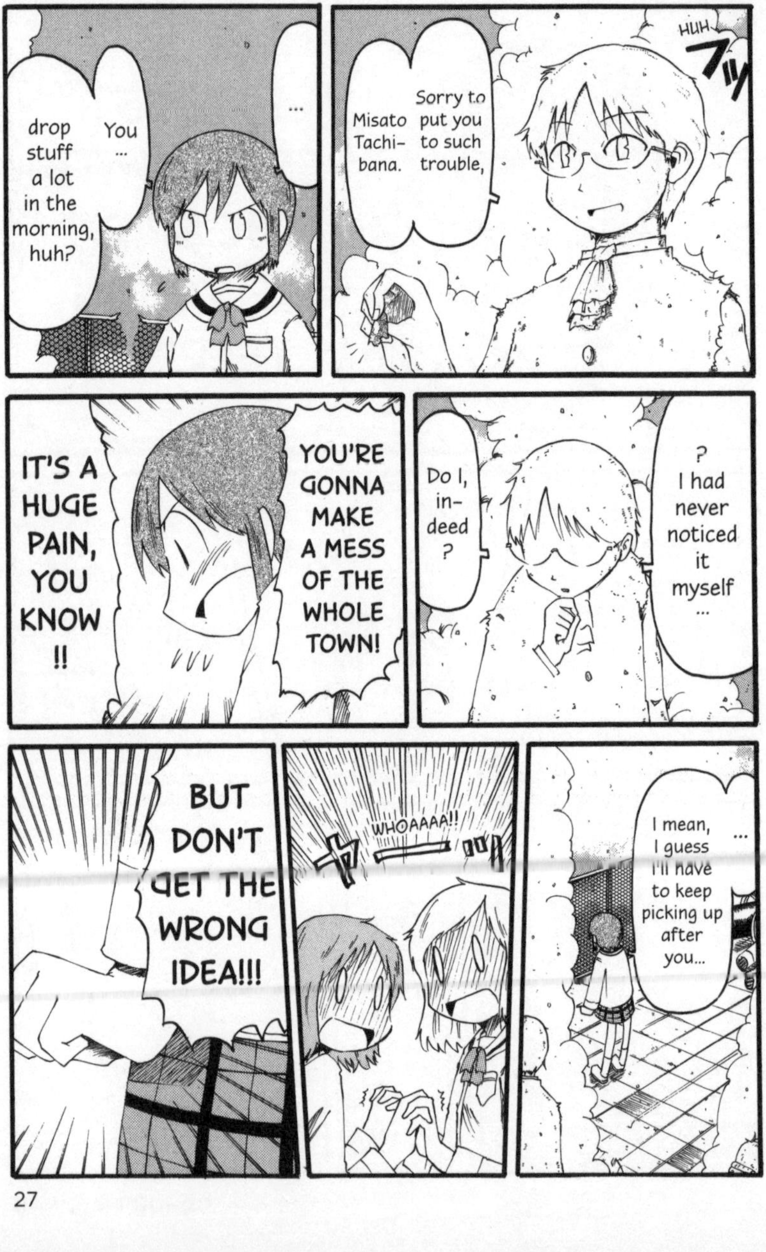
HUH
Sorry to put you to such trouble,
Misato Tachibana.
...
You ...
drop stuff a lot in the morning, huh?
? I had never noticed it myself ...
Do I, indeed?
YOU'RE GONNA MAKE A MESS OF THE WHOLE TOWN!
IT'S A HUGE PAIN, YOU KNOW!!
...
I mean, I guess I'll have to keep picking up after you...
WHOAAAA!!
BUT DON'T GET THE WRONG IDEA!!!

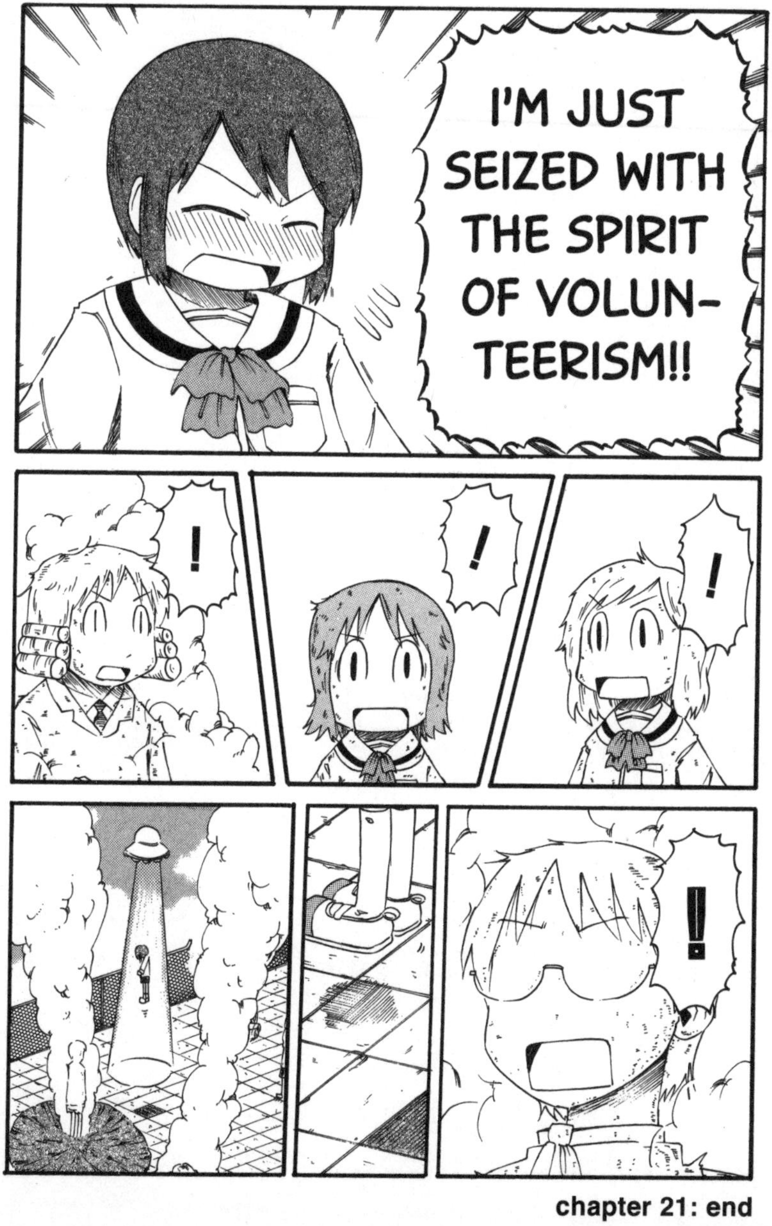
I'M JUST SEIZED WITH THE SPIRIT OF VOLUN-TEERISM!!
!
!
!
!

chapter 21: end

chapter 22

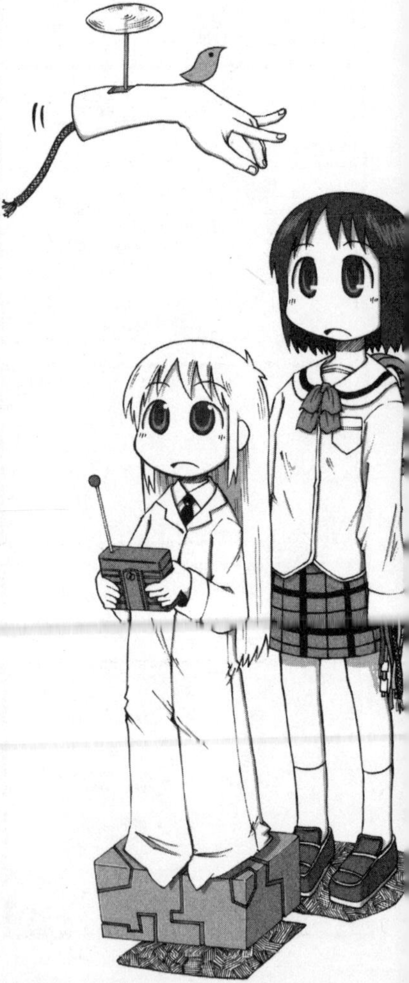

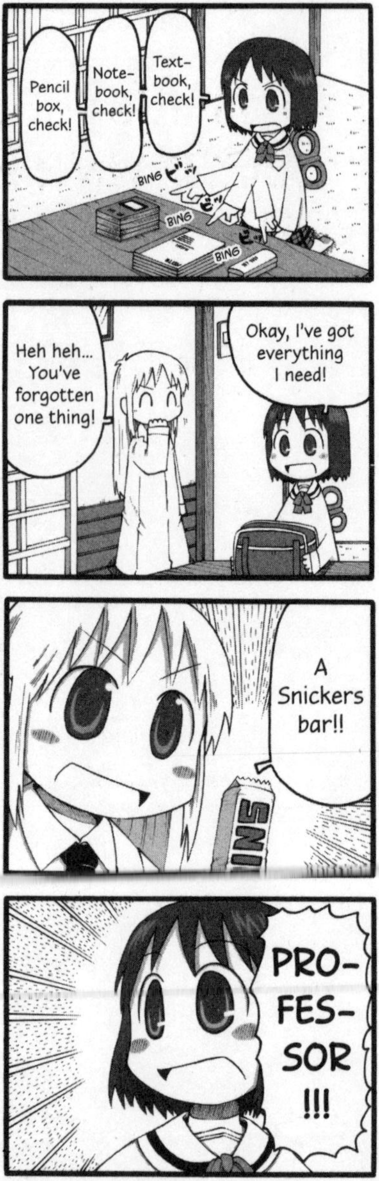
Text-book, check!
Note-book, check!
Pencil box, check!
BING
BING
BING
Okay, I've got everything I need!
Heh heh... You've forgotten one thing!
A Snickers bar!!
PRO-FES-SOR !!!

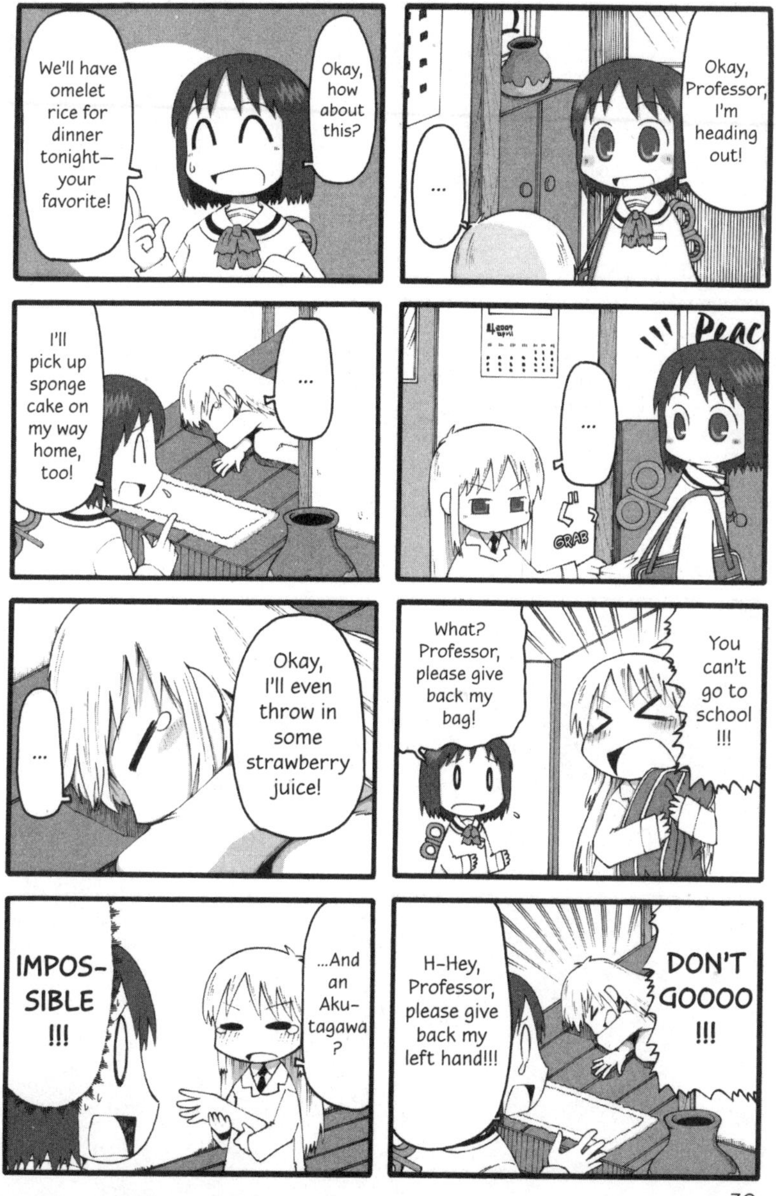
Okay, Professor, I'm heading out!
...
Okay, how about this?
We'll have omelet rice for dinner tonight—your favorite!
PEAC
...
GRAB
...
I'll pick up sponge cake on my way home, too!
You can't go to school!!!
What? Professor, please give back my bag!
Okay, I'll even throw in some strawberry juice!
...
DON'T GOOOO!!!
H-Hey, Professor, please give back my left hand!!!
...And an Aku-tagawa?
IMPOS-SIBLE!!!

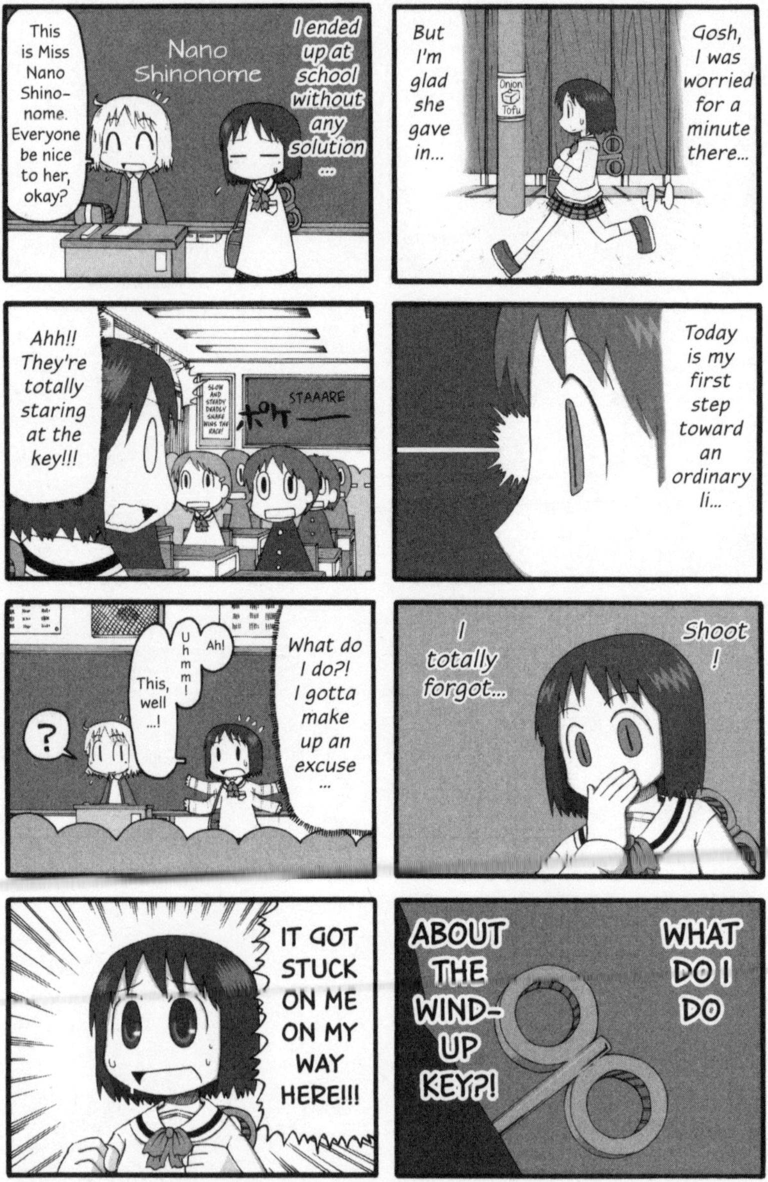
Gosh, I was worried for a minute there...
But I'm glad she gave in...
Onion Tofu
I ended up at school without any solution...
Nano Shinonome
This is Miss Nano Shinonome. Everyone be nice to her, okay?
Today is my first step toward an ordinary li...
Ahh!! They're totally staring at the key!!!
STAAARE
SLOW AND STEADY DEADLY SNAKE WINS THE RACE!
Shoot!
I totally forgot...
What do I do?! I gotta make up an excuse...
Uhmm!
Ah!
This, well...!
?
WHAT DO I DO
ABOUT THE WIND-UP KEY?!
IT GOT STUCK ON ME ON MY WAY HERE!!!

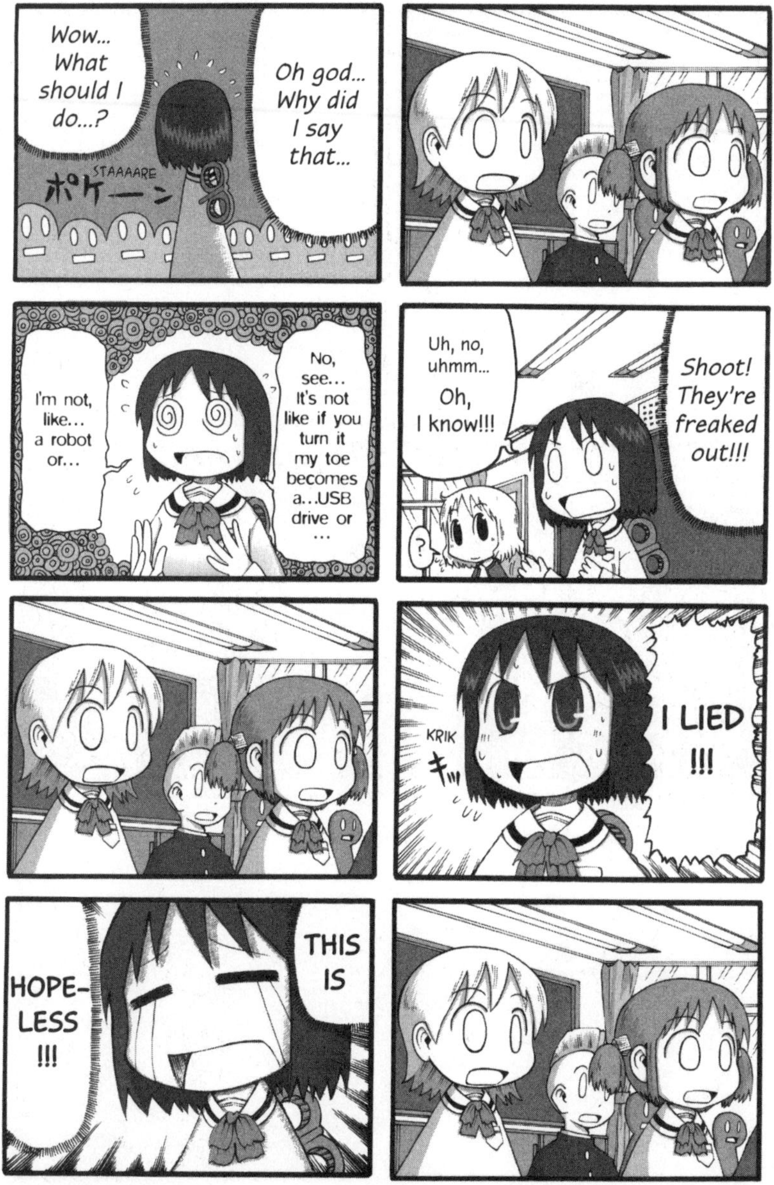
Oh god... Why did I say that...
Wow... What should I do...?
STAAAARE
ポケーン
Shoot! They're freaked out!!!
Uh, no, uhmm... Oh, I know!!!
?
No, see... It's not like if you turn it my toe becomes a...USB drive or ...
I'm not, like... a robot or...
I LIED !!!
KRIK
キッ
THIS IS
HOPE-LESS !!!

chapter 22: end

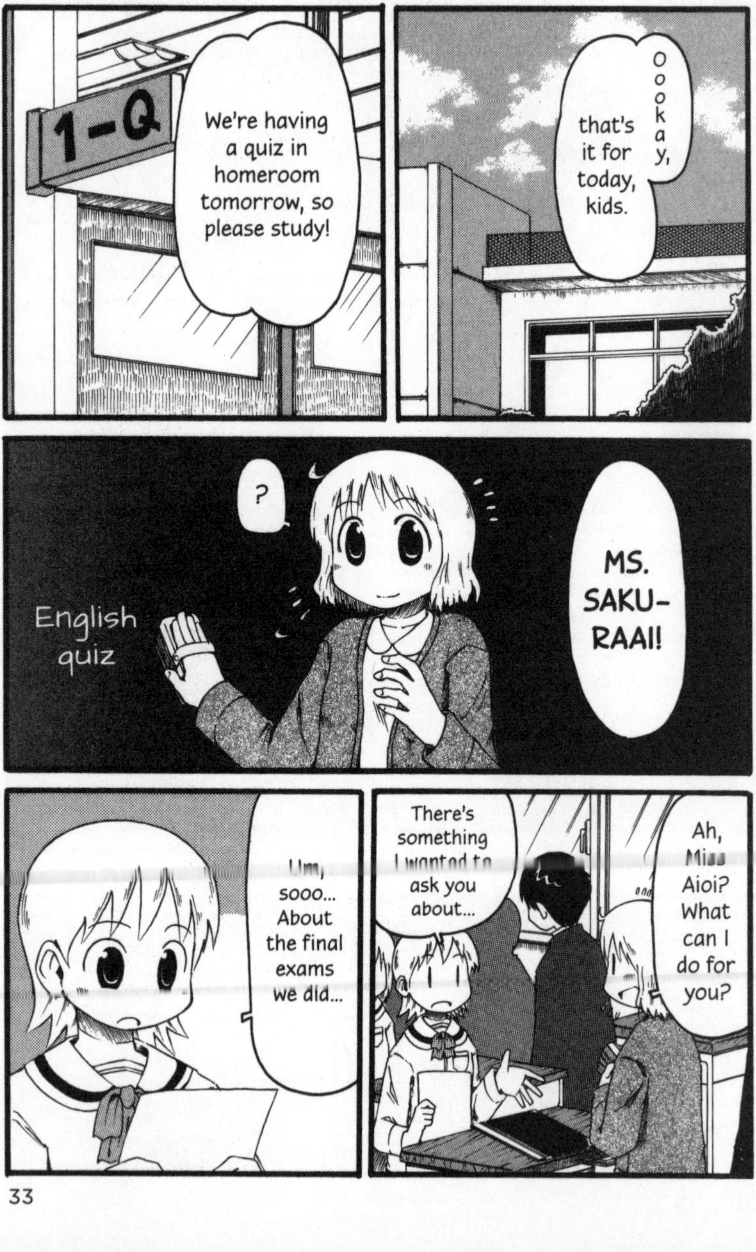
Ooookay, that's it for today, kids.
We're having a quiz in homeroom tomorrow, so please study!
MS. SAKU-RAAI!
?
English quiz
Ah, Miss Aioi? What can I do for you?
There's something I wanted to ask you about...
Um, sooo... About the final exams we did...

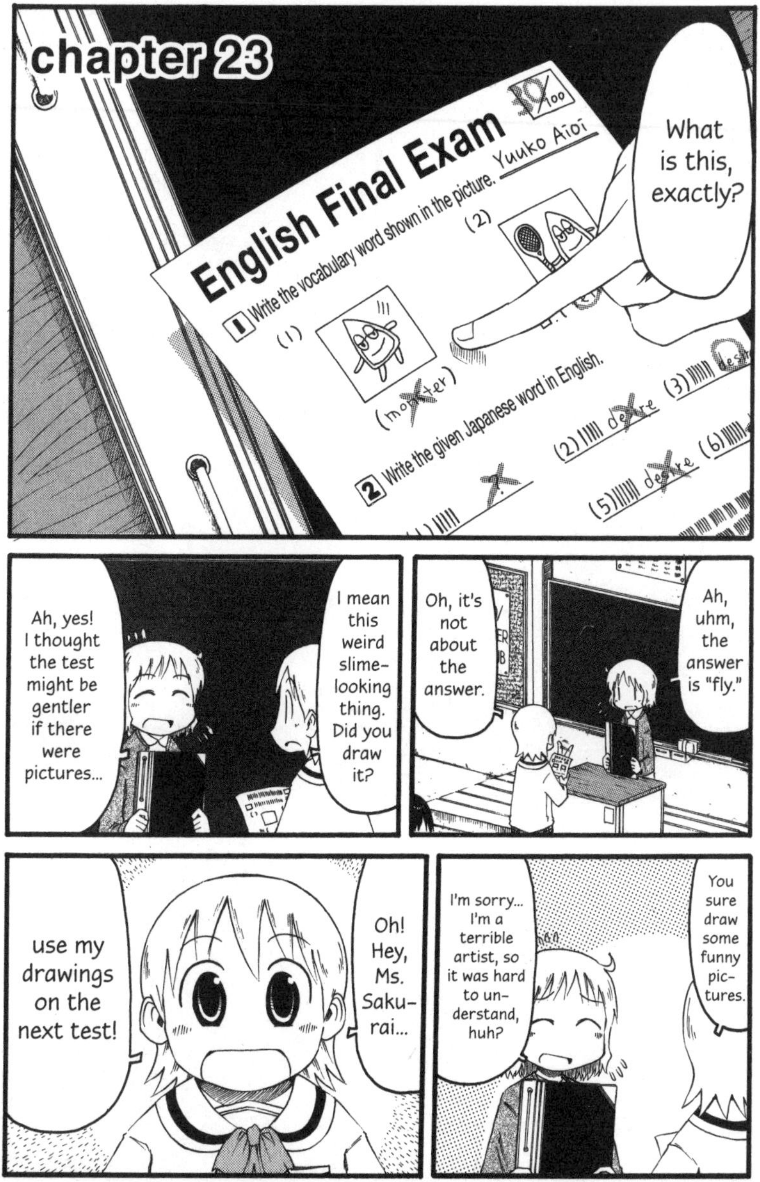
chapter 23
English Final Exam
Yuuko Aioi
1 Write the vocabulary word shown in the picture.
2 Write the given Japanese word in English.
What is this, exactly?
Ah, uhm, the answer is "fly."
Oh, it's not about the answer.
I mean this weird slime-looking thing. Did you draw it?
Ah, yes! I thought the test might be gentler if there were pictures...
You sure draw some funny pictures.
I'm sorry... I'm a terrible artist, so it was hard to understand, huh?
Oh! Hey, Ms. Sakurai...
use my drawings on the next test!

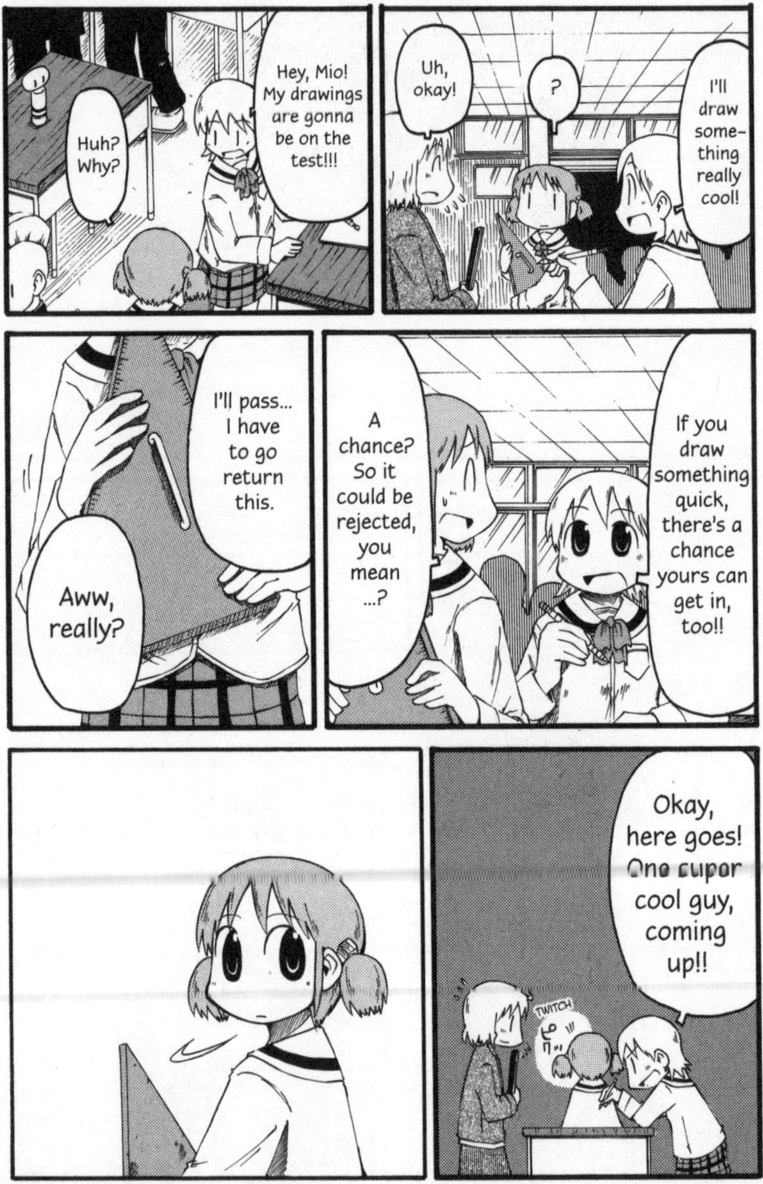
I'll draw some-thing really cool!
?
Uh, okay!
Hey, Mio! My drawings are gonna be on the test!!!
Huh? Why?
If you draw something quick, there's a chance yours can get in, too!!
A chance? So it could be rejected, you mean ...?
I'll pass... I have to go return this.
Aww, really?
Okay, here goes! One super cool guy, coming up!!
TWITCH

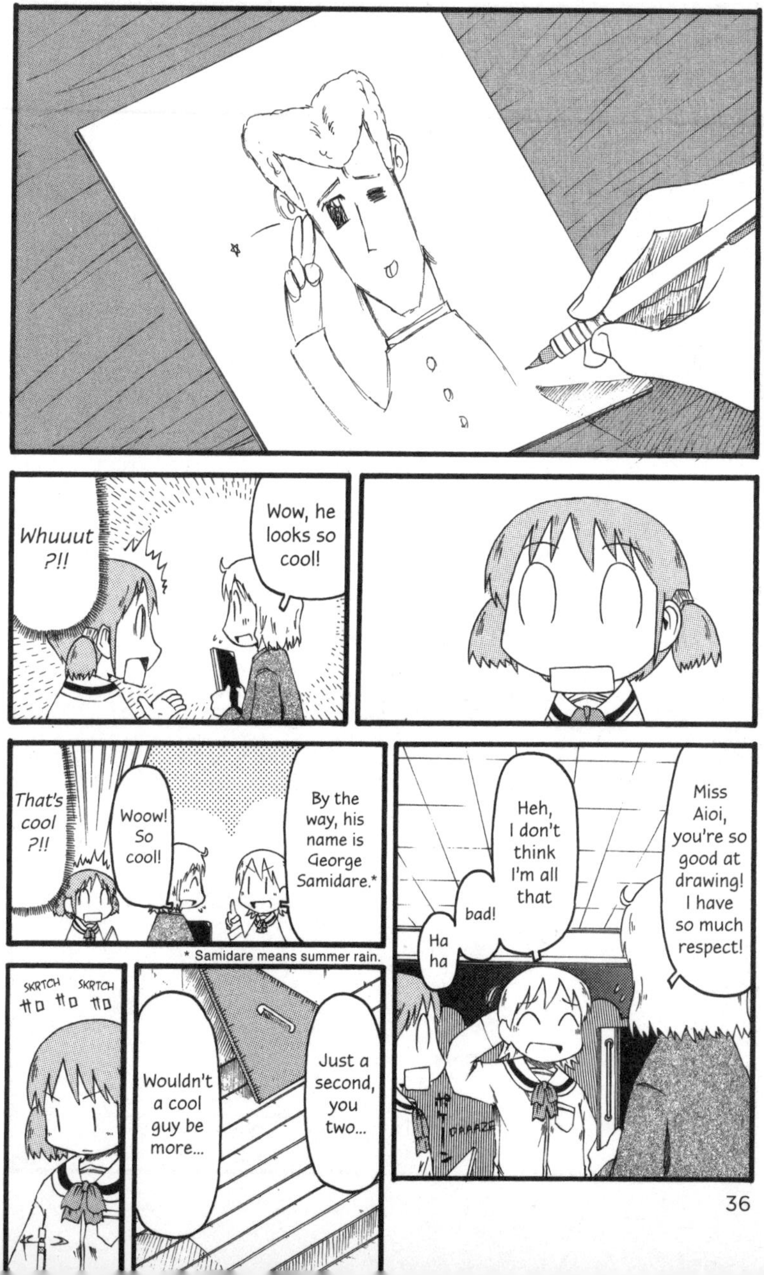
Wow, he looks so cool!
Whuuut ?!!
Miss Aioi, you're so good at drawing! I have so much respect!
Heh, I don't think I'm all that bad!
Ha ha
DAAAZE
By the way, his name is George Samidare.*
Woow! So cool!
That's cool ?!!
Just a second, you two...
Wouldn't a cool guy be more...
SKRTCH SKRTCH

* Samidare means summer rain.

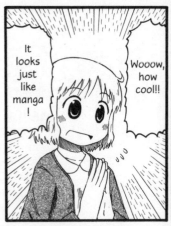

like this?
Dull.
Wooow, how cool!!
It looks just like manga!
Miss Nagano-hara, do you draw manga?
ちやほや
FLATTER
Oh, no way! Well, maybe a little...
ちやほや
FLATTER
Oh, lovely! I'd like to see it sometime!
Uh, well... that'd be a bit, uhm...
GRRRRRRR
LEMME SEE THAT!!
GRAB
Whoa!
Mine is gonna be way cooler!
Dull.

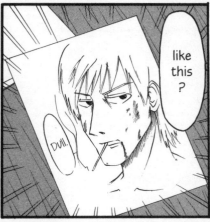

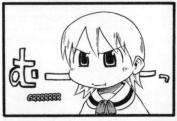

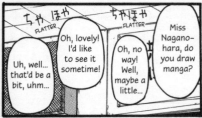

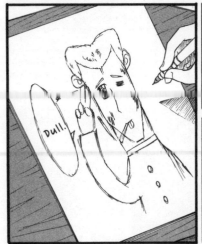

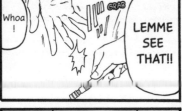

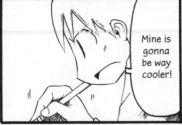

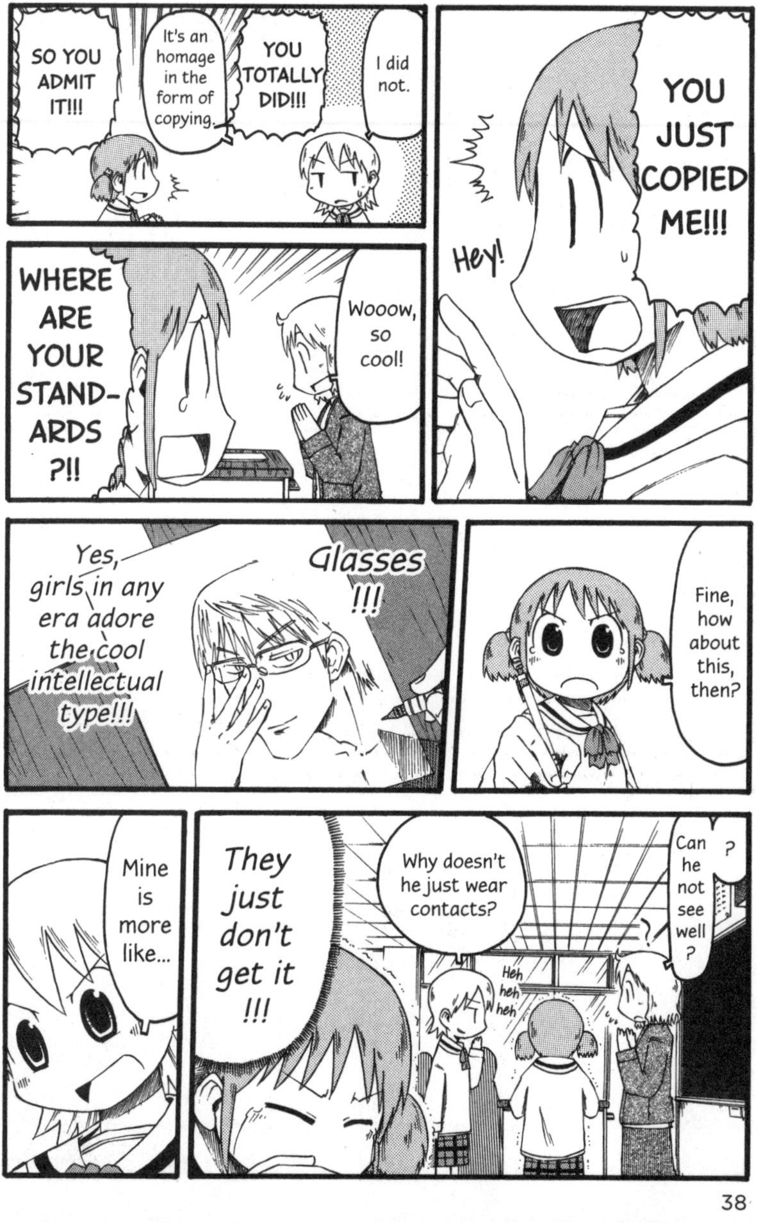
YOU JUST COPIED ME!!!
Hey!
I did not.
YOU TOTALLY DID!!!
It's an homage in the form of copying.
SO YOU ADMIT IT!!!
Wooow, so cool!
WHERE ARE YOUR STAND-ARDS?!!
Fine, how about this, then?
Glasses!!!
Yes, girls in any era adore the cool intellectual type!!!
Can he not see well?
?
?
Why doesn't he just wear contacts?
Heh heh heh
They just don't get it!!!
Mine is more like...

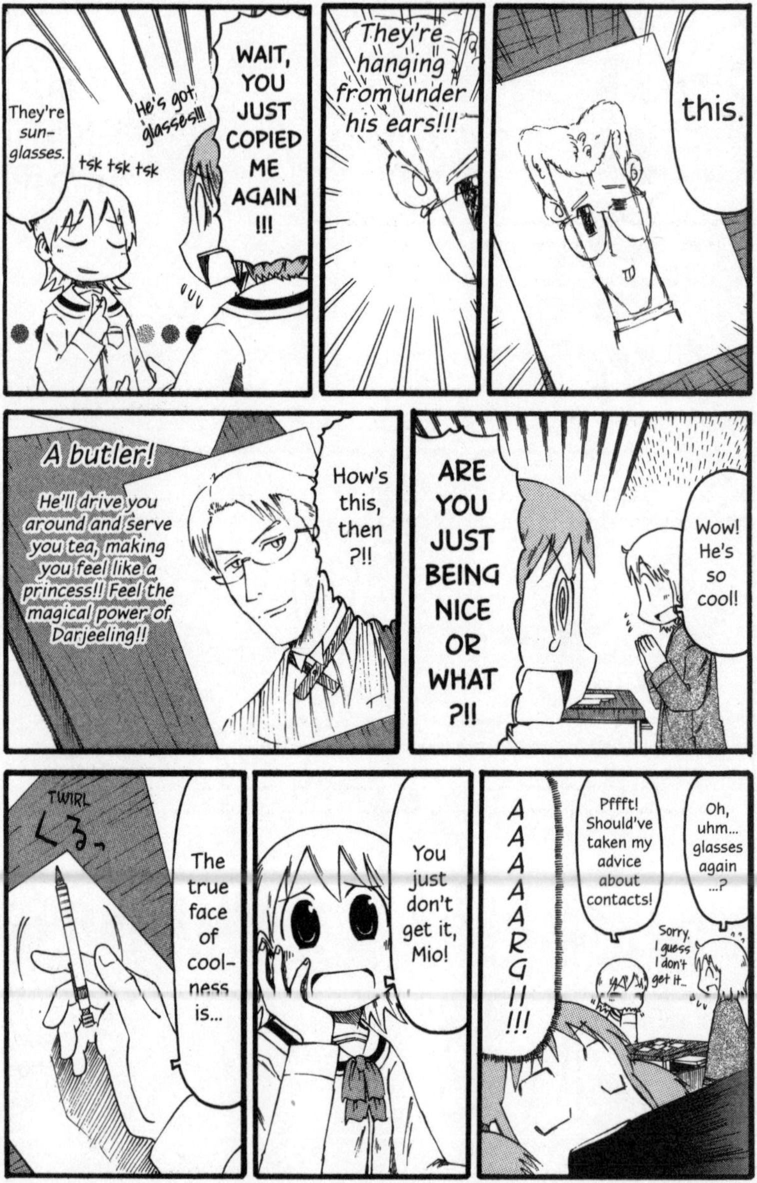
this.
They're hanging from under his ears!!!
WAIT, YOU JUST COPIED ME AGAIN!!!
He's got glasses!!!
They're sun-glasses.
tsk tsk tsk
Wow! He's so cool!
ARE YOU JUST BEING NICE OR WHAT?!!
How's this, then?!!
A butler!
He'll drive you around and serve you tea, making you feel like a princess!! Feel the magical power of Darjeeling!!
Oh, uhm... glasses again ...?
Pffft! Should've taken my advice about contacts!
AAAAARG!!!
Sorry. I guess I don't get it...
You just don't get it, Mio!
The true face of cool-ness is...
TWIRL

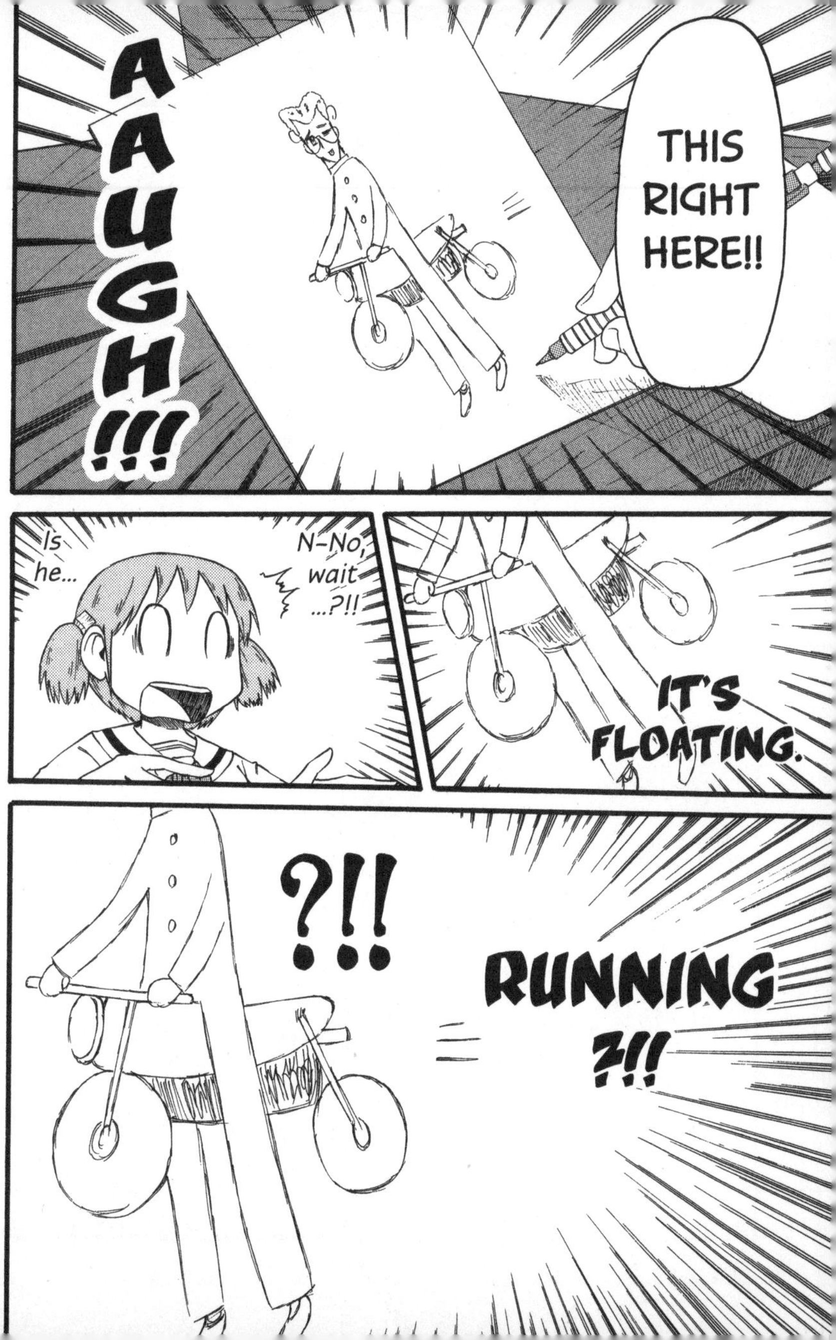
THIS RIGHT HERE!!
AAUGH!!!
IT'S FLOATING.
N-No, wait ...?!!
Is he...
RUNNING ?!!
?!!

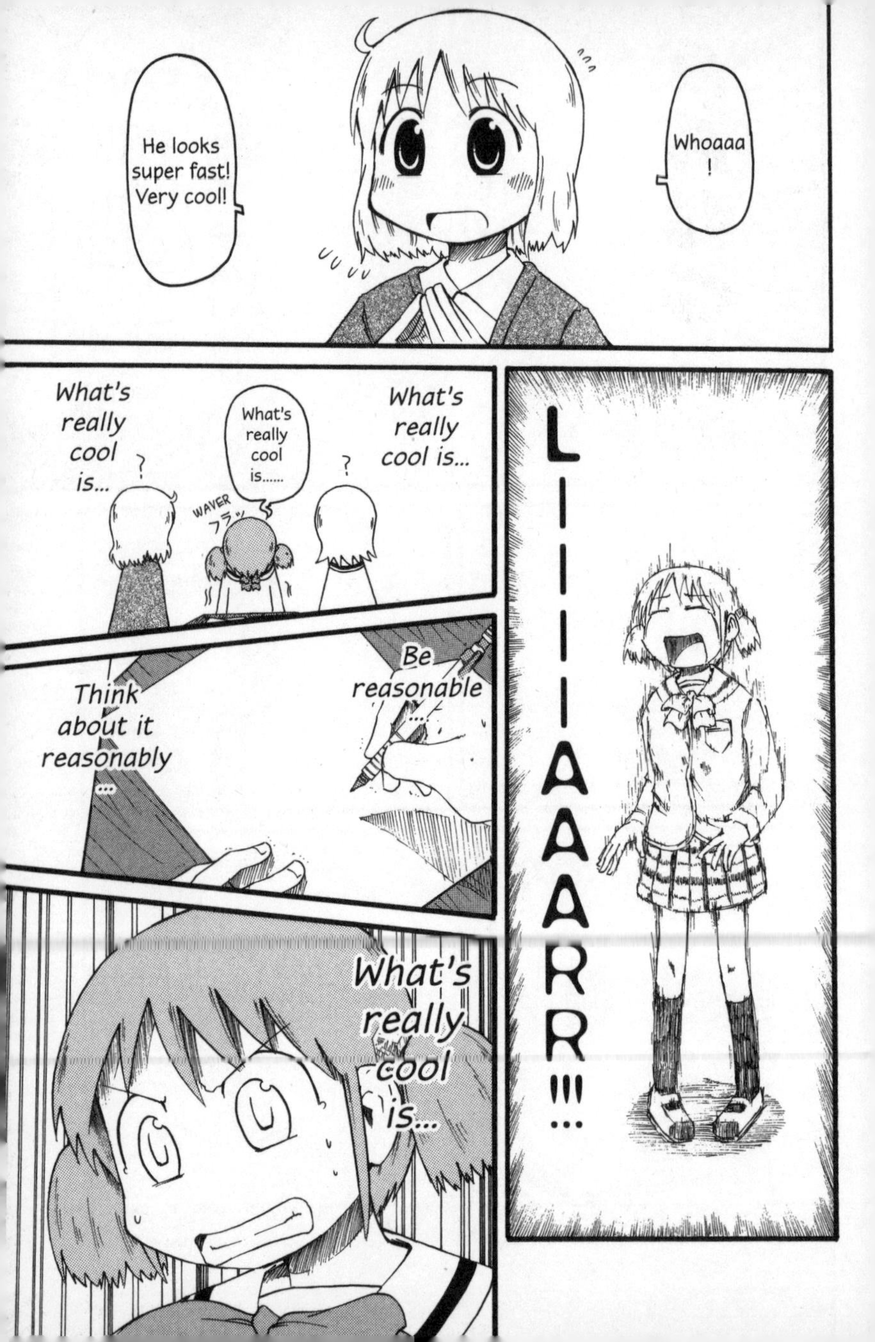
Whoaaa !
He looks super fast! Very cool!
LIIIAAARR!!!...
What's really cool is...
WAVER フラッ
What's really cool is......
What's really cool is...
Be reasonable ...
Think about it reasonably ...
What's really cool is...

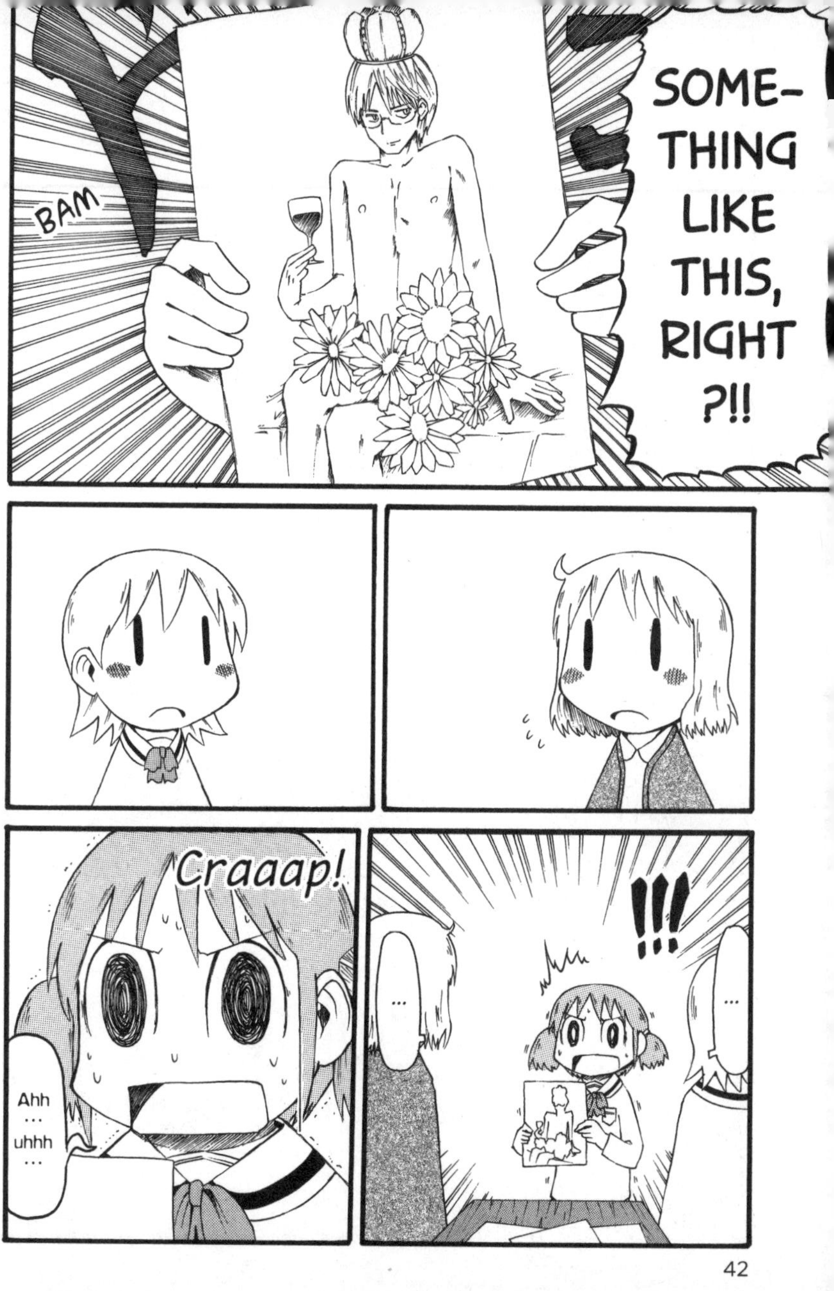
SOME-THING LIKE THIS, RIGHT?!!
BAM
!!!
...
...
Craaap!
Ahh... uhhh...

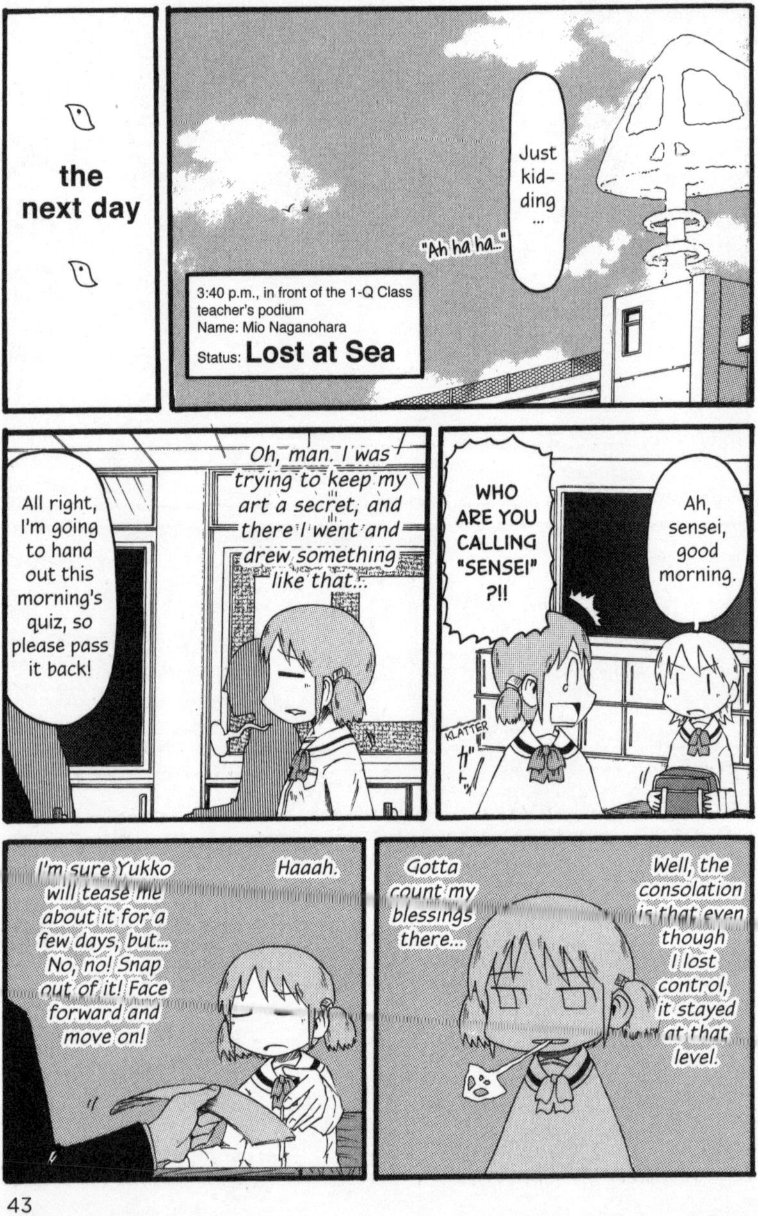
Just kid-ding ...
"Ah ha ha.."
3:40 p.m., in front of the 1-Q Class teacher's podium
Name: Mio Naganohara
Status: Lost at Sea
the next day
Ah, sensei, good morning.
WHO ARE YOU CALLING "SENSEI" ?!!
KLATTER
Oh, man. I was trying to keep my art a secret, and there I went and drew something like that...
All right, I'm going to hand out this morning's quiz, so please pass it back!
Well, the consolation is that even though I lost control, it stayed at that level.
Gotta count my blessings there...
Haaah.
I'm sure Yukko will tease me about it for a few days, but... No, no! Snap out of it! Face forward and move on!

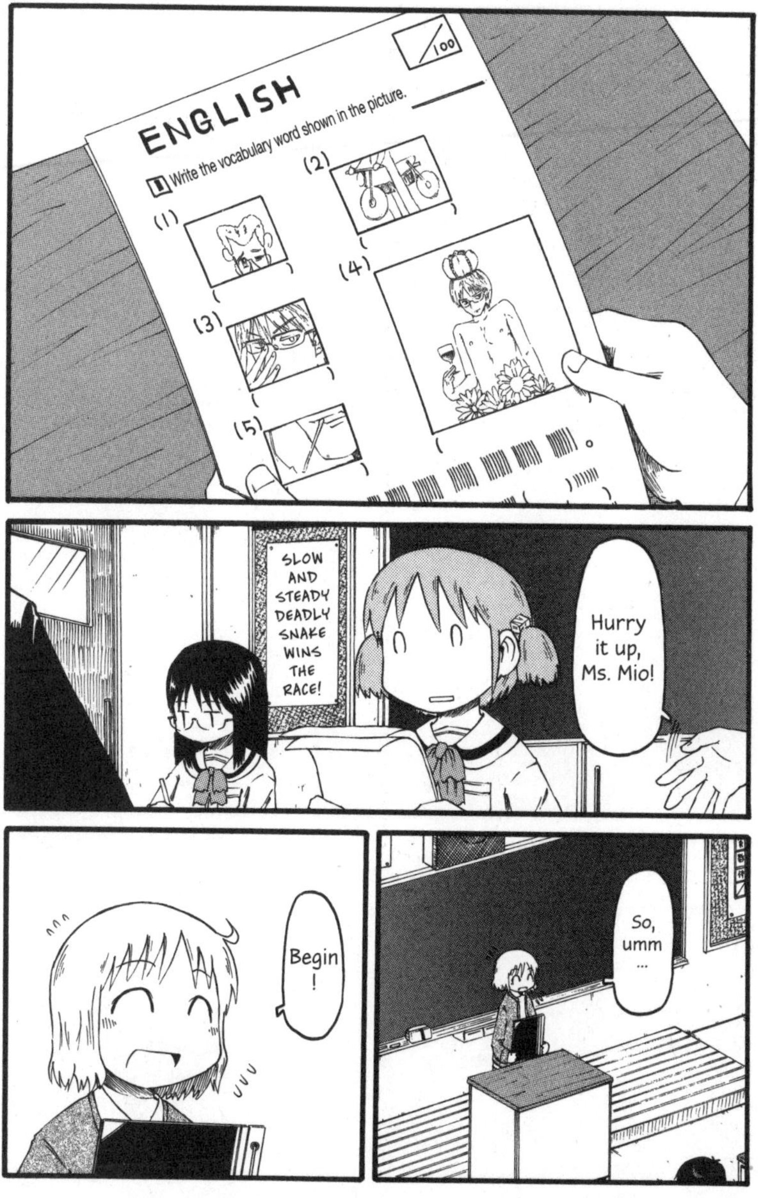

100
ENGLISH
Write the vocabulary word shown in the picture.
(1)
(2)
(3)
(4)
(5)
Hurry it up, Ms. Mio!
SLOW AND STEADY DEADLY SNAKE WINS THE RACE!
So, umm ...
Begin !

chapter 23: end

chapter 24

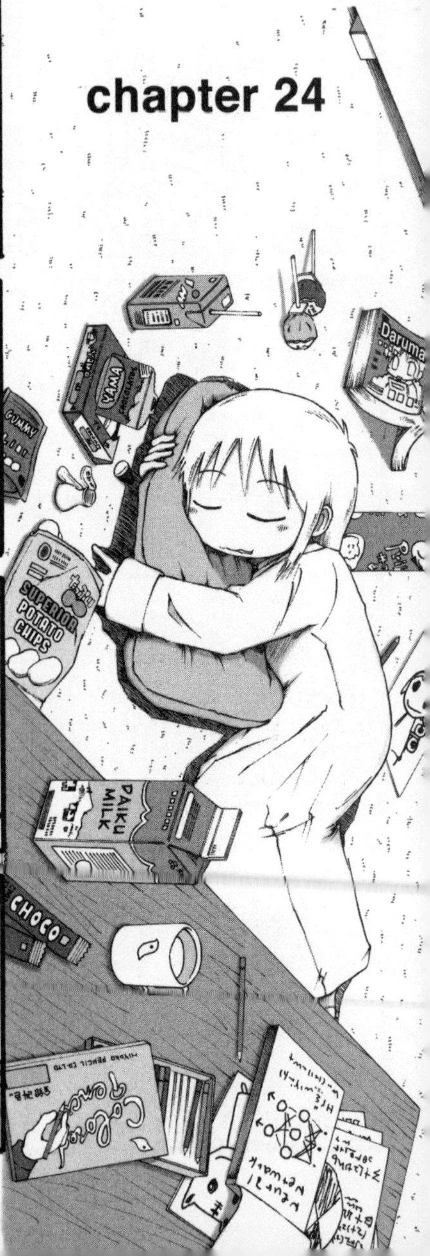
Daruma
YAMA
GUMMY
SUPERIOR POTATO CHIPS
DAIKU MILK
CHOCO

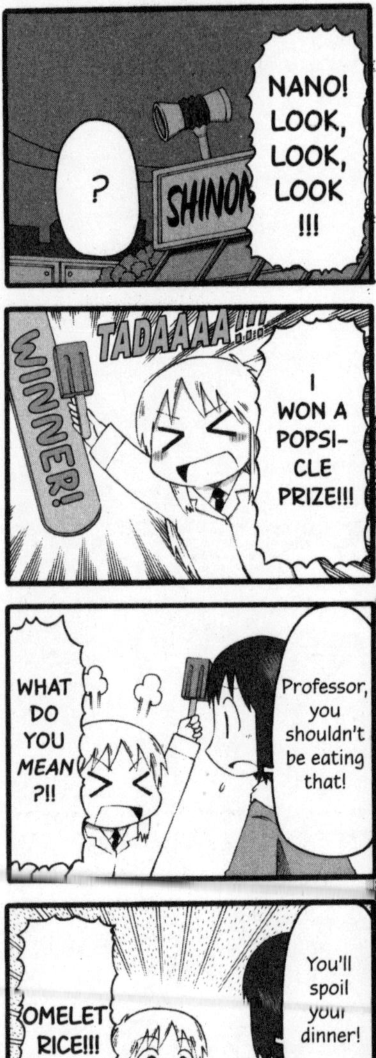
NANO! LOOK, LOOK, LOOK !!!
?
SHINON
TADAAAA!!!
I WON A POPSI-CLE PRIZE!!!
WINNER!
Professor, you shouldn't be eating that!
WHAT DO YOU MEAN ?!!
You'll spoil your dinner!
OMELET RICE!!!

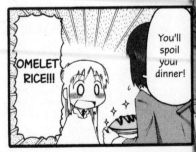

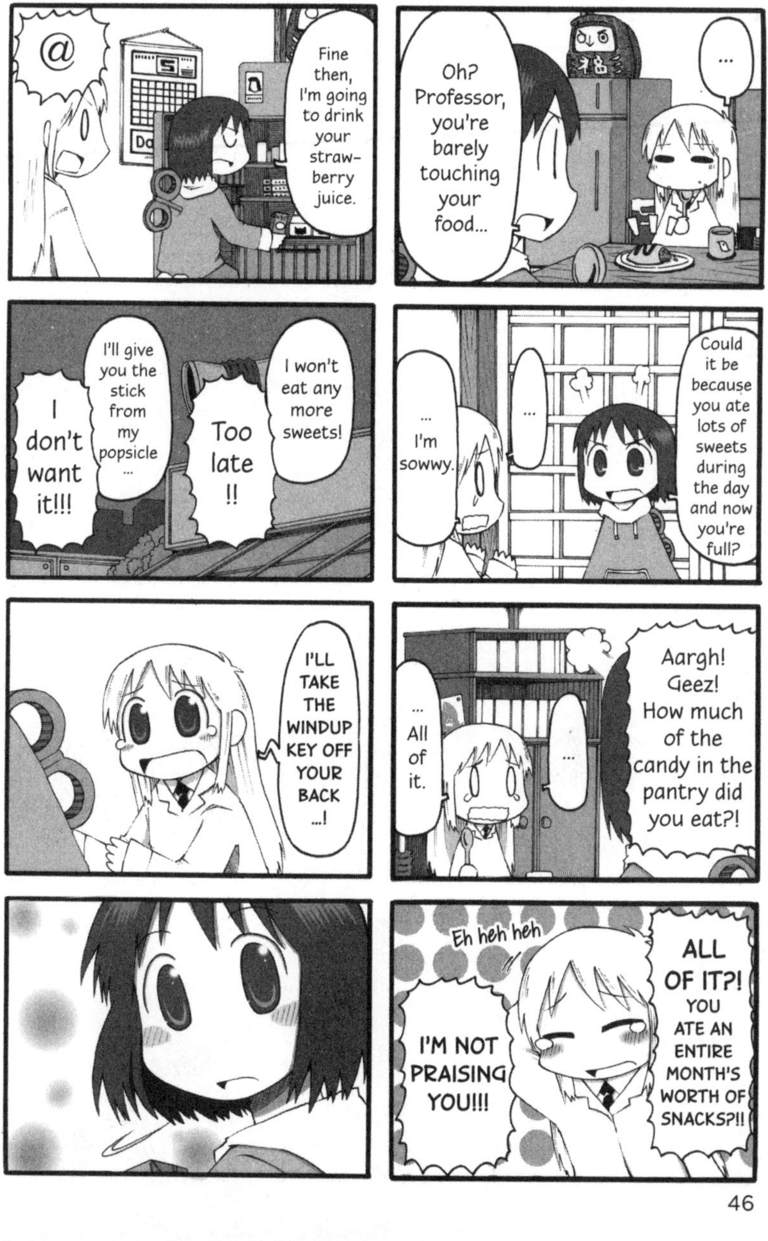
...
Oh? Professor, you're barely touching your food...
Fine then, I'm going to drink your strawberry juice.
@
Could it be because you ate lots of sweets during the day and now you're full?
...
... I'm sowwy.
I won't eat any more sweets!
Too late!!
I'll give you the stick from my popsicle ...
I don't want it!!!
Aargh! Geez! How much of the candy in the pantry did you eat?!
...
... All of it.
I'LL TAKE THE WINDUP KEY OFF YOUR BACK ...!
ALL OF IT?! YOU ATE AN ENTIRE MONTH'S WORTH OF SNACKS?!!
Eh heh heh
I'M NOT PRAISING YOU!!!

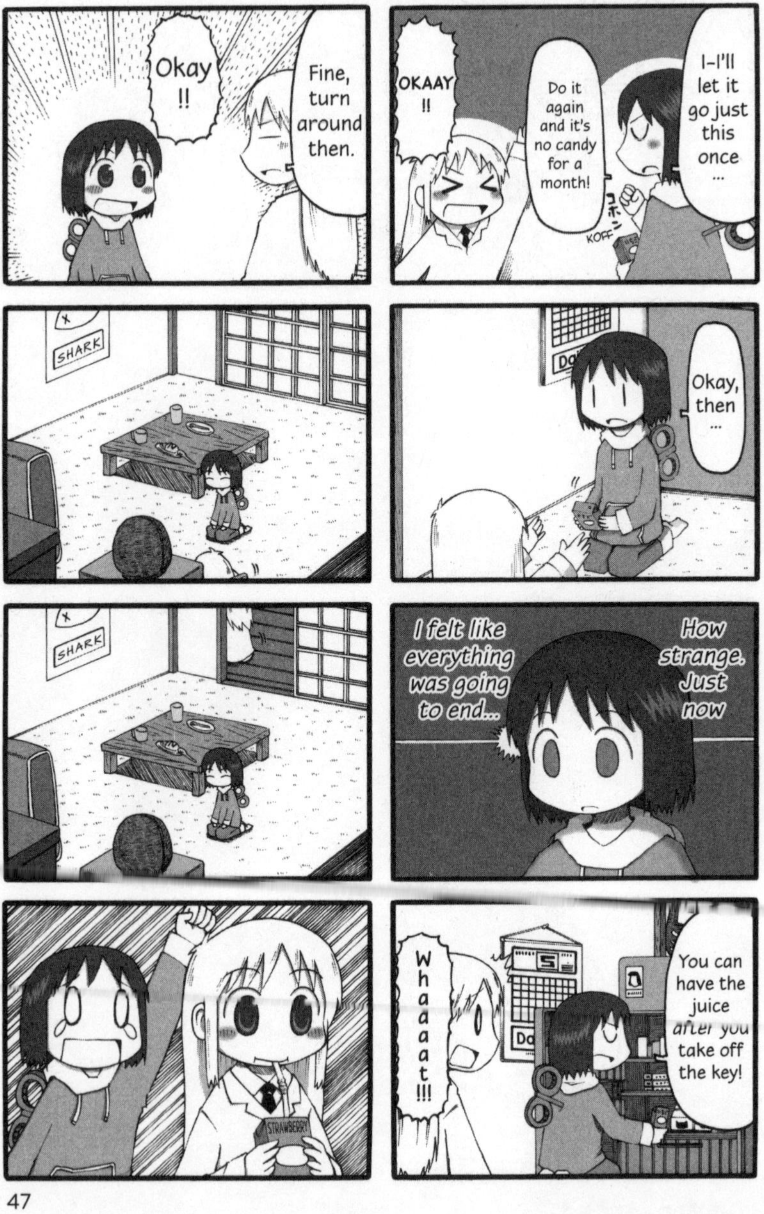
I-I'll let it go just this once ...
Do it again and it's no candy for a month!
コホン
KOFF
OKAAY !!
Fine, turn around then.
Okay !!
Okay, then ...
X
SHARK
How strange. Just now
I felt like everything was going to end...
X
SHARK
You can have the juice after you take off the key!
Whaaaat!!!
STRAWBERRY

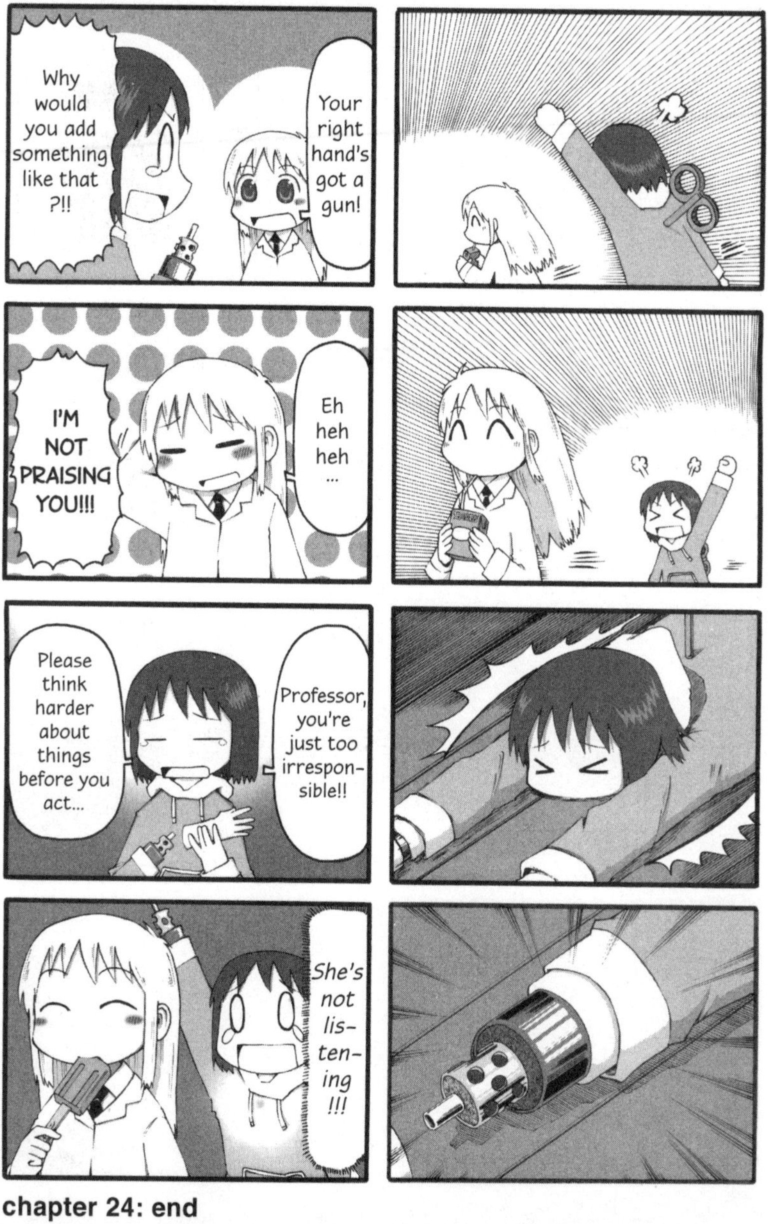
Your right hand's got a gun!
Why would you add something like that?!!
Eh heh heh...
I'M NOT PRAISING YOU!!!
Professor, you're just too irresponsible!!
Please think harder about things before you act...
She's not listening!!!

chapter 24: end

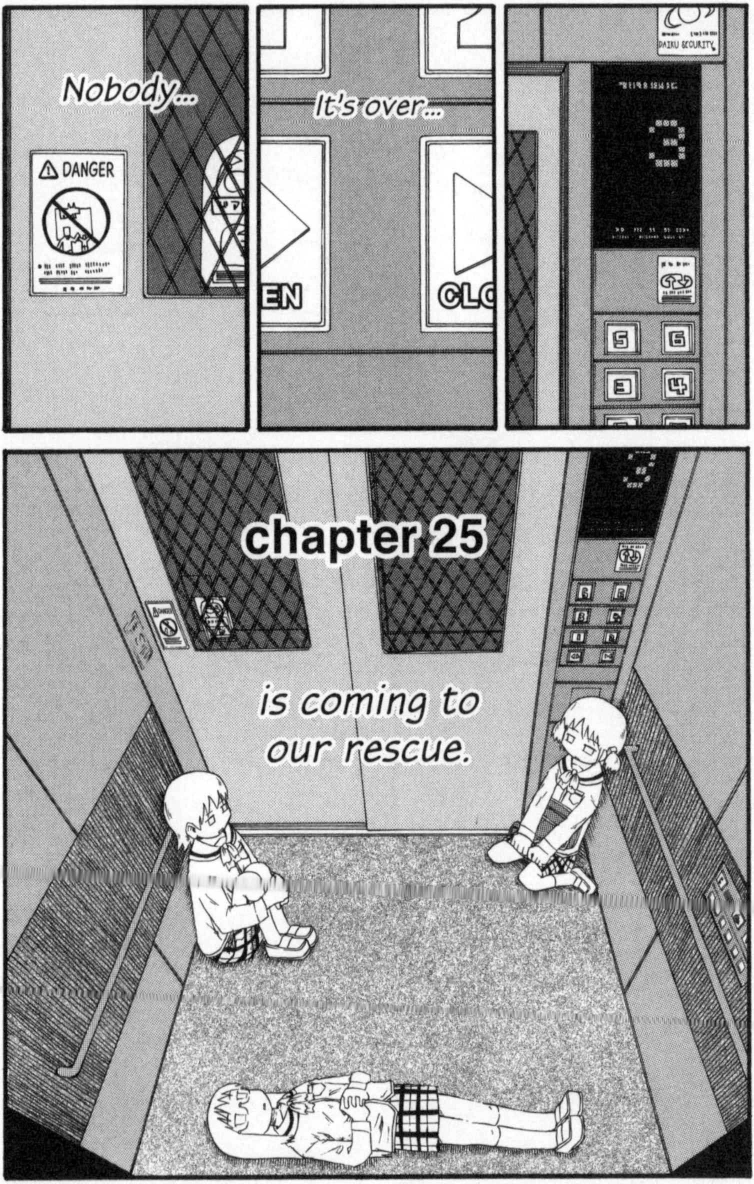
DAIKU SECURITY
It's over...
Nobody...
DANGER
chapter 25
is coming to our rescue.

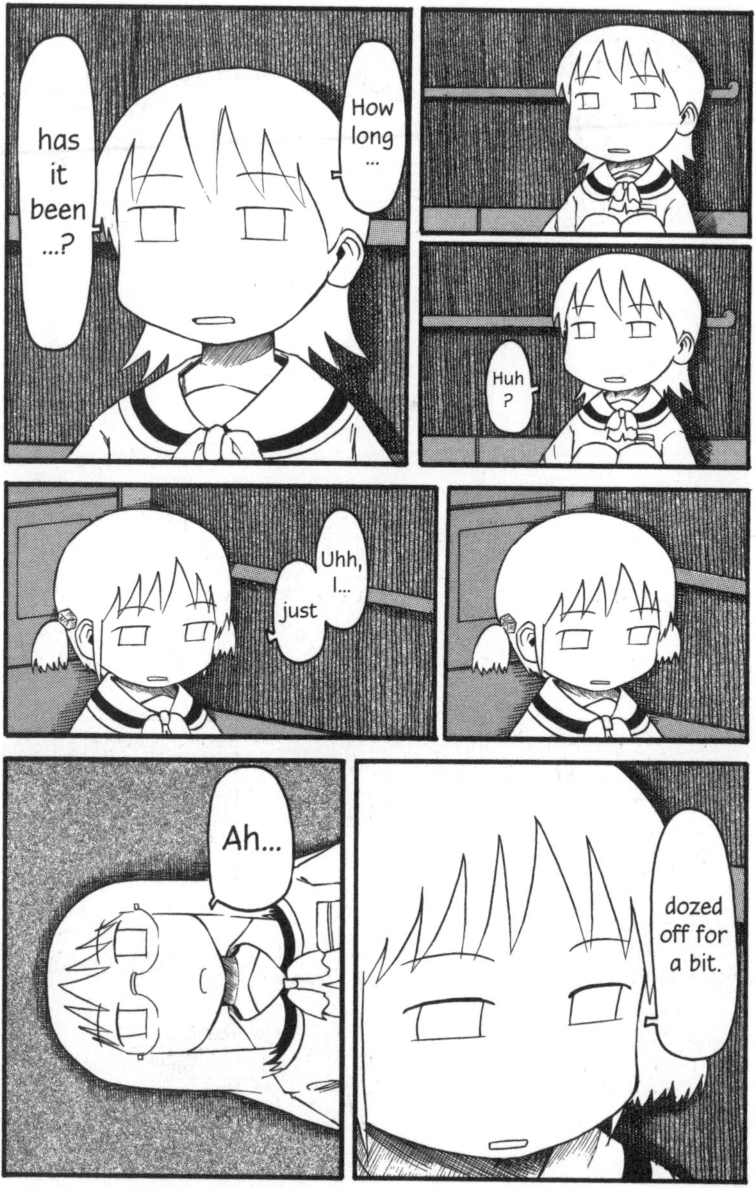
Huh?
How long...
has it been...?
Uhh, I...
just
dozed off for a bit.
Ah...

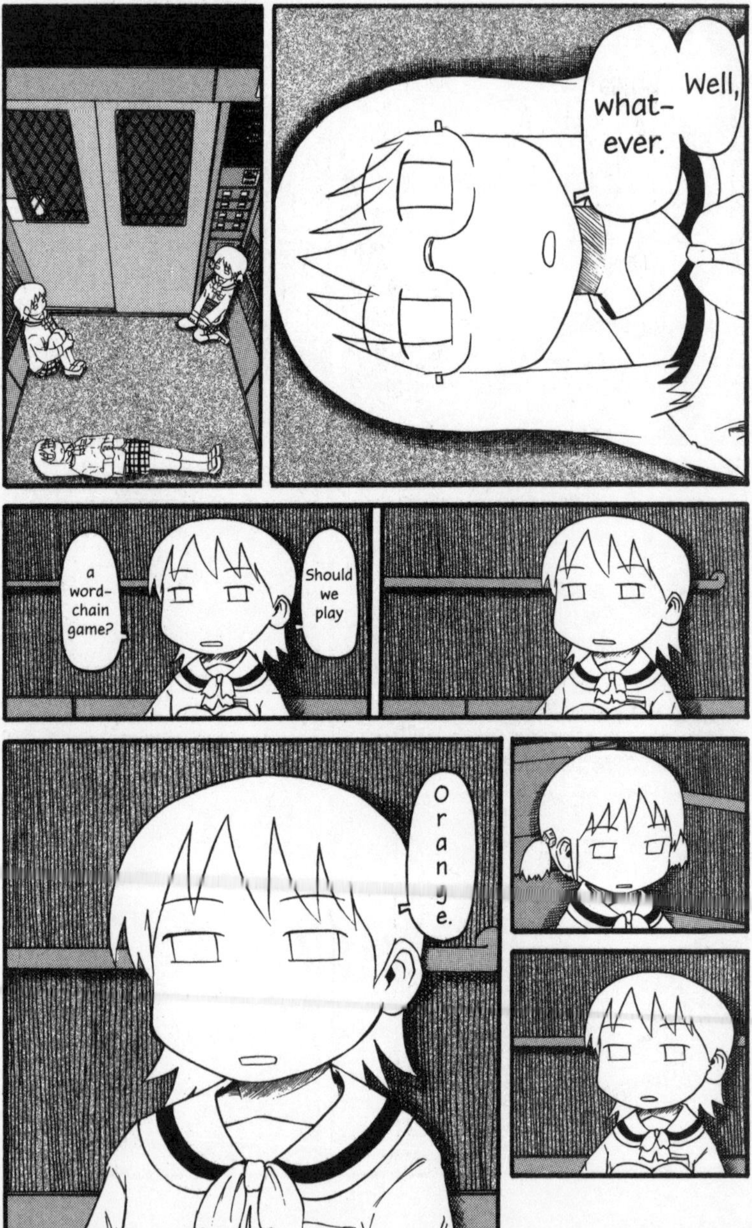
Well, whatever.
Should we play
a word-chain game?
Orange.

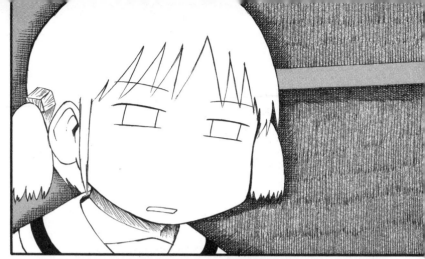

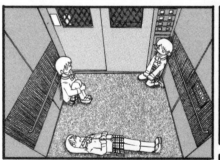

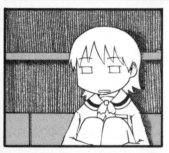

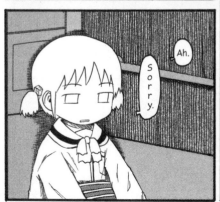

Ah.

Sorry.

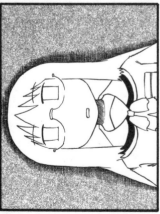

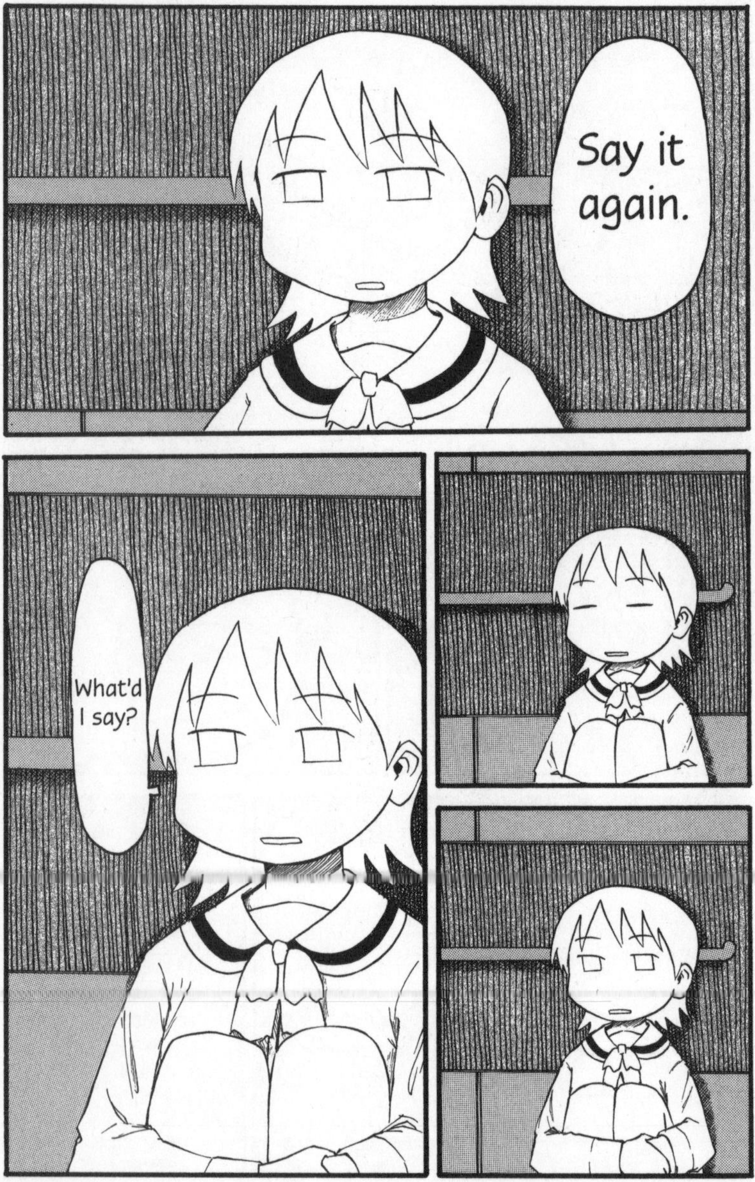
Say it again.
What'd I say?

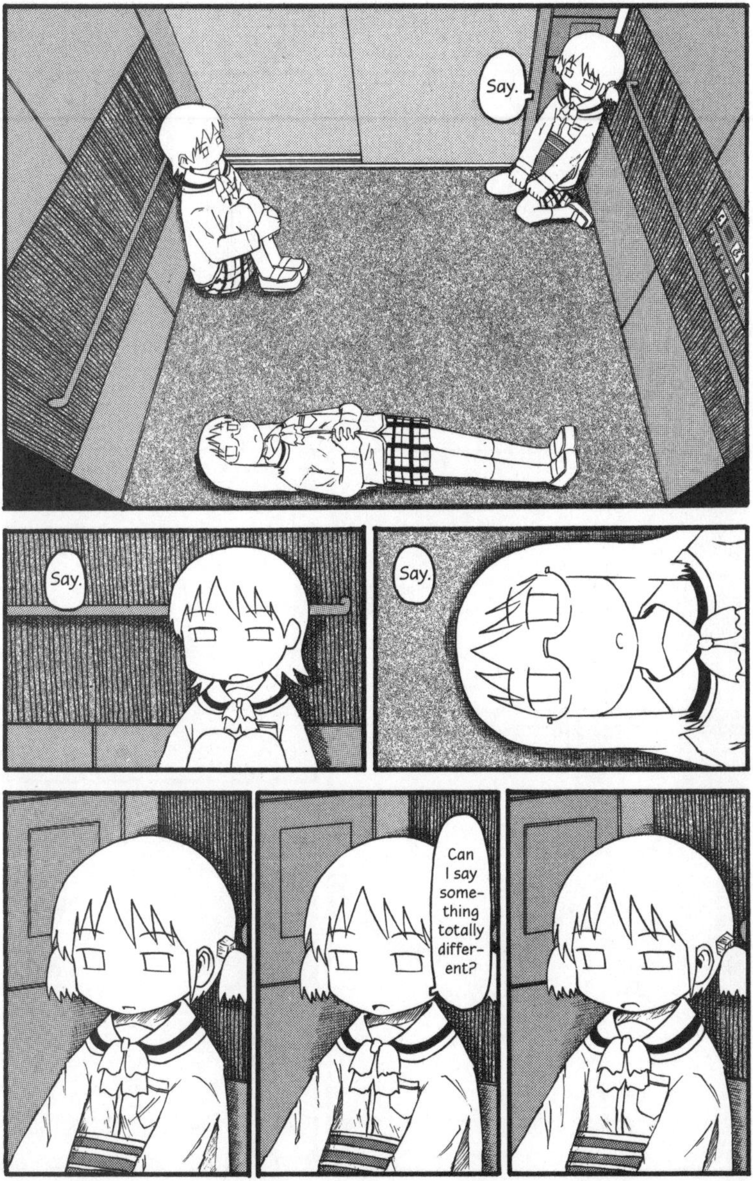
Say.
Say.
Say.
Can I say something totally different?

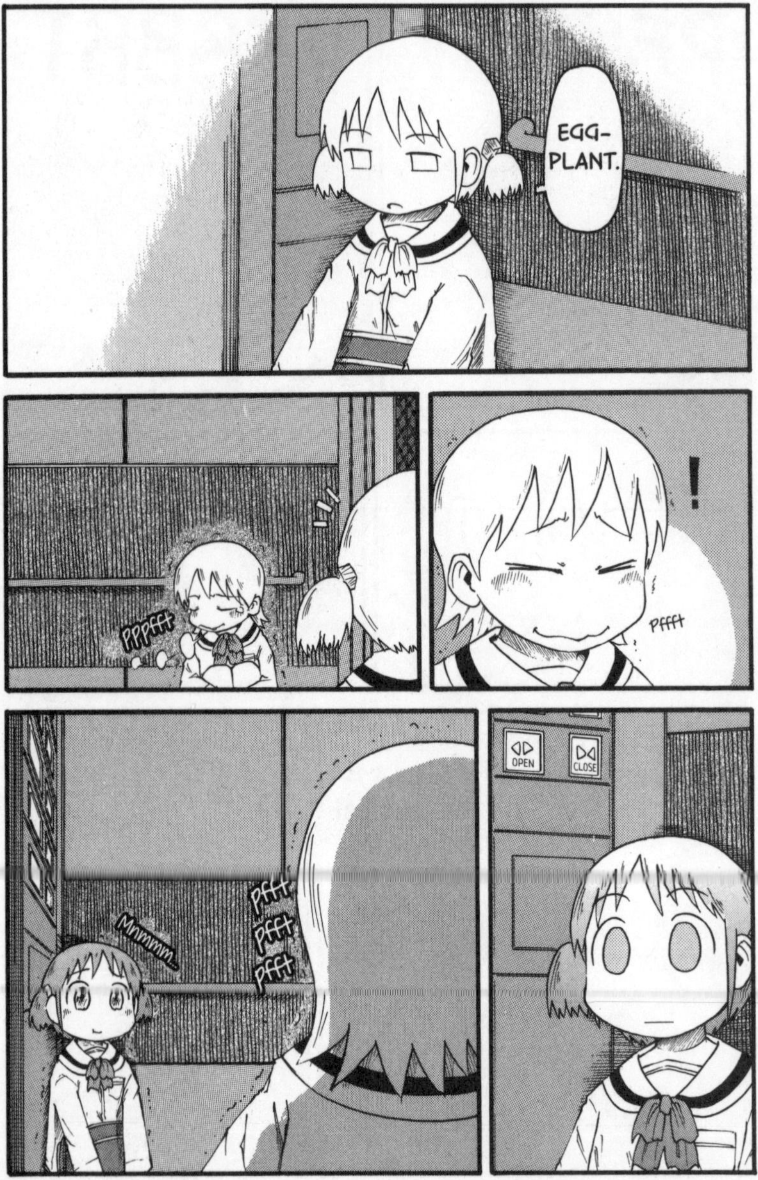
EGG-PLANT.
!
Pffft
Pppffft
OPEN
CLOSE
Mnmmm...
Pfft
Pfft
Pfft

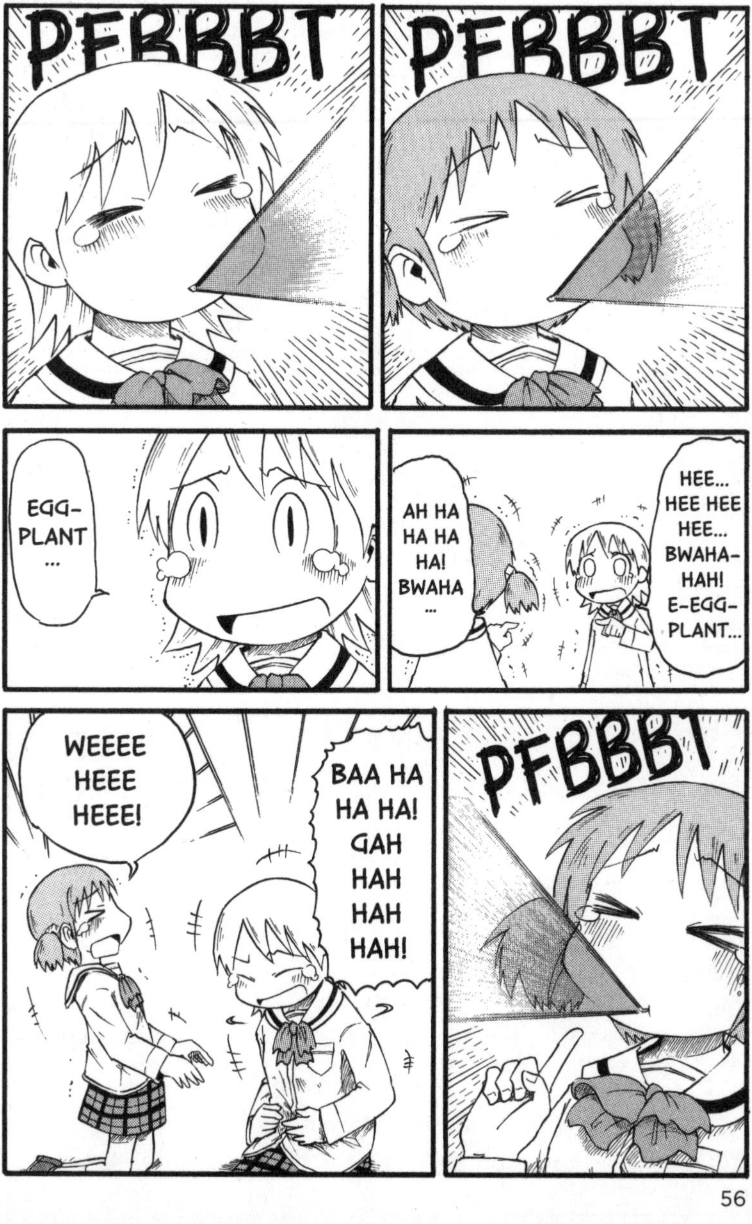
PFBBBT
PFBBBT
HEE... HEE HEE HEE... BWAHA-HAH! E-EGG-PLANT...
AH HA HA HA HA! BWAHA ...
EGG-PLANT ...
PFBBBT
BAA HA HA HA! GAH HAH HAH HAH!
WEEEE HEEE HEEE!

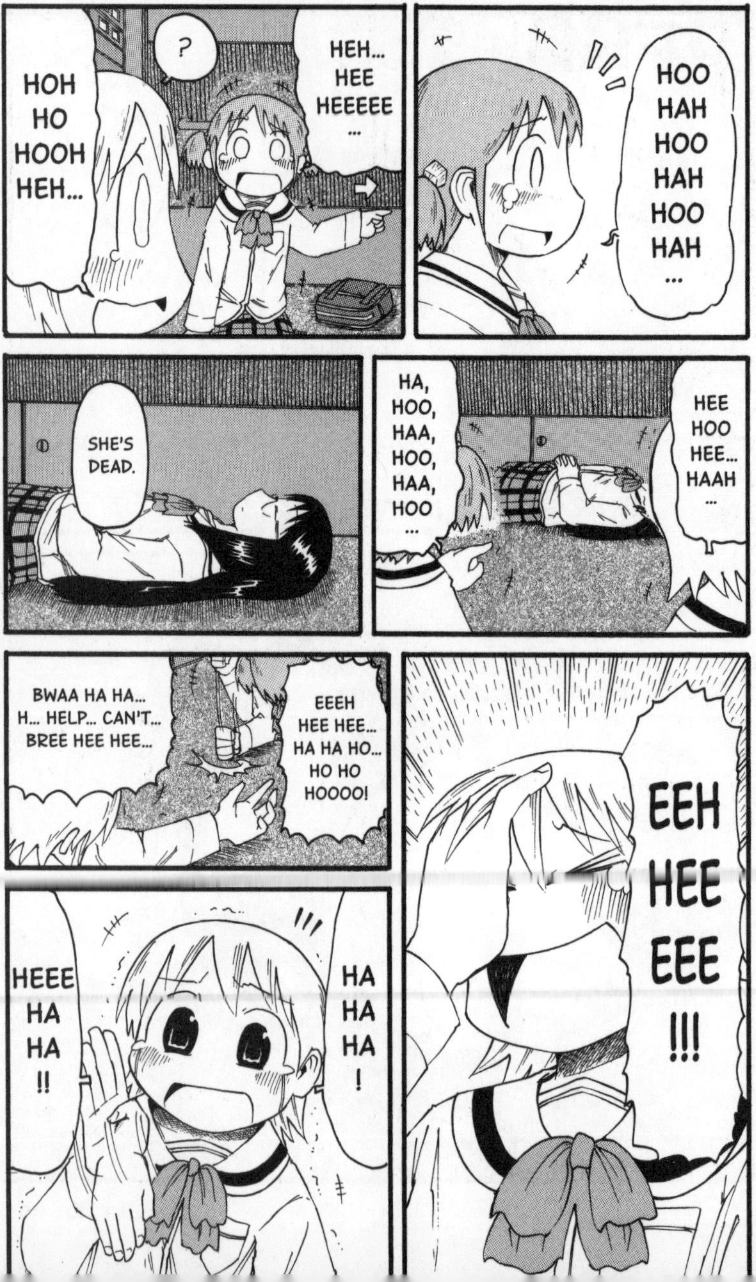
HOO HAH HOO HAH HOO HAH ...
HEH... HEE HEEEEE ...
?
HOH HO HOOH HEH...
HEE HOO HEE... HAAH ...
HA, HOO, HAA, HOO, HAA, HOO ...
SHE'S DEAD.
EEH HEE EEE !!!
EEEH HEE HEE... HA HA HO... HO HO HOOOO!
BWAA HA HA... H... HELP... CAN'T... BREE HEE HEE...
HA HA HA !
HEEE HA HA !!

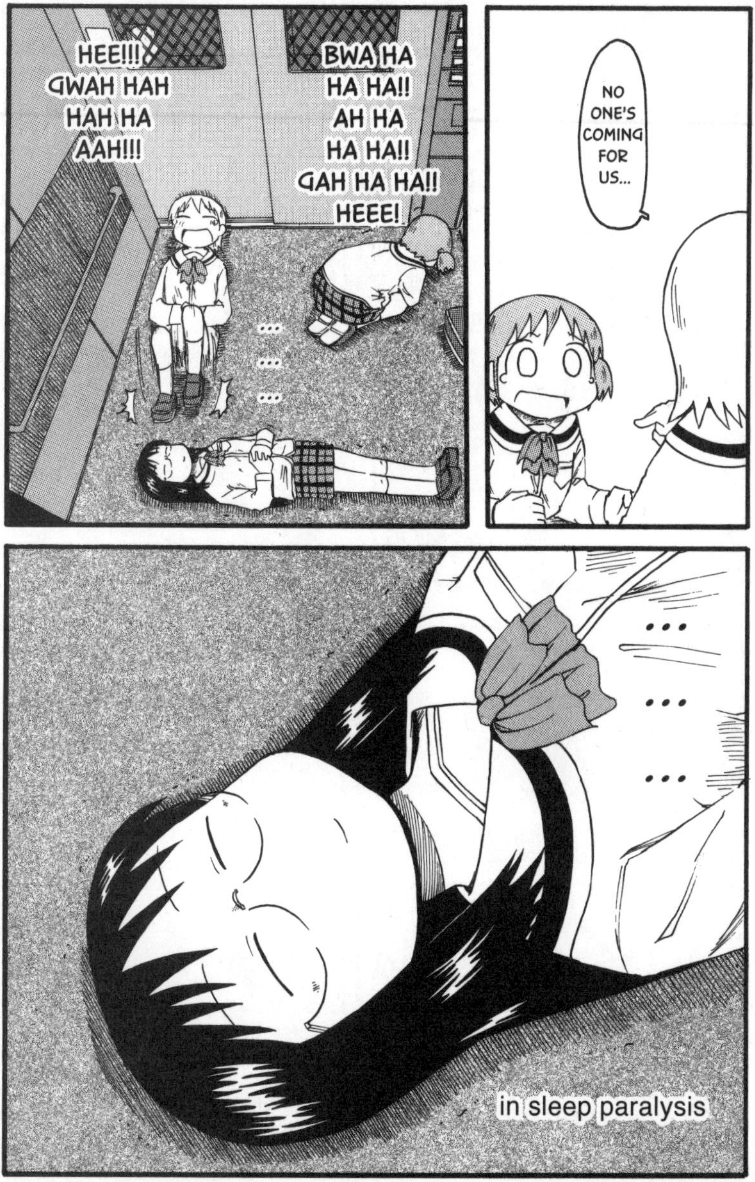
NO ONE'S COMING FOR US...
HEE!!! GWAH HAH HAH HA AAH!!!
BWA HA HA HA!! AH HA HA HA!! GAH HA HA!! HEEE!
...
...
...
...
...
...
in sleep paralysis

chapter 25: end

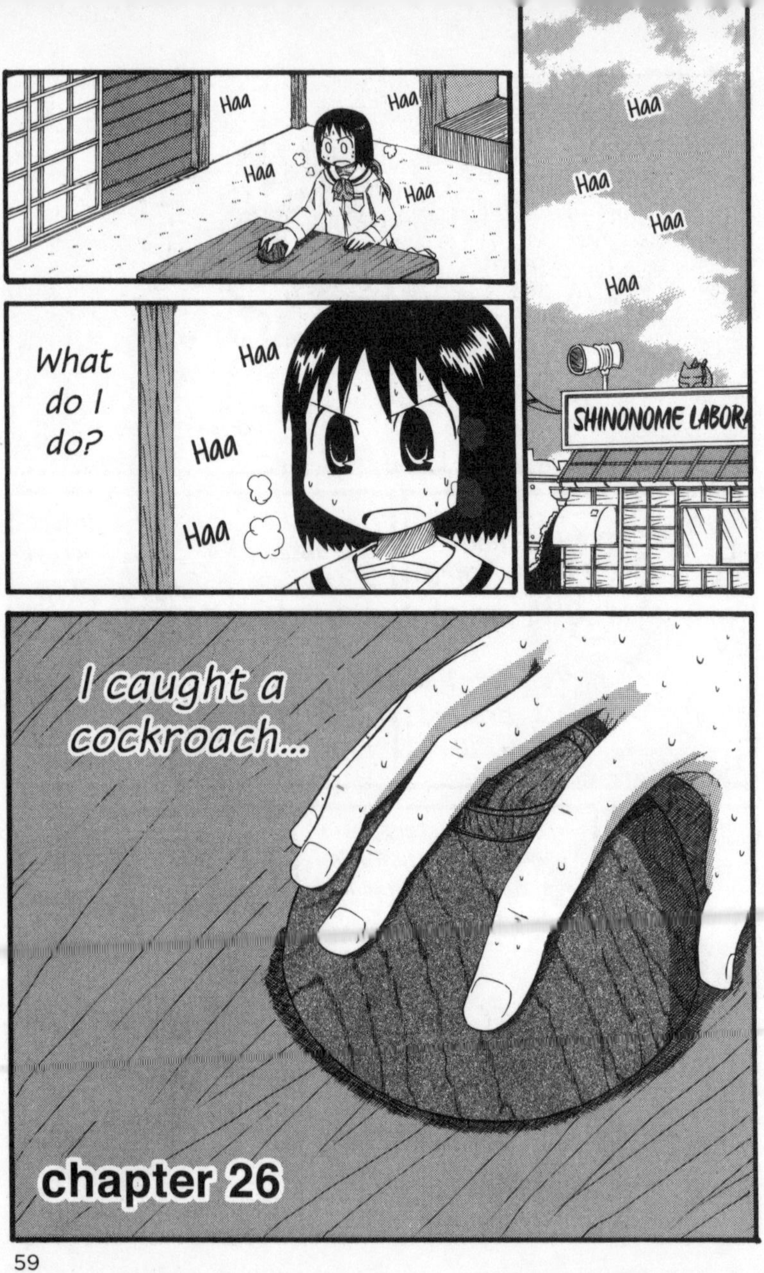
Haa
Haa
Haa
Haa
SHINONOME LABORA
Haa
Haa
Haa
Haa
What do I do?
Haa
Haa
Haa
I caught a cockroach...
chapter 26

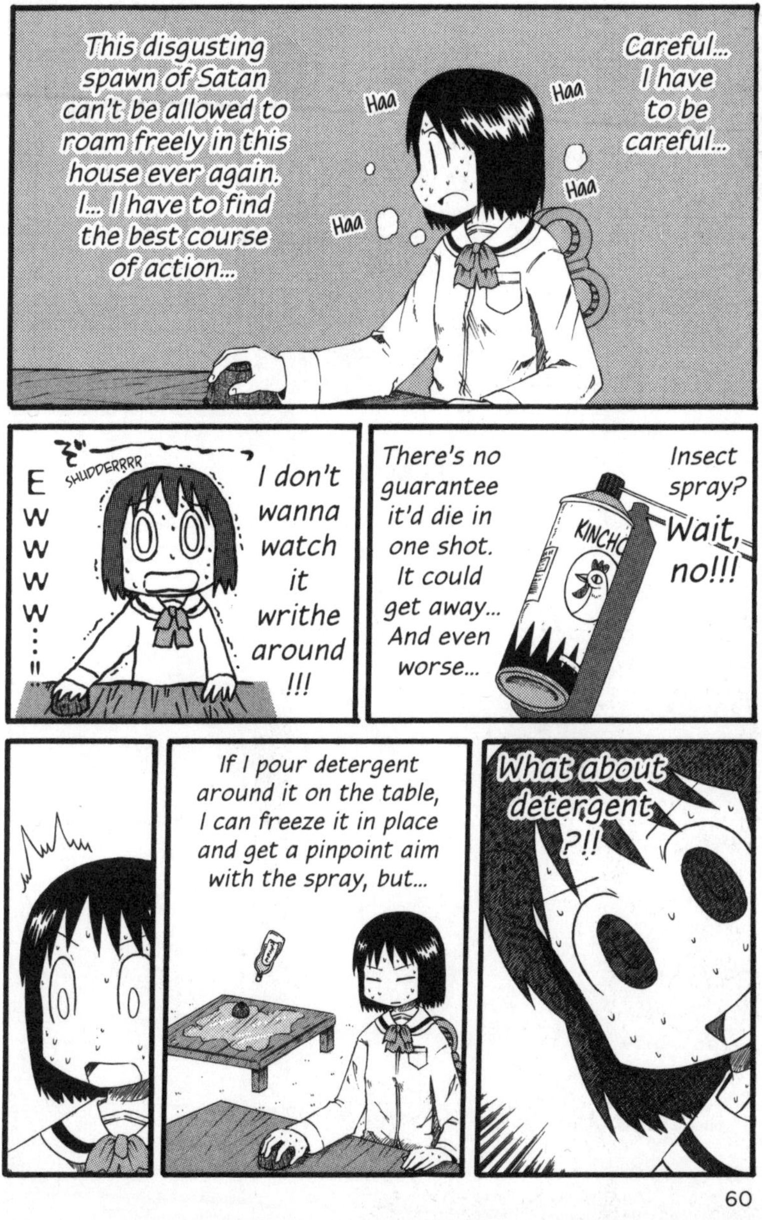
Careful... I have to be careful...
Haa
Haa
Haa
Haa
This disgusting spawn of Satan can't be allowed to roam freely in this house ever again. I... I have to find the best course of action...
Insect spray?
Wait, no!!!
KINCHO
There's no guarantee it'd die in one shot. It could get away... And even worse...
SHUDDERRRR
I don't wanna watch it writhe around!!!
Ewwww...!!
What about detergent?!!
If I pour detergent around it on the table, I can freeze it in place and get a pinpoint aim with the spray, but...

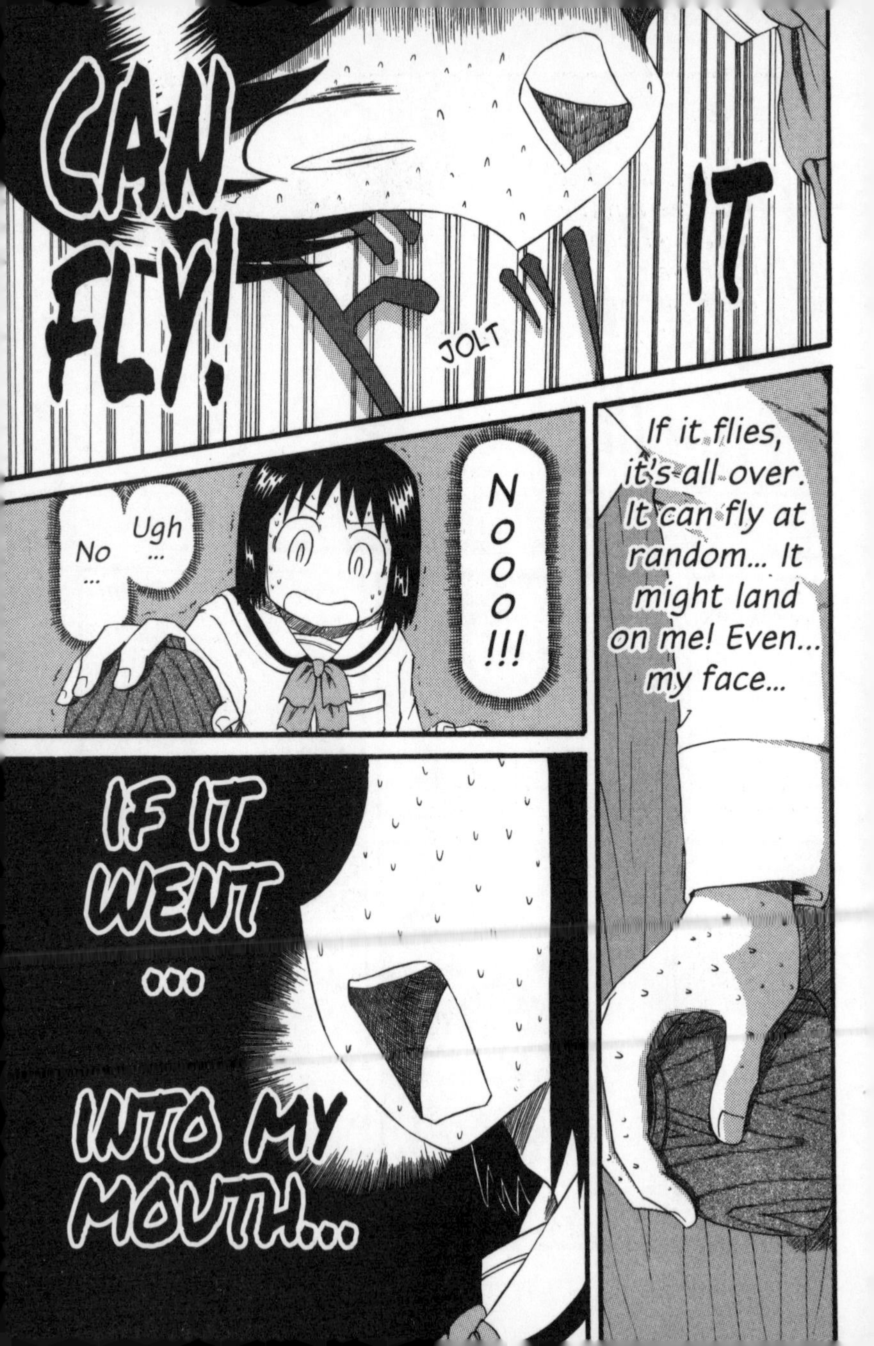
IT
JOLT
CAN FLY!
If it flies, it's all over. It can fly at random... It might land on me! Even... my face...
NOOOO!!!
Ugh ...
No ...
IF IT WENT ...
INTO MY MOUTH...

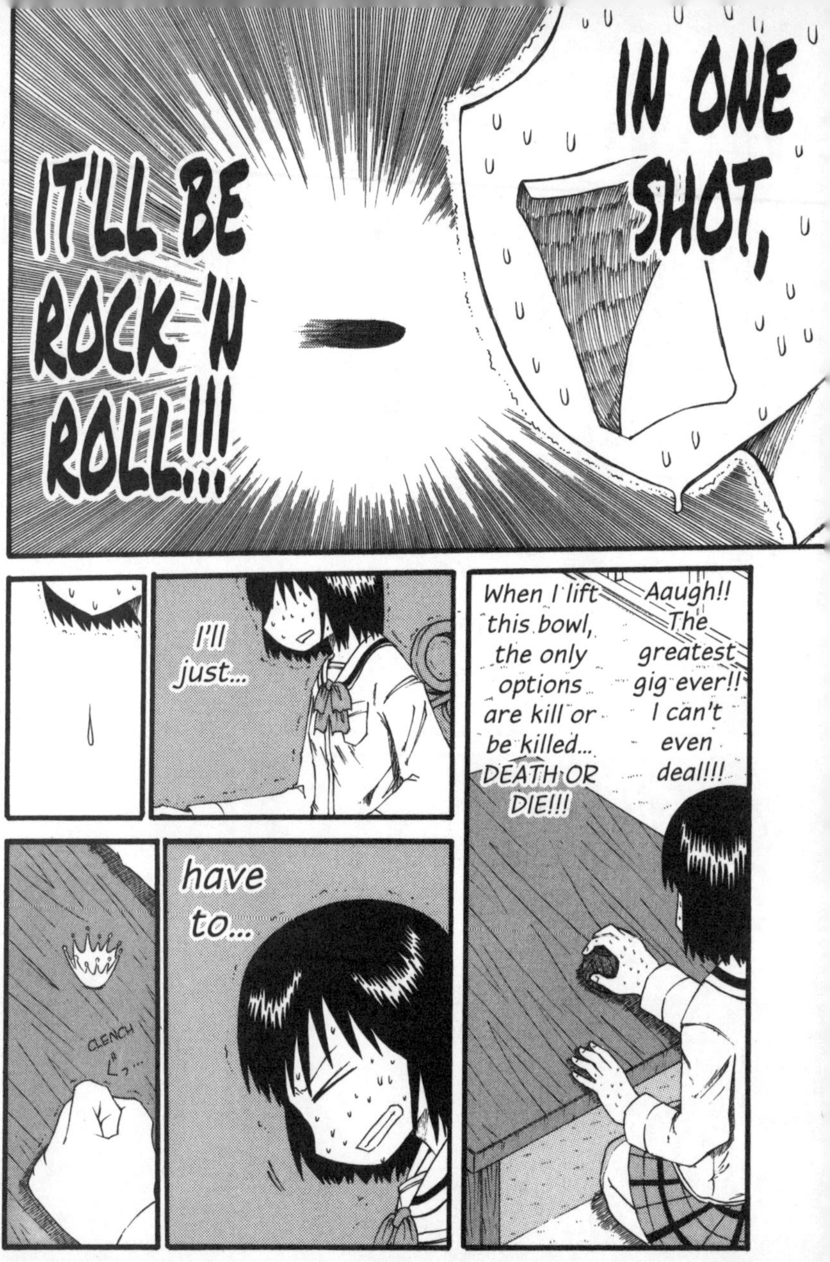
IN ONE SHOT,
IT'LL BE ROCK 'N ROLL!!!
Aaugh!! The greatest gig ever!! I can't even deal!!!
When I lift this bowl, the only options are kill or be killed... DEATH OR DIE!!!
I'll just...
have to...
CLENCH

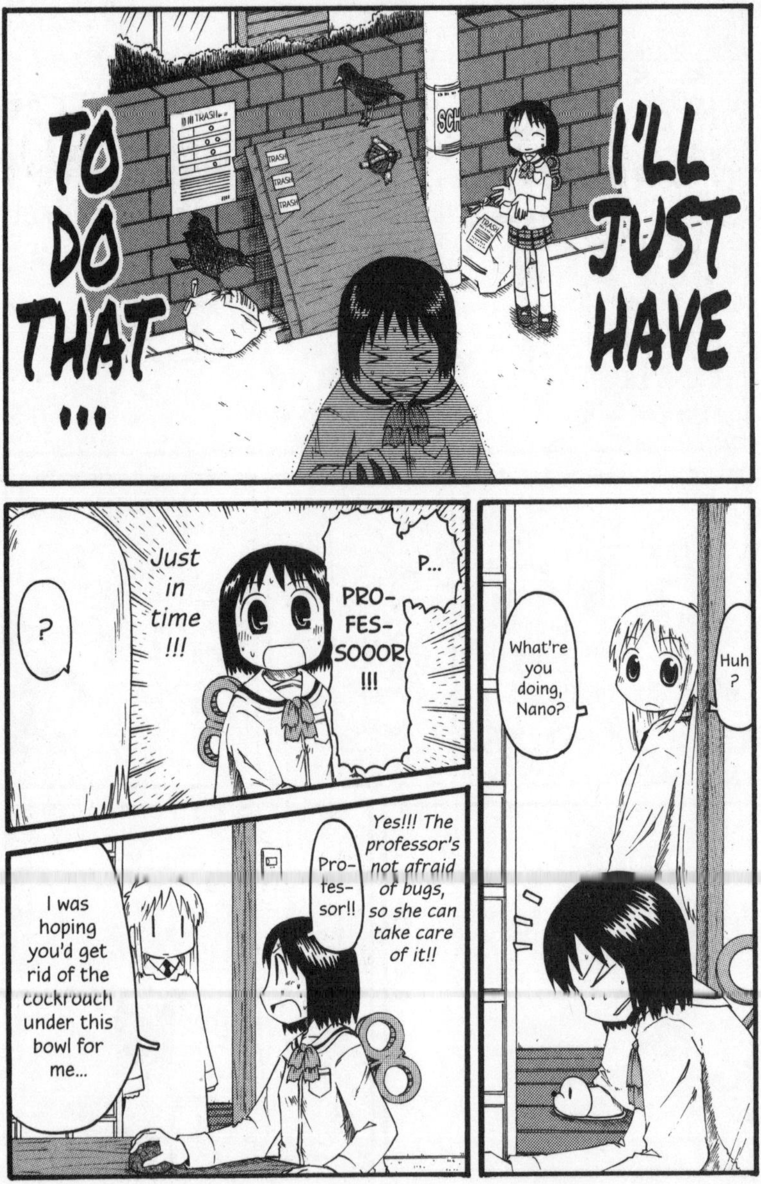
I'LL JUST HAVE
TO DO THAT...
Huh?
What're you doing, Nano?
P... PRO-FES-SOOOR!!!
Just in time!!!
?
Yes!!! The professor's not afraid of bugs, so she can take care of it!!
Pro-fes-sor!!
I was hoping you'd get rid of the cockroach under this bowl for me...

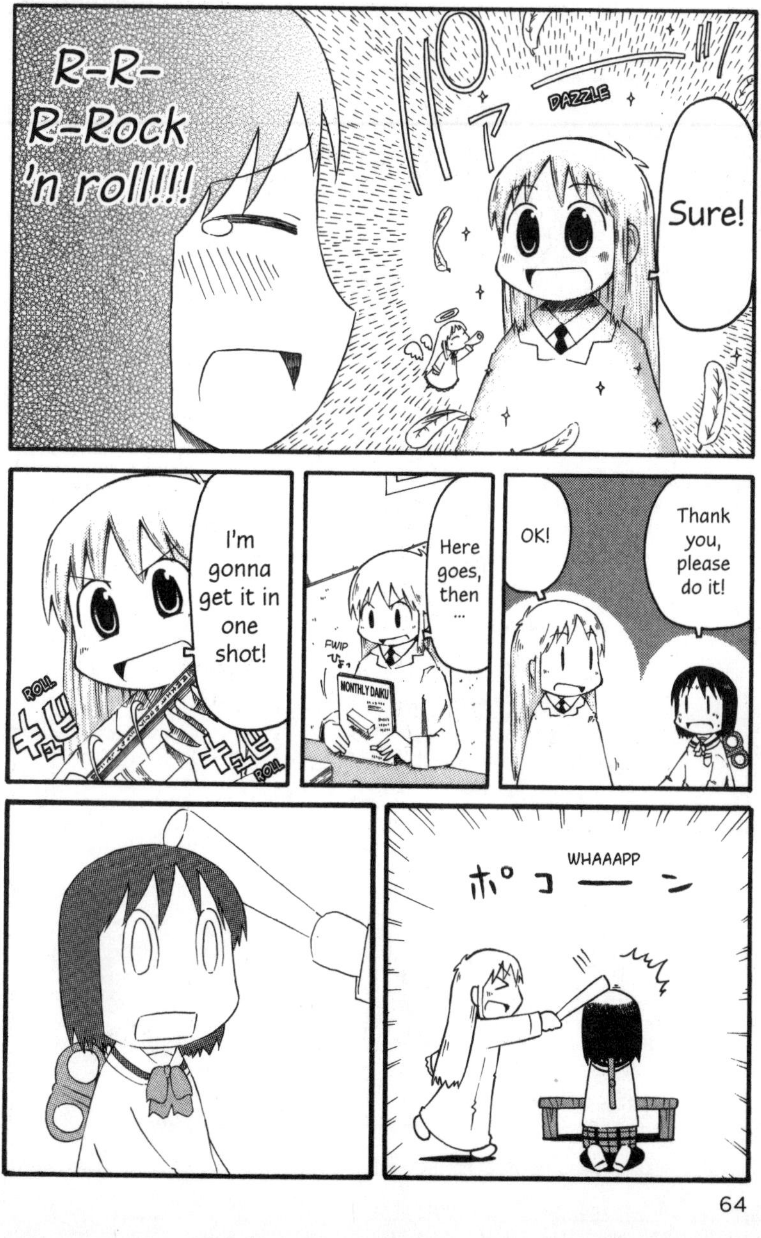
Sure!
DAZZLE
R-R-R-Rock 'n roll!!!
Thank you, please do it!
OK!
Here goes, then ...
FWIP
I'm gonna get it in one shot!
ROLL
ROLL
WHAAAPP

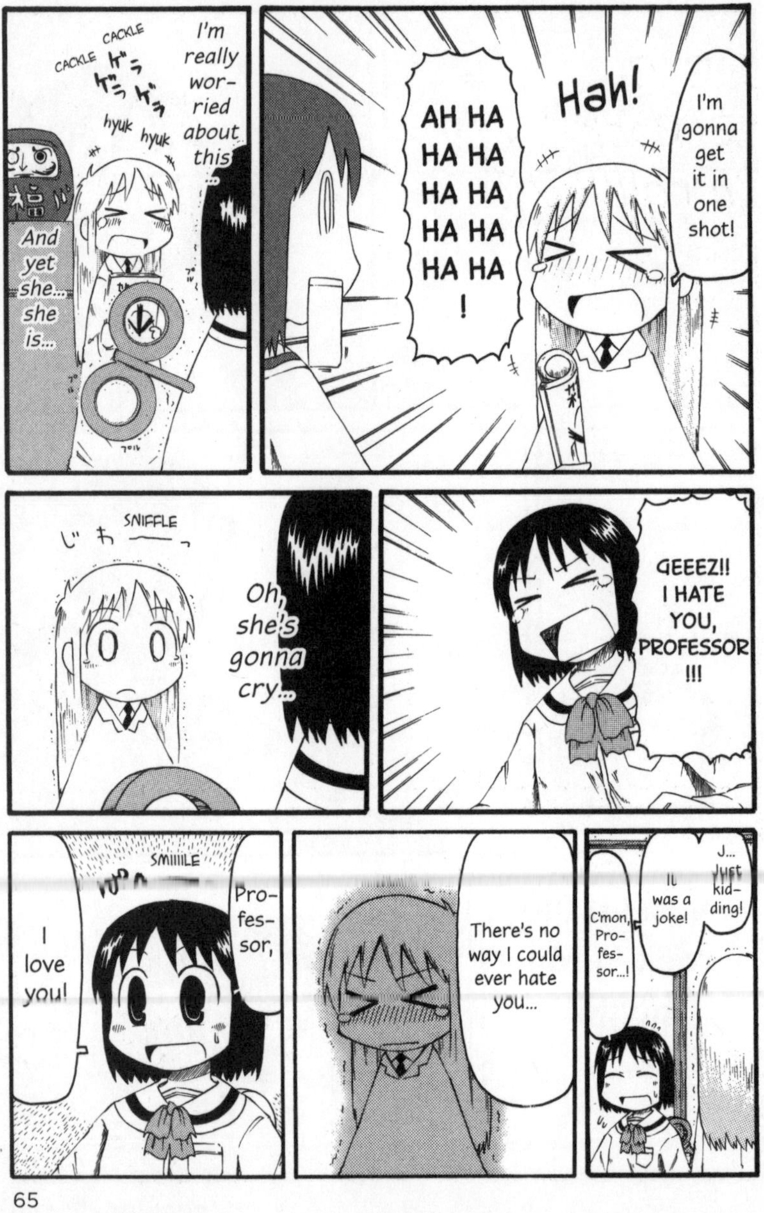
Hah!
I'm gonna get it in one shot!
AH HA HA HA HA HA HA HA HA HA!
CACKLE
CACKLE
I'm really wor-ried about this…
hyuk
hyuk
And yet she... she is...
GEEEZ!! I HATE YOU, PROFESSOR!!!
SNIFFLE
Oh, she's gonna cry...
J... Just kid-ding!
It was a joke!
C'mon, Pro-fes-sor...!
There's no way I could ever hate you...
SMIIIILE
Pro-fes-sor,
I love you!

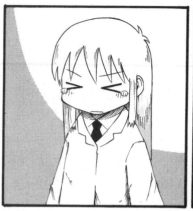

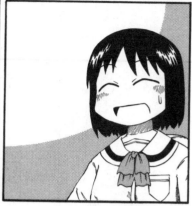

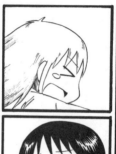

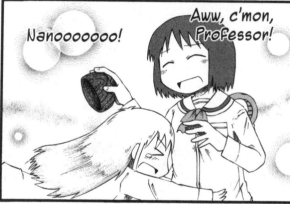

Nanoooooooo!

Aww, c'mon, Professor!

Now let the rock 'n roll begin.

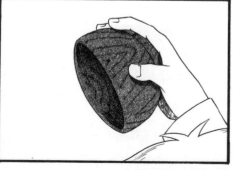

chapter 26: end

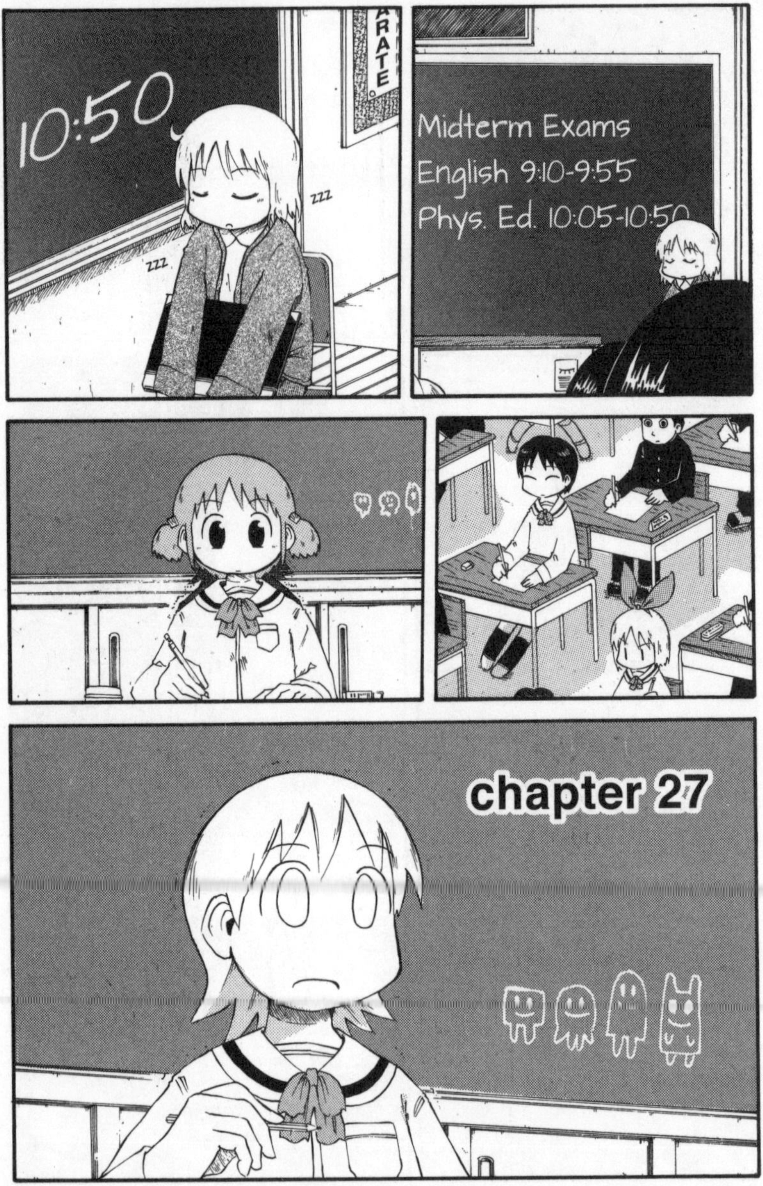
Midterm Exams
English 9:10-9:55
Phys. Ed. 10:05-10:50
10:50
zzz
zzz
zzz
chapter 27

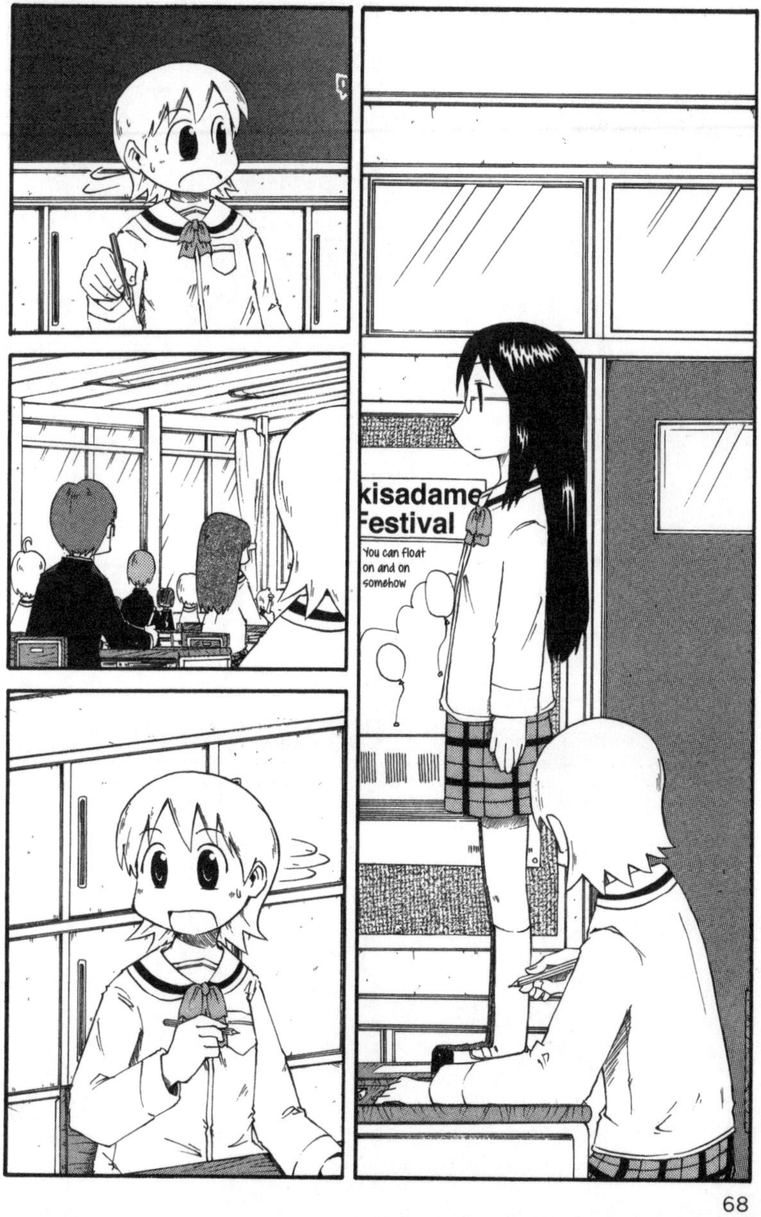
kisadame
Festival
You can float on and on somehow

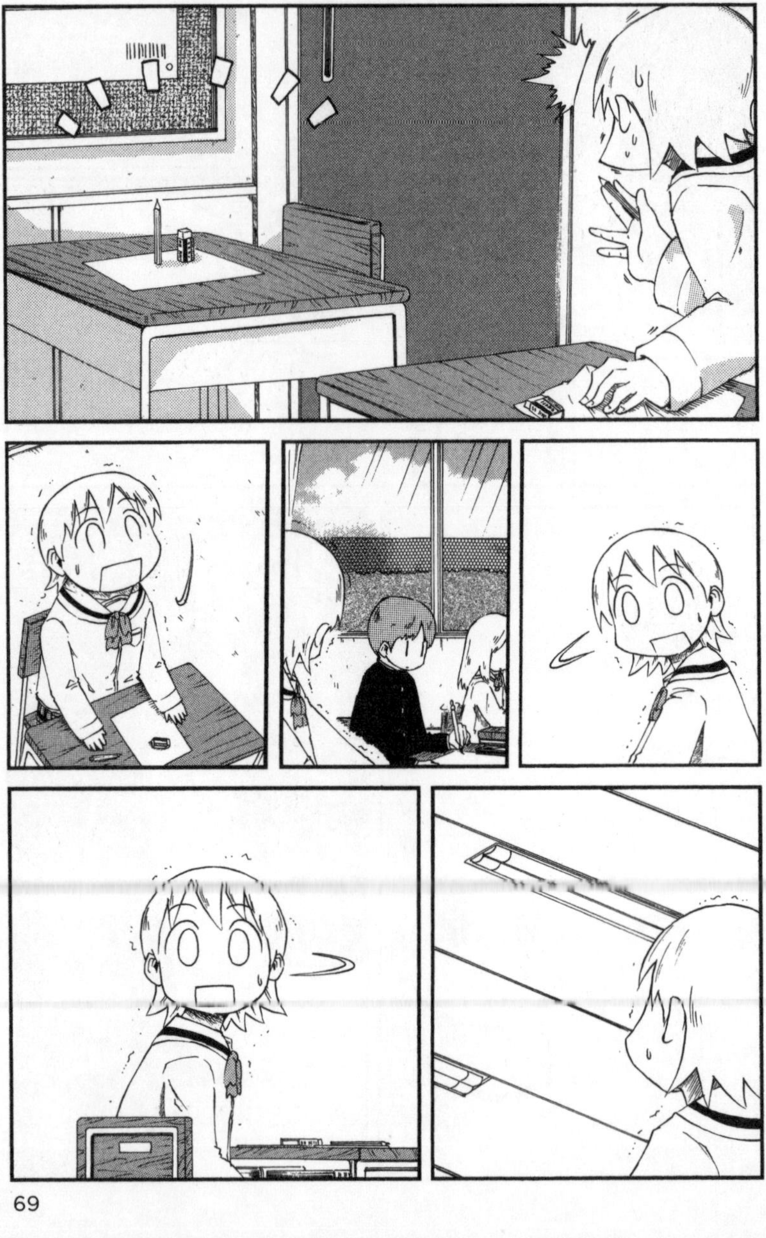

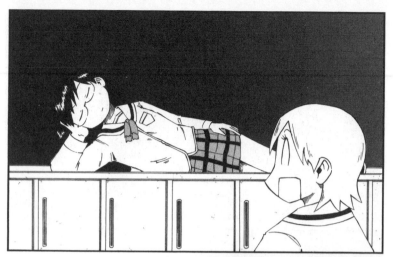

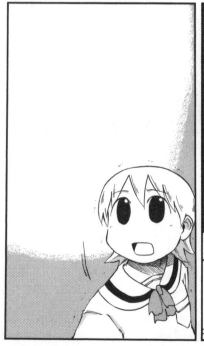

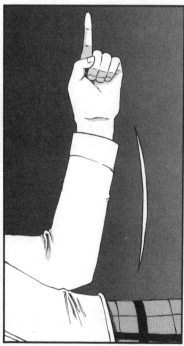

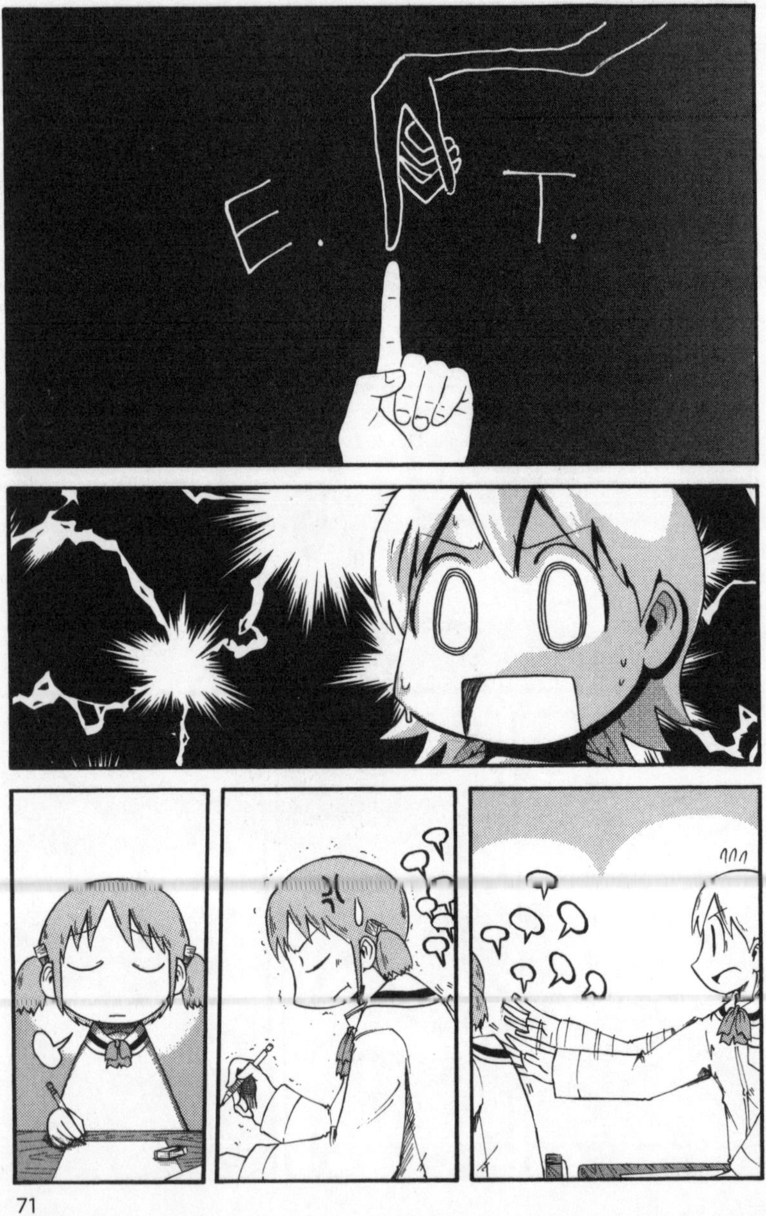
E. T.

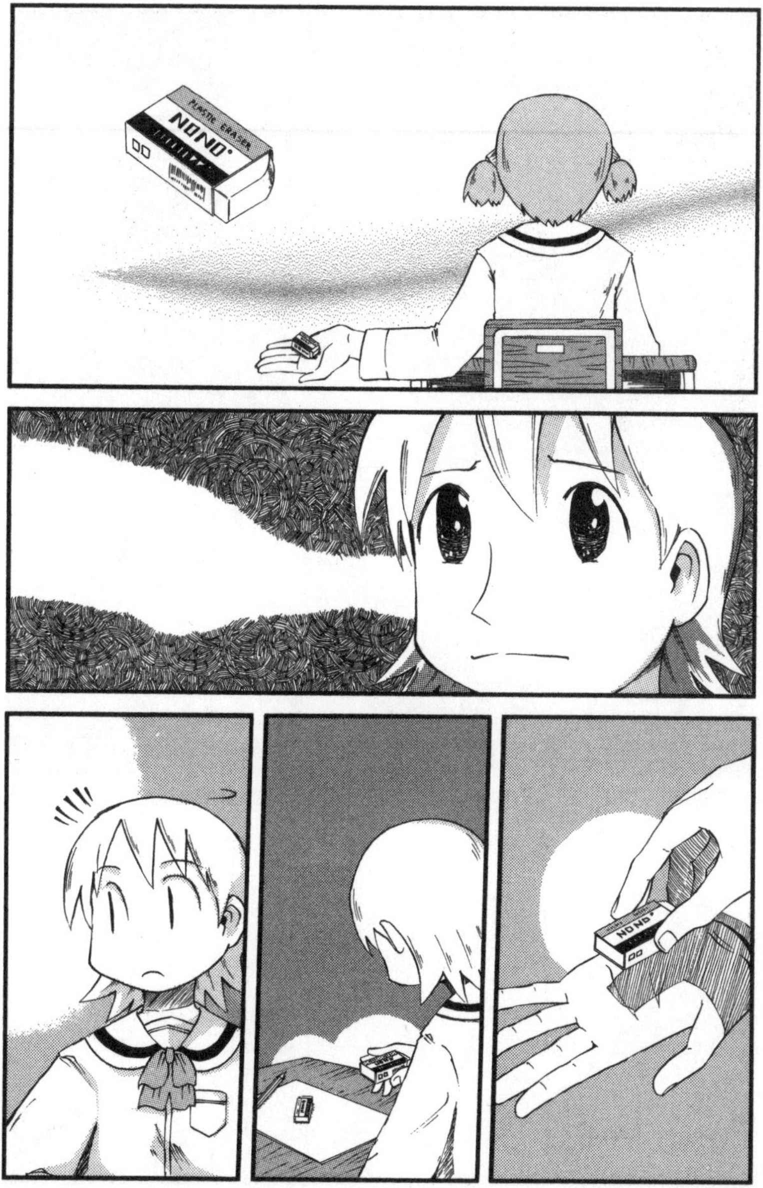
PLASTIC ERASER
NONO

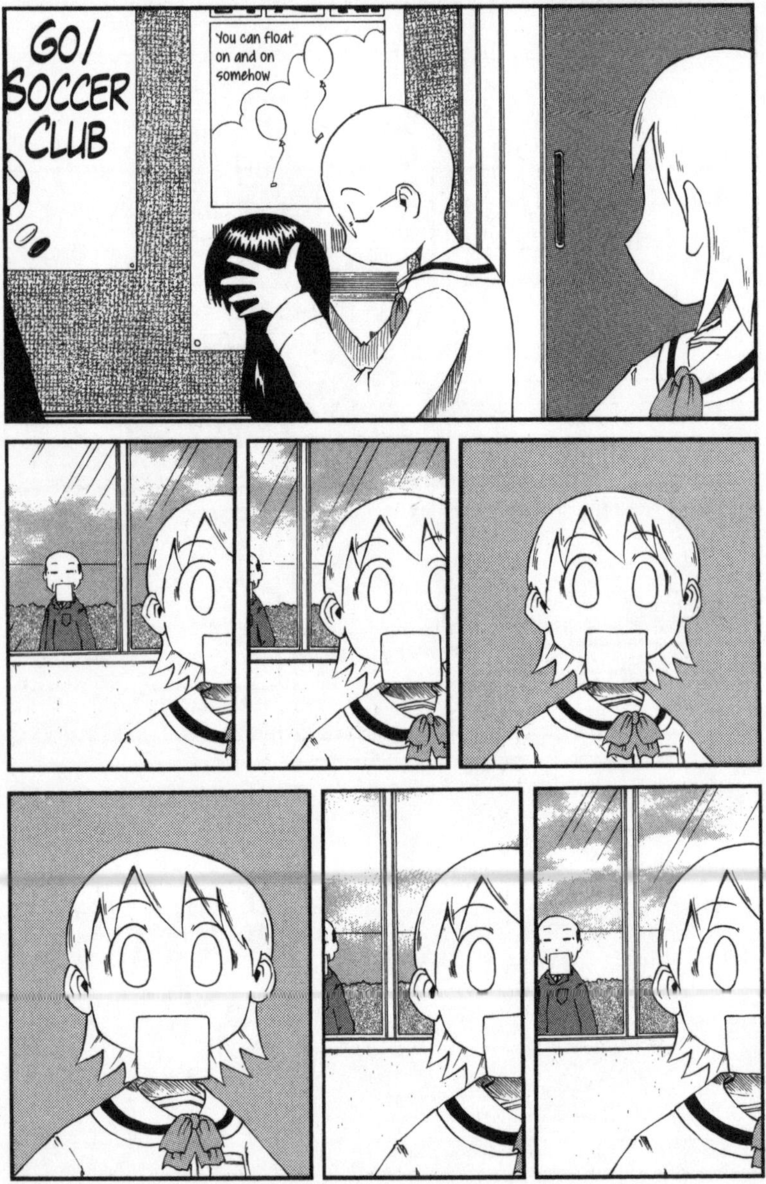
You can float on and on somehow
GO! SOCCER CLUB

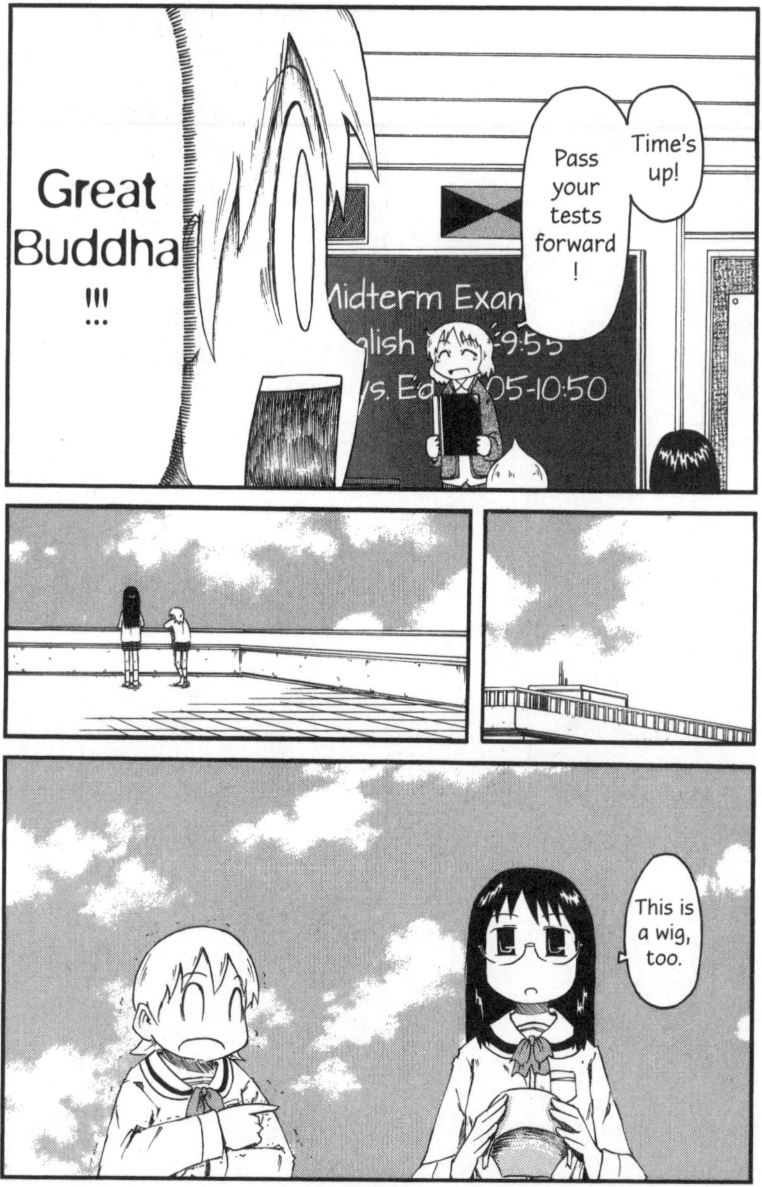

Time's up!
Pass your tests forward!
Great Buddha!!!...
This is a wig, too.

chapter 27: end

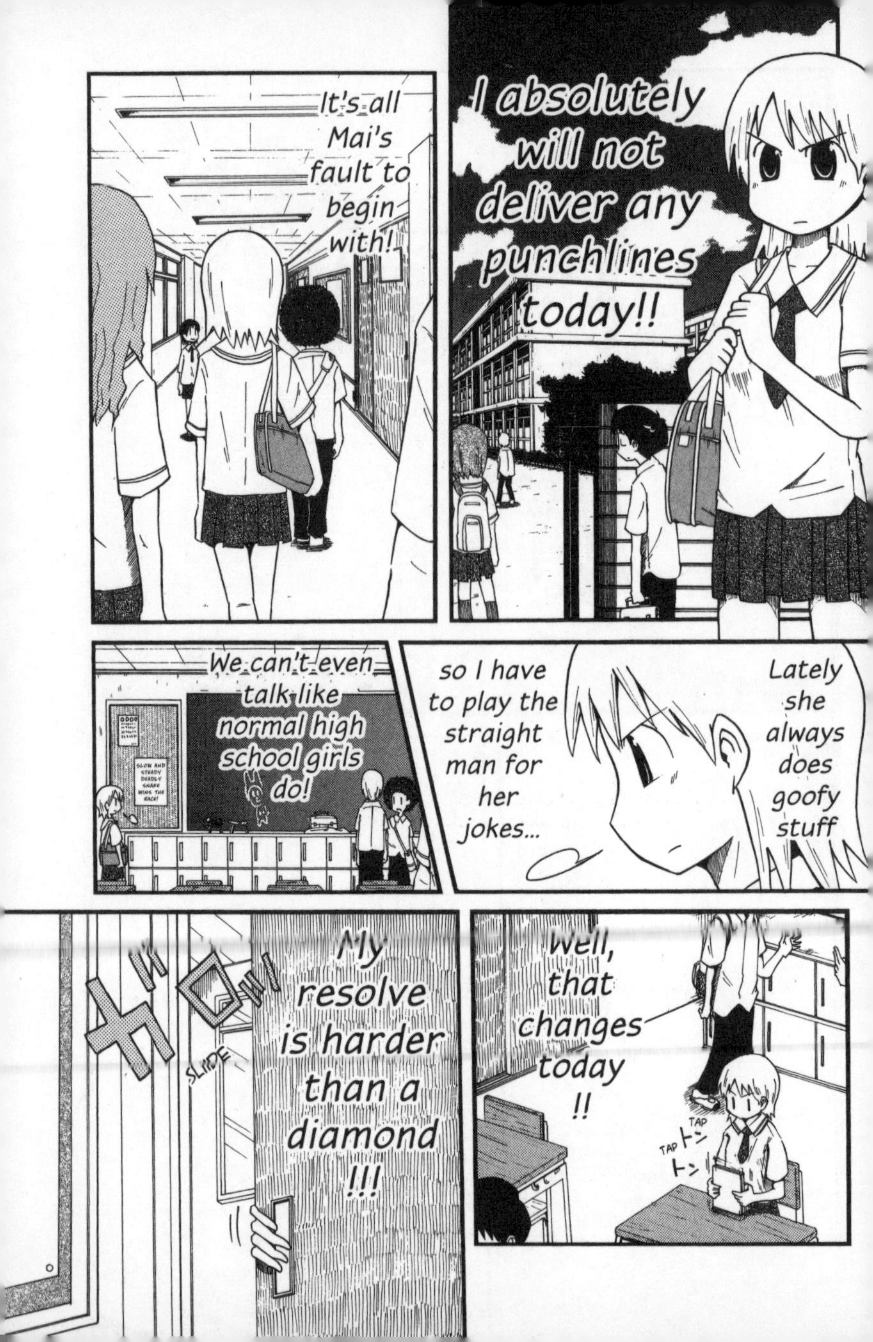
I absolutely will not deliver any punchlines today!!
It's all Mai's fault to begin with!
Lately she always does goofy stuff
so I have to play the straight man for her jokes...
We can't even talk like normal high school girls do!
SLOW AND STEADY DEADLY SNAKE WINS THE RACE!
Well, that changes today !!
TAP トン
TAP トン
SLIDE
My resolve is harder than a diamond !!!

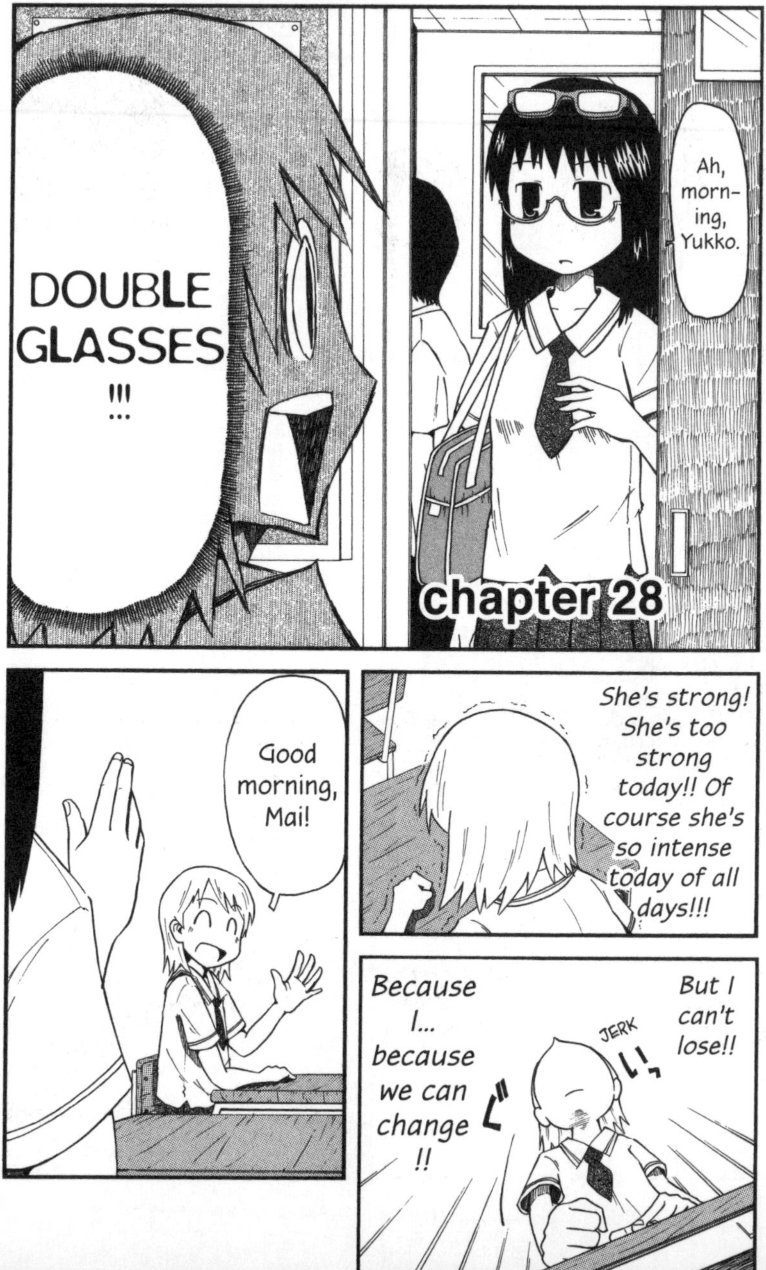

Ah, morning, Yukko.
chapter 28
DOUBLE GLASSES !!!...
She's strong! She's too strong today!! Of course she's so intense today of all days!!!
But I can't lose!!
JERK
Because I... because we can change !!
Good morning, Mai!

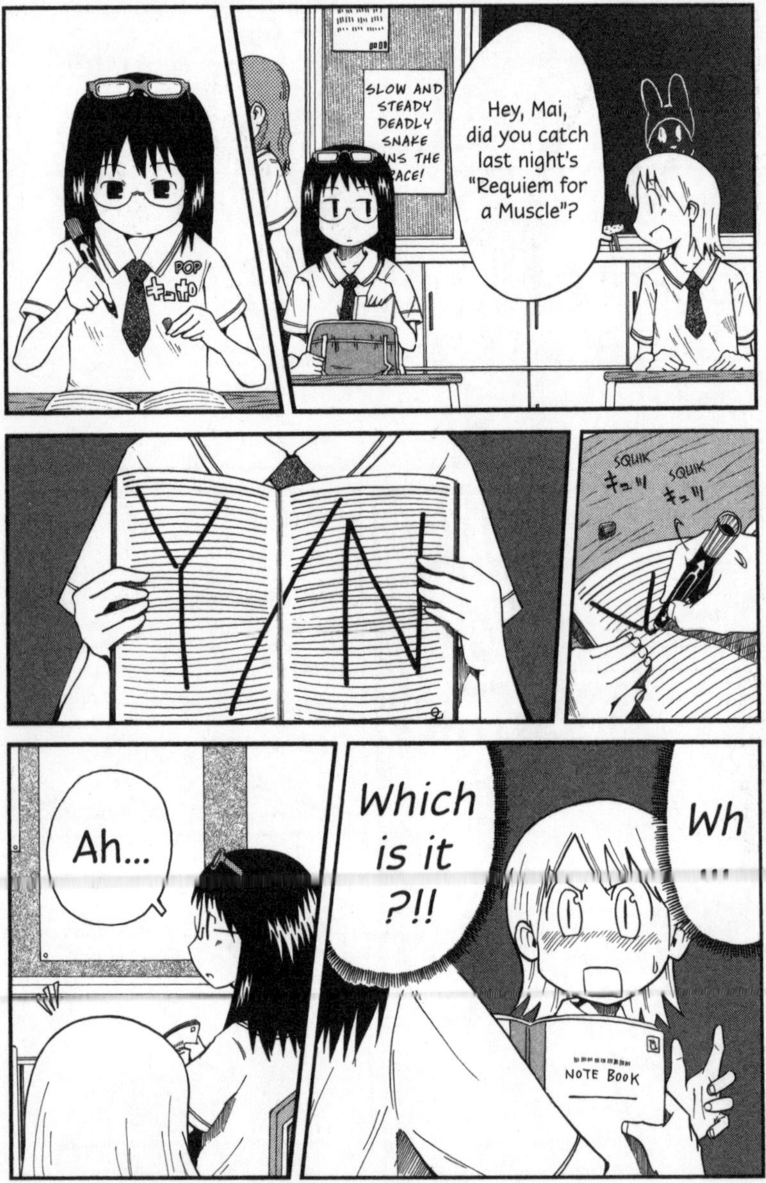
Hey, Mai, did you catch last night's "Requiem for a Muscle"?
SLOW AND
STEADY
DEADLY
SNAKE
NS THE
ACE!
SQUIK
キュッ
SQUIK
キュッ
Y
N
Wh...
Which is it?!!
NOTE BOOK
Ah...

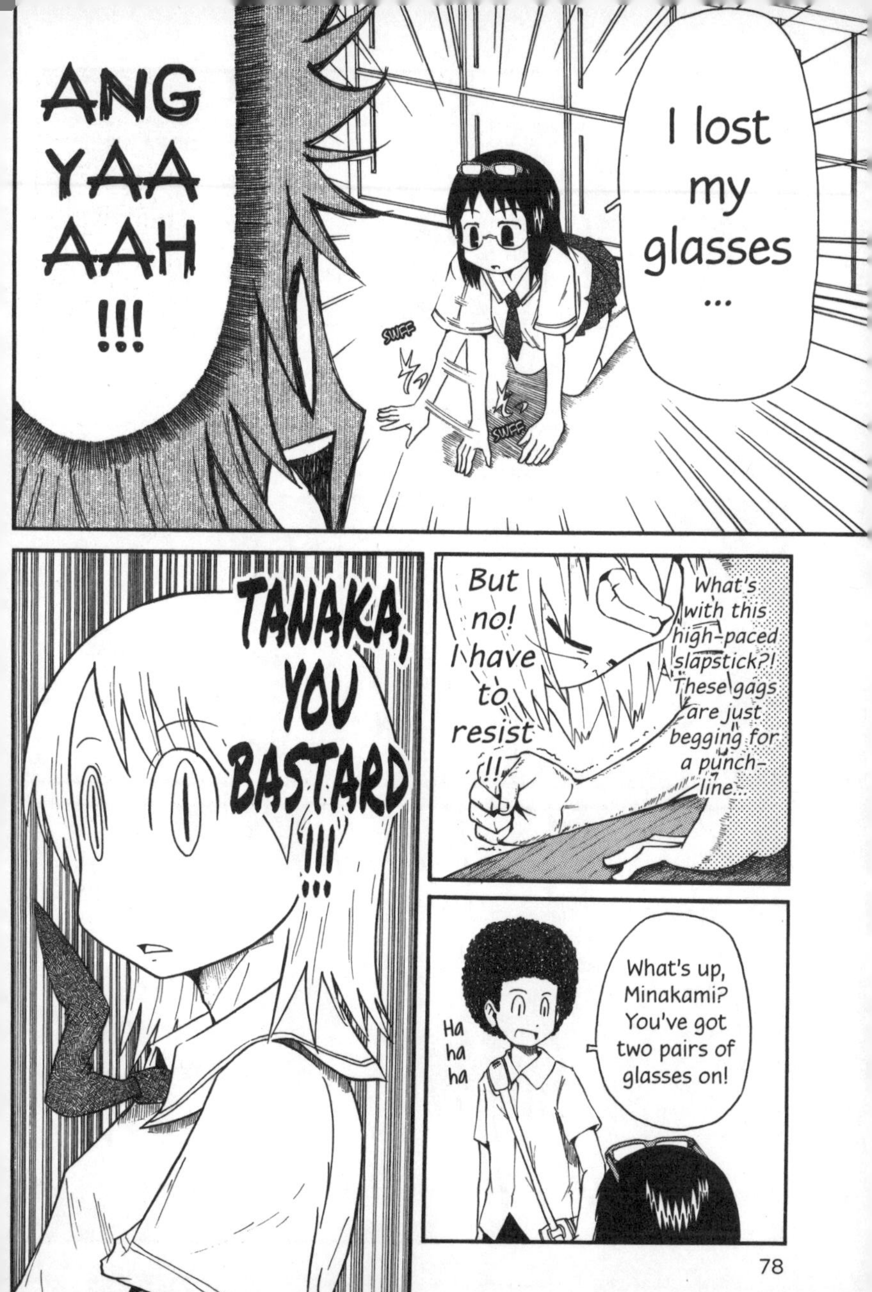
I lost my glasses ...
ANG YAA AAH !!!
SWFF
SWFF
What's with this high-paced slapstick?! These gags are just begging for a punch-line...
But no! I have to resist !!
What's up, Minakami? You've got two pairs of glasses on!
Ha ha ha
TANAKA, YOU BASTARD !!!

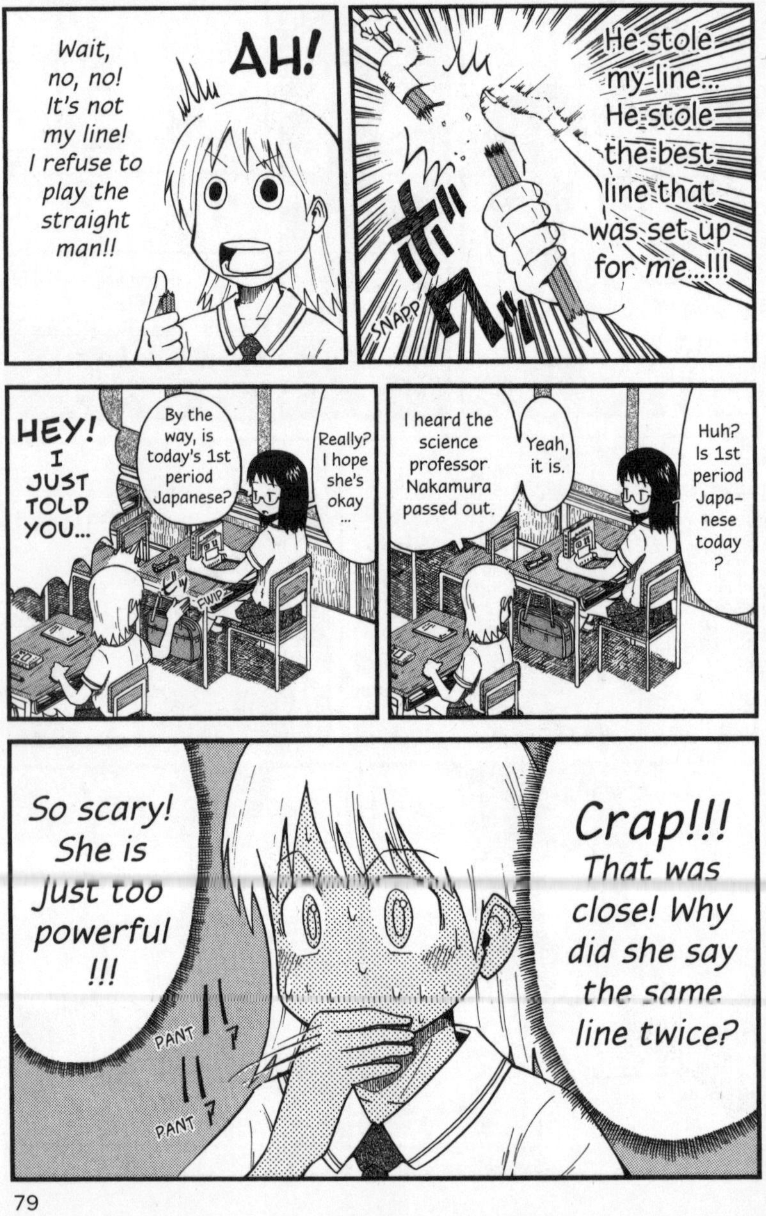
He stole my line... He stole the best line that was set up for me...!!!
SNAPP
AH!
Wait, no, no! It's not my line! I refuse to play the straight man!!
Huh? Is 1st period Japanese today?
Yeah, it is.
I heard the science professor Nakamura passed out.
Really? I hope she's okay ...
By the way, is today's 1st period Japanese?
FWIP
HEY! I JUST TOLD YOU...
Crap!!! That was close! Why did she say the same line twice?
So scary! She is just too powerful !!!
PANT
PANT

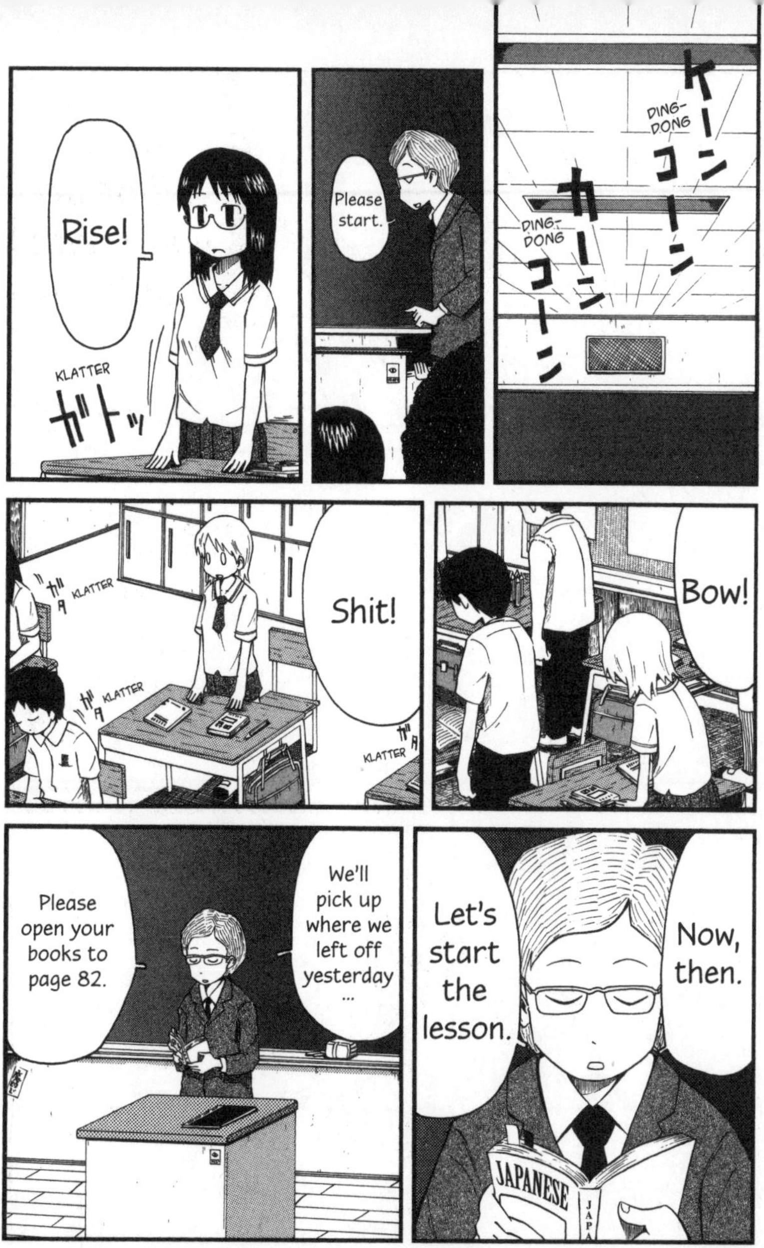

キーンコーン
DING-DONG
カーンコーン
DING-DONG
Please start.
Rise!
ガトッ
KLATTER
Bow!
Shit!
ガタ
KLATTER
ガタ
KLATTER
ガタ
KLATTER
Now, then.
Let's start the lesson.
JAPANESE
We'll pick up where we left off yesterday ...
Please open your books to page 82.

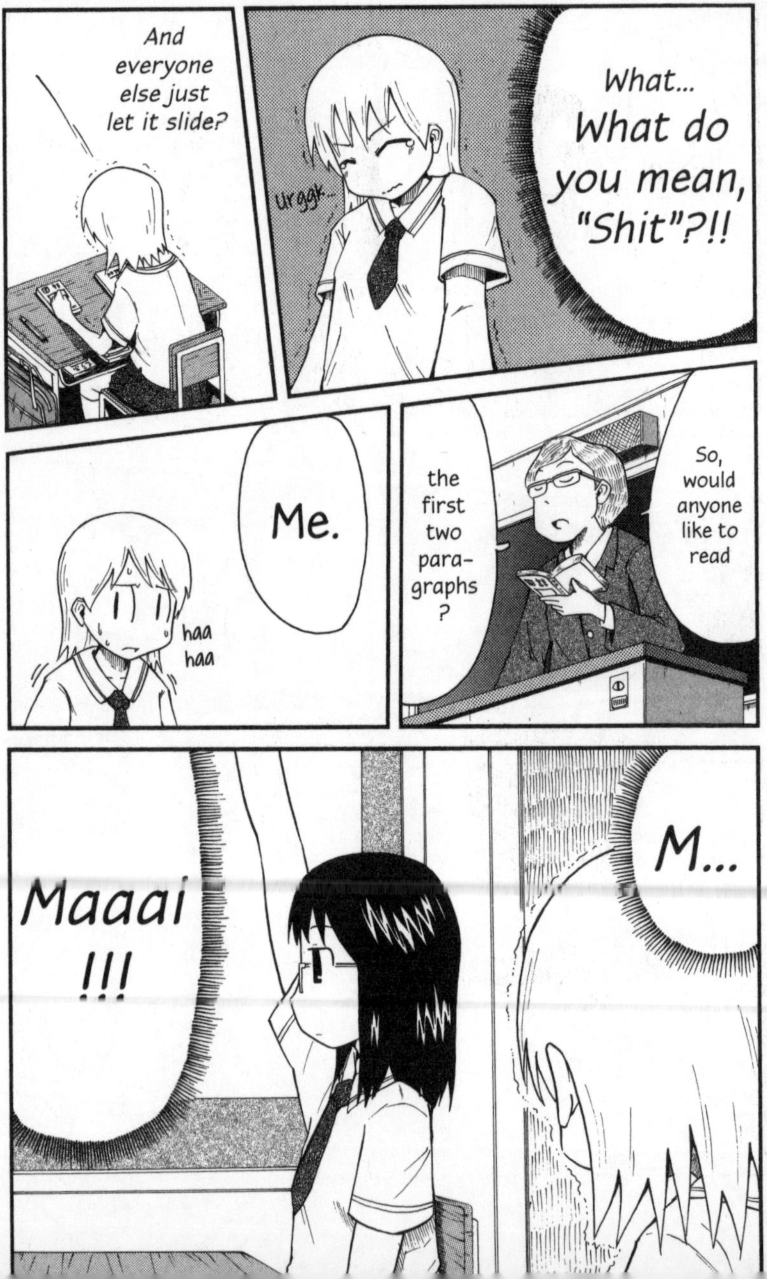
What...
What do you mean, "Shit"?!!
Urggk...
And everyone else just let it slide?
So, would anyone like to read
the first two para-graphs?
Me.
haa haa
M...
Maaai !!!

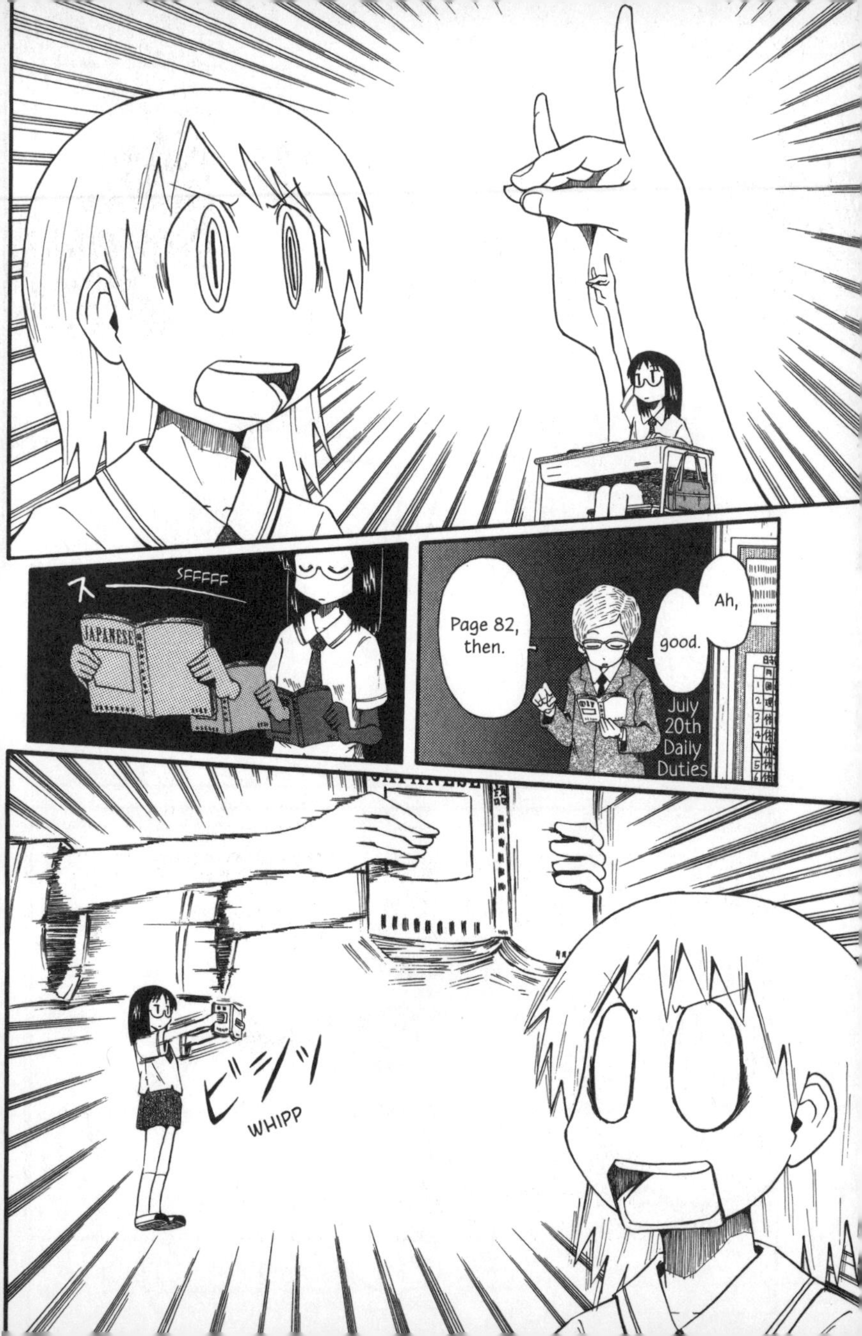
Ah, good.
Page 82, then.
July 20th Daily Duties
ス
SFFFFF
ビシッ
WHIPP

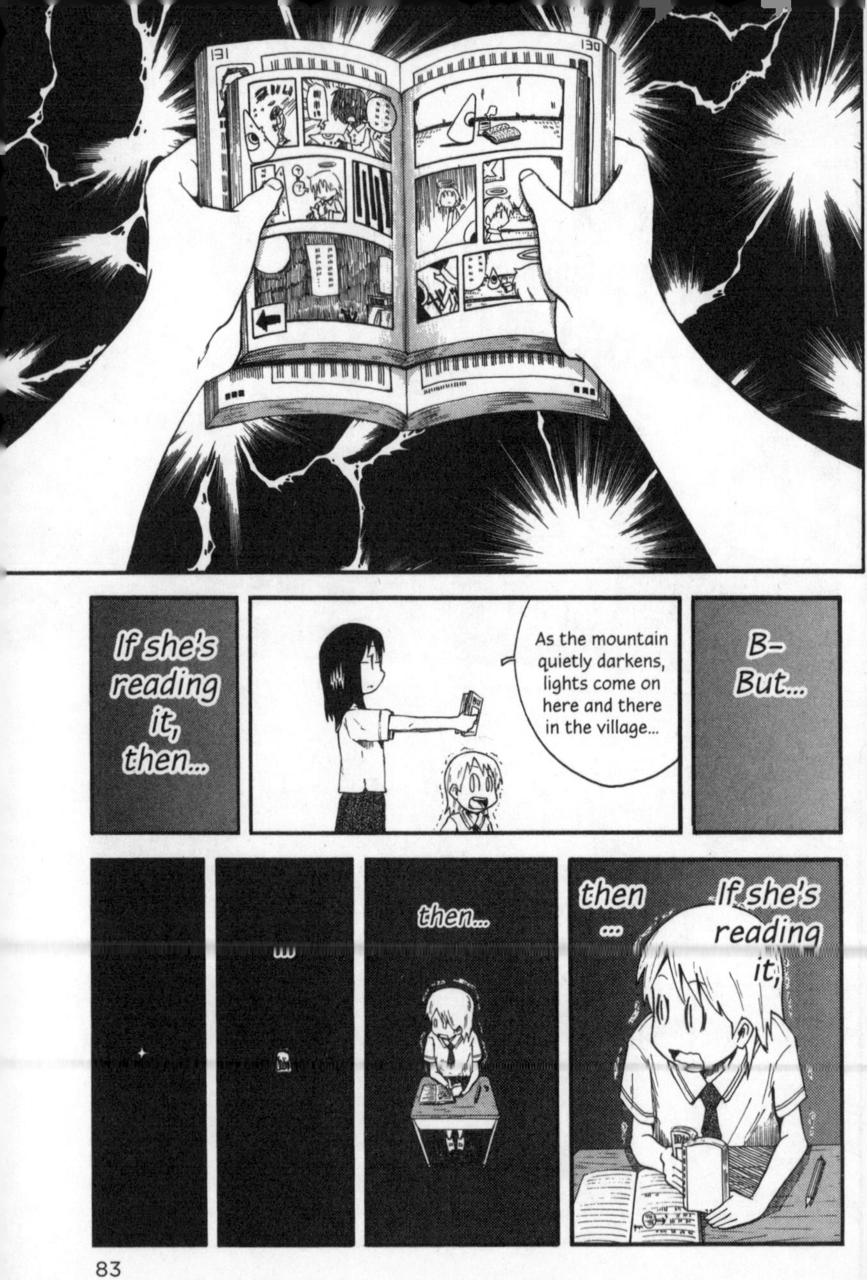
B– But...
As the mountain quietly darkens, lights come on here and there in the village...
If she's reading it, then...
If she's reading it,
then ...
then...

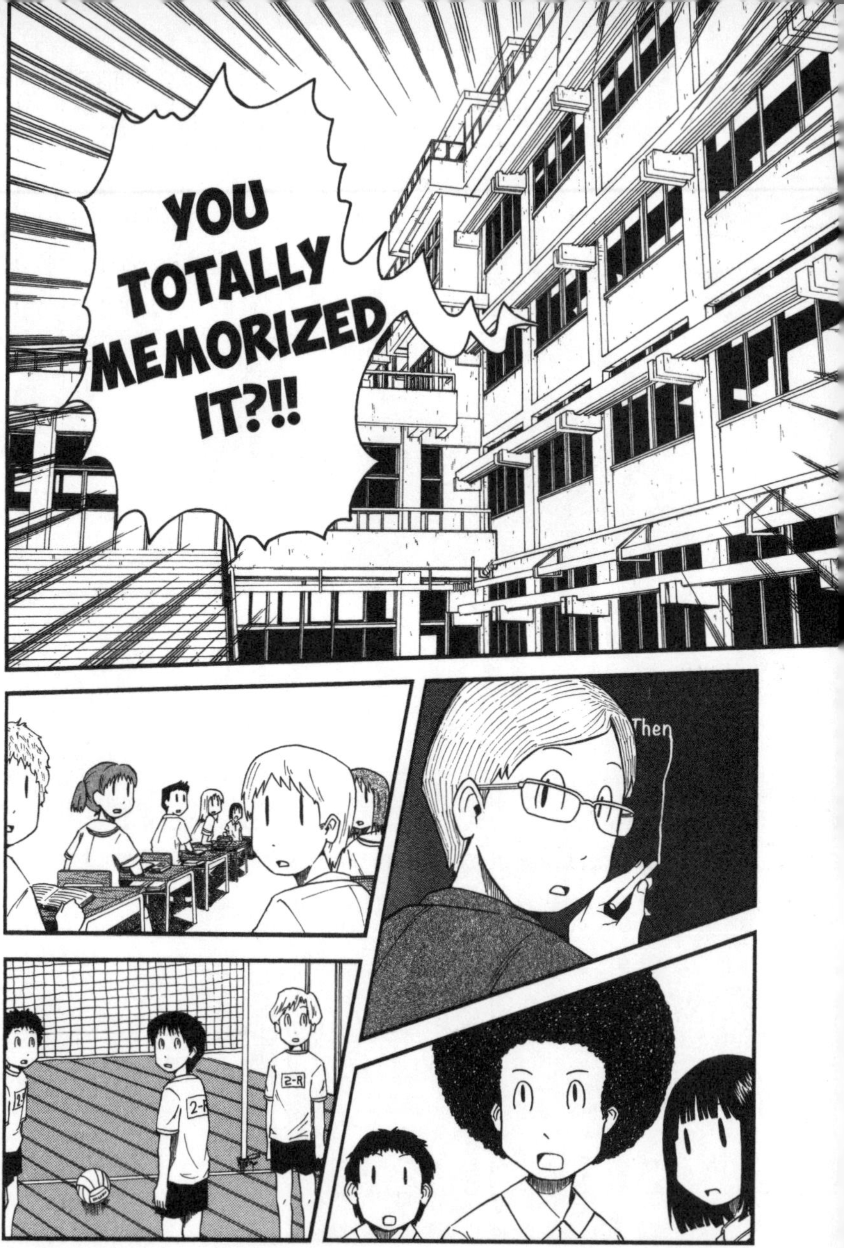
YOU TOTALLY MEMORIZED IT?!!
Then
2-R
2-R

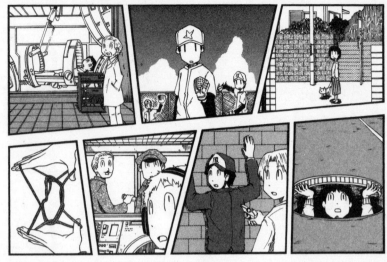

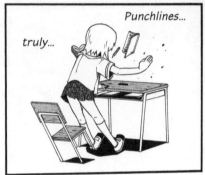

Punchlines...

truly...

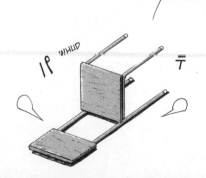

WHUD

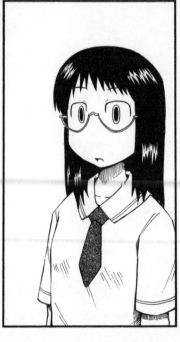

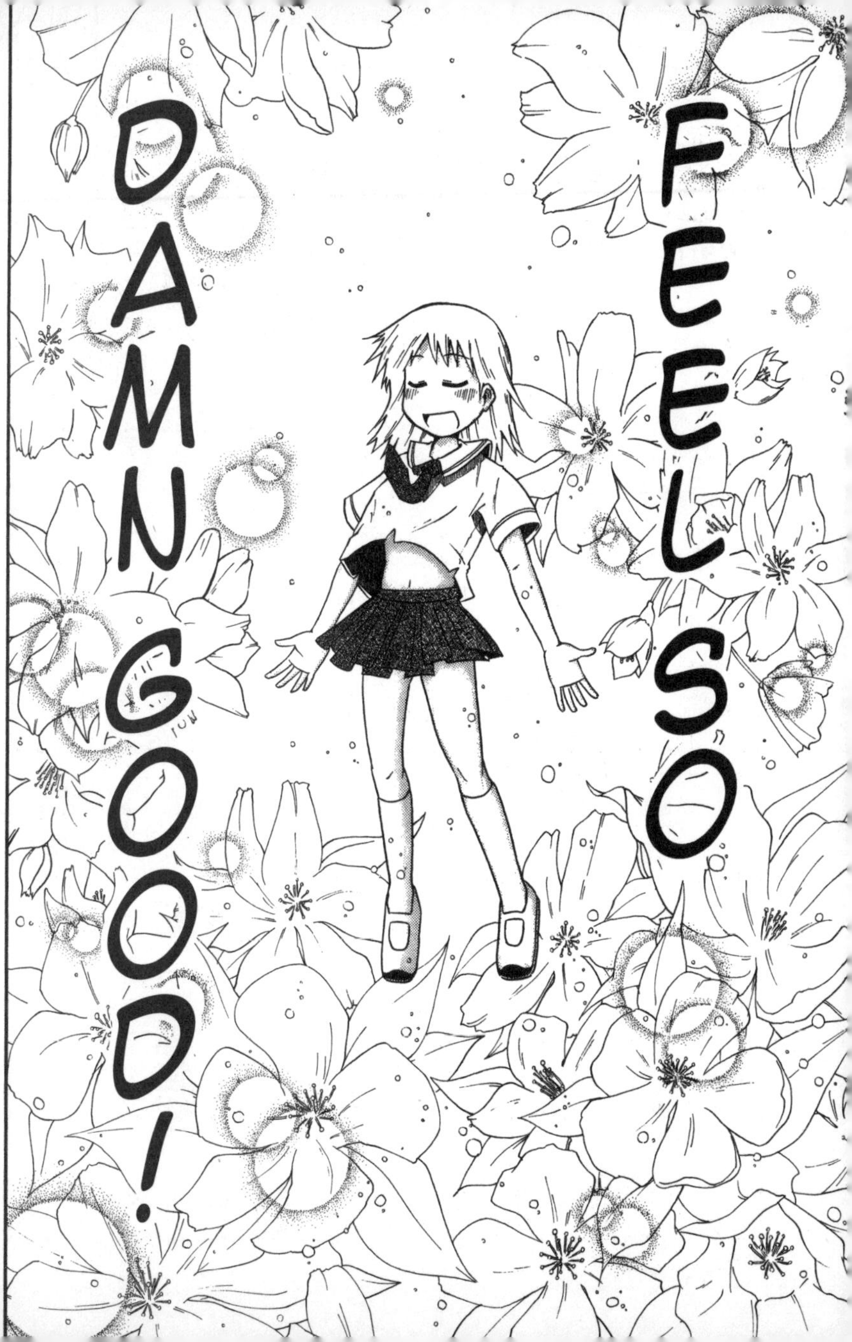
FEEL SO
DAMN GOOD!

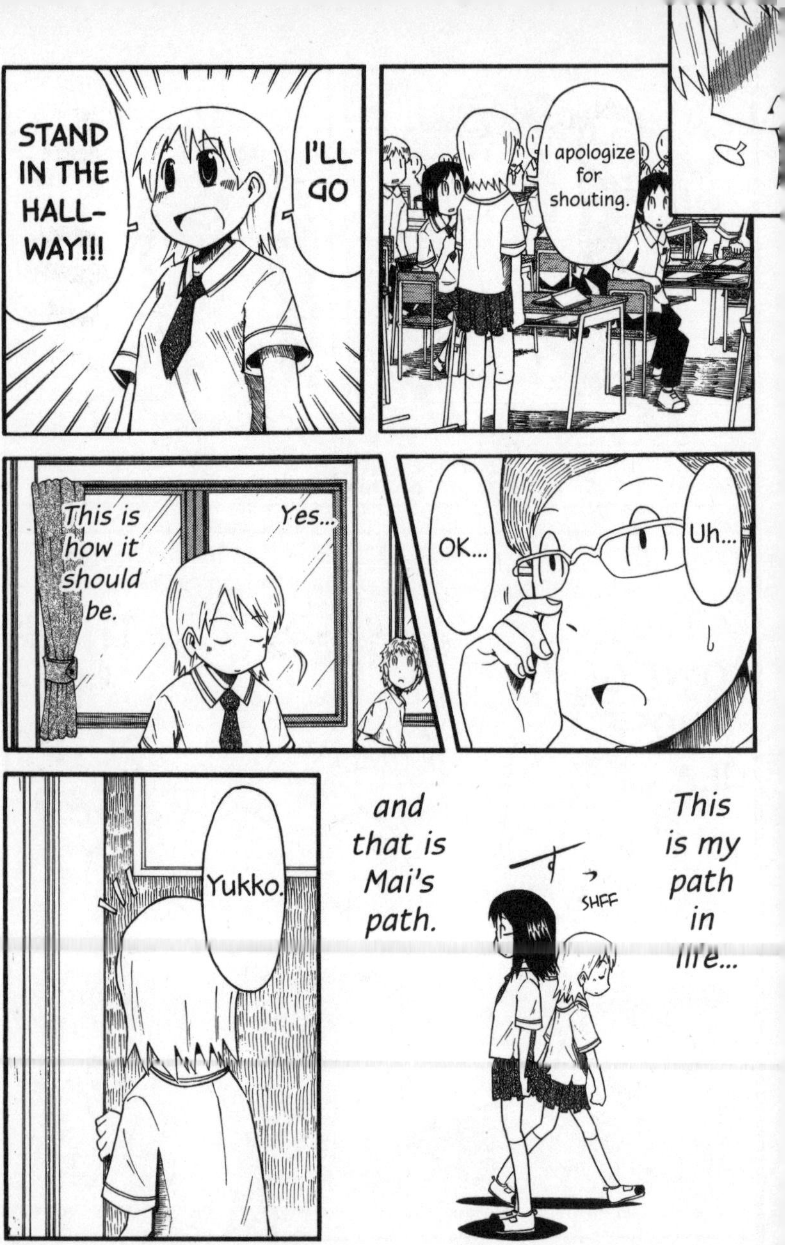
I apologize for shouting.
I'LL GO
STAND IN THE HALL-WAY!!!
Uh...
OK...
Yes...
This is how it should be.
This is my path in life...
SHFF
and that is Mai's path.
Yukko.

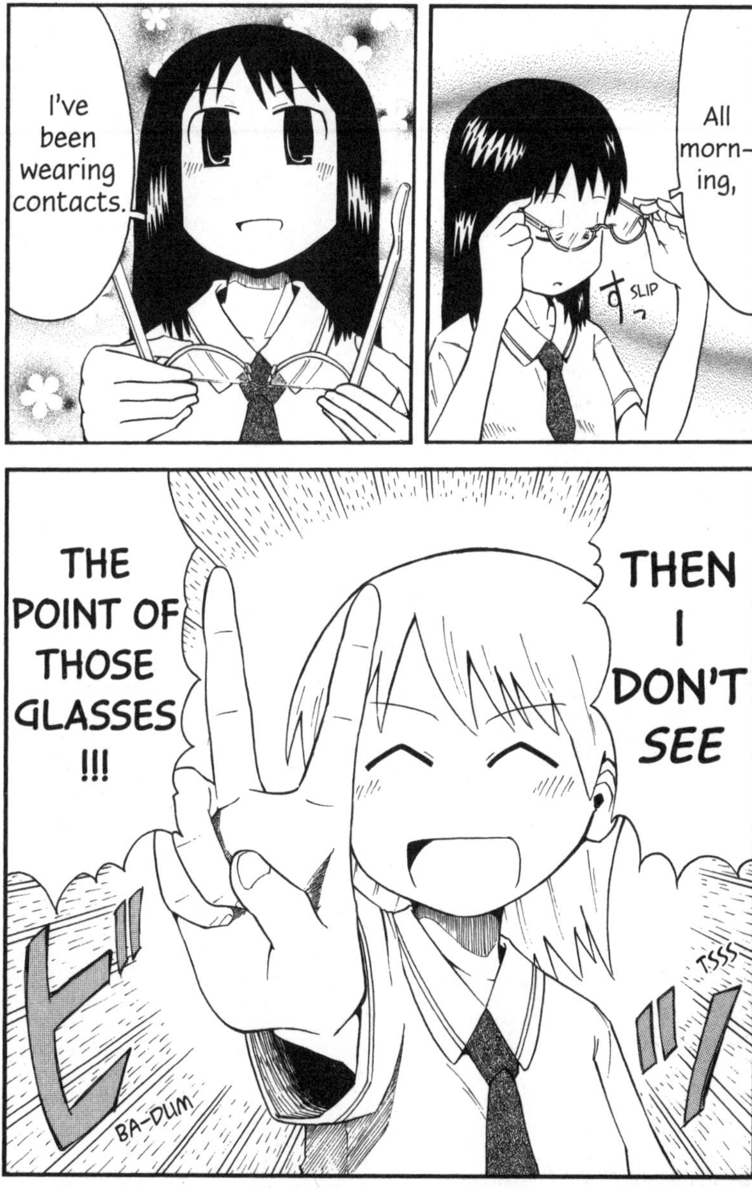
All morning,
す SLIP
I've been wearing contacts.
THEN I DON'T SEE
THE POINT OF THOSE GLASSES !!!
TSSS
BA-DUM

chapter 28: end

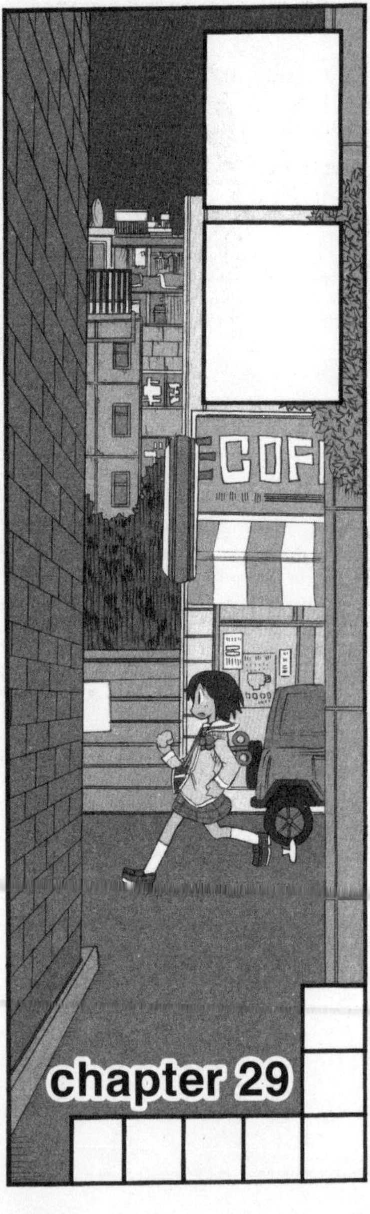
chapter 29

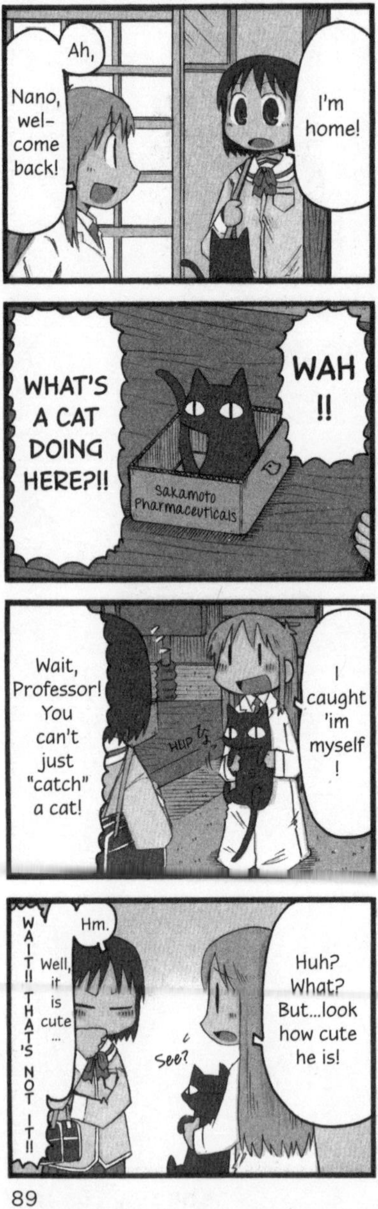
I'm home!
Ah, Nano, wel- come back!
WAH !!
WHAT'S A CAT DOING HERE?!!
Sakamoto Pharmaceuticals
I caught 'im myself !
HUP
Wait, Professor! You can't just "catch" a cat!
Huh? What? But...look how cute he is!
See?
Hm.
Well, it is cute ...
WAIT!! THAT'S NOT IT!!

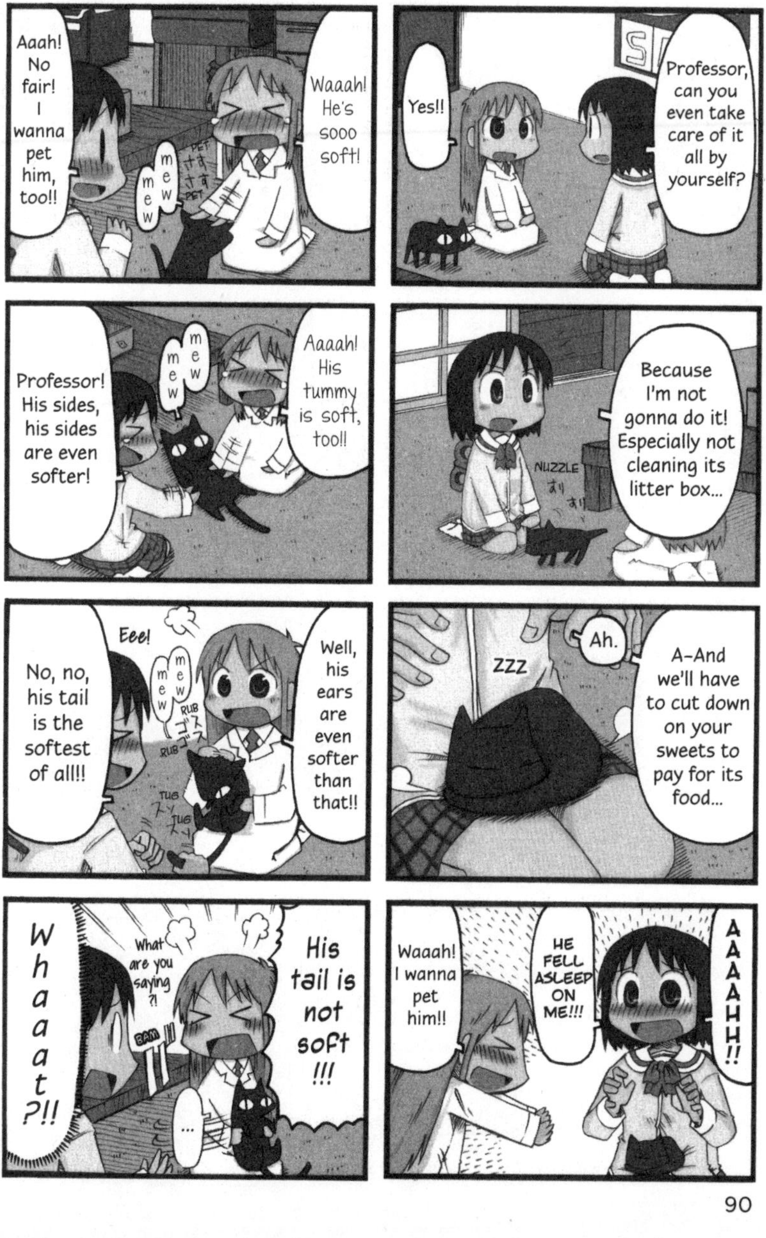
Professor, can you even take care of it all by yourself?
Yes!!
Waaah! He's sooo soft!
PET
PET
mew mew
Aaah! No fair! I wanna pet him, too!!
Because I'm not gonna do it! Especially not cleaning its litter box...
NUZZLE
Aaaah! His tummy is soft, too!!
mew mew mew
Professor! His sides, his sides are even softer!
Ah.
A-And we'll have to cut down on your sweets to pay for its food...
ZZZ
Well, his ears are even softer than that!!
Eee!
mew mew
RUB
RUB
TUG
TUG
No, no, his tail is the softest of all!!
AAAAAHH!!
HE FELL ASLEEP ON ME!!!
Waaah! I wanna pet him!!
His tail is not soft!!!
What are you saying?!
BAM
...
Whaaaat?!!

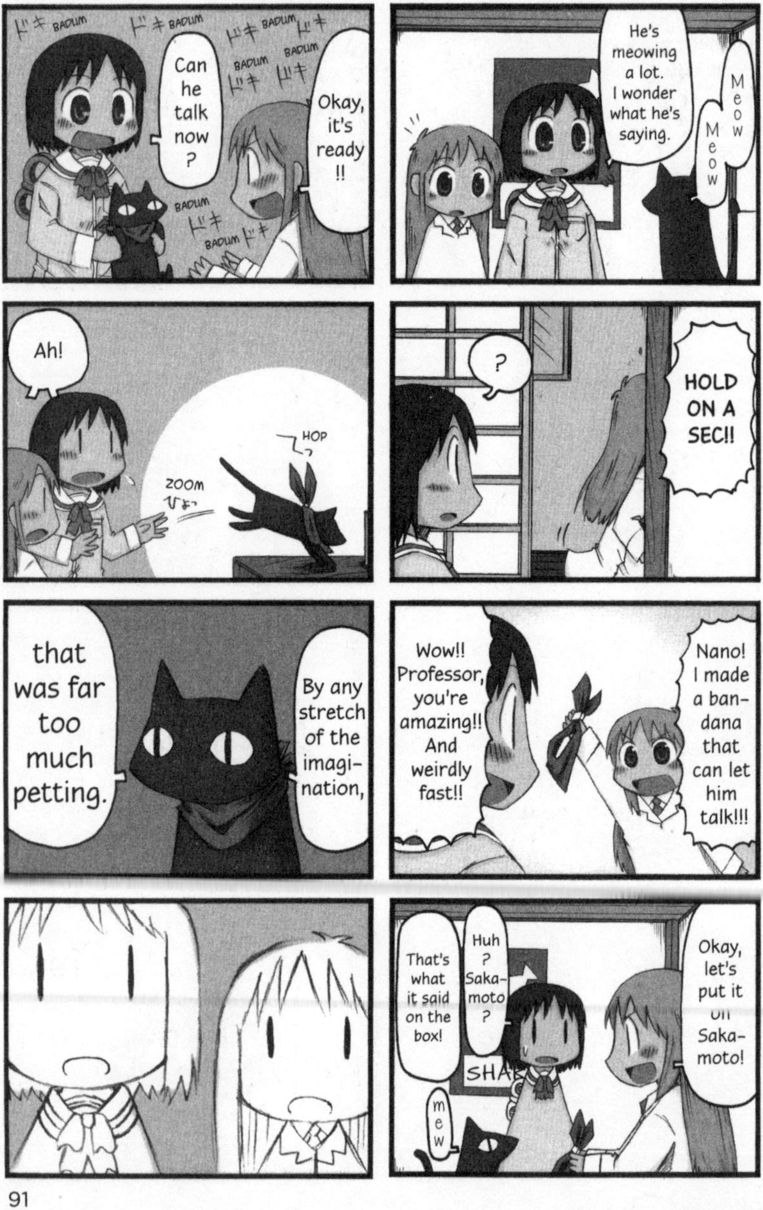
He's meowing a lot. I wonder what he's saying.
Meow
Meow
Okay, it's ready!!
Can he talk now?
ドキ BADUM
ドキ BADUM
ドキ BADUM
ドキ BADUM
ドキ BADUM
ドキ BADUM
HOLD ON A SEC!!
?
Ah!
HOP
ZOOM ぴょっ
Nano! I made a ban-dana that can let him talk!!!
Wow!! Professor, you're amazing!! And weirdly fast!!
By any stretch of the imagi-nation,
that was far too much petting.
Okay, let's put it on Saka-moto!
Huh? Saka-moto?
That's what it said on the box!
SHA
mew

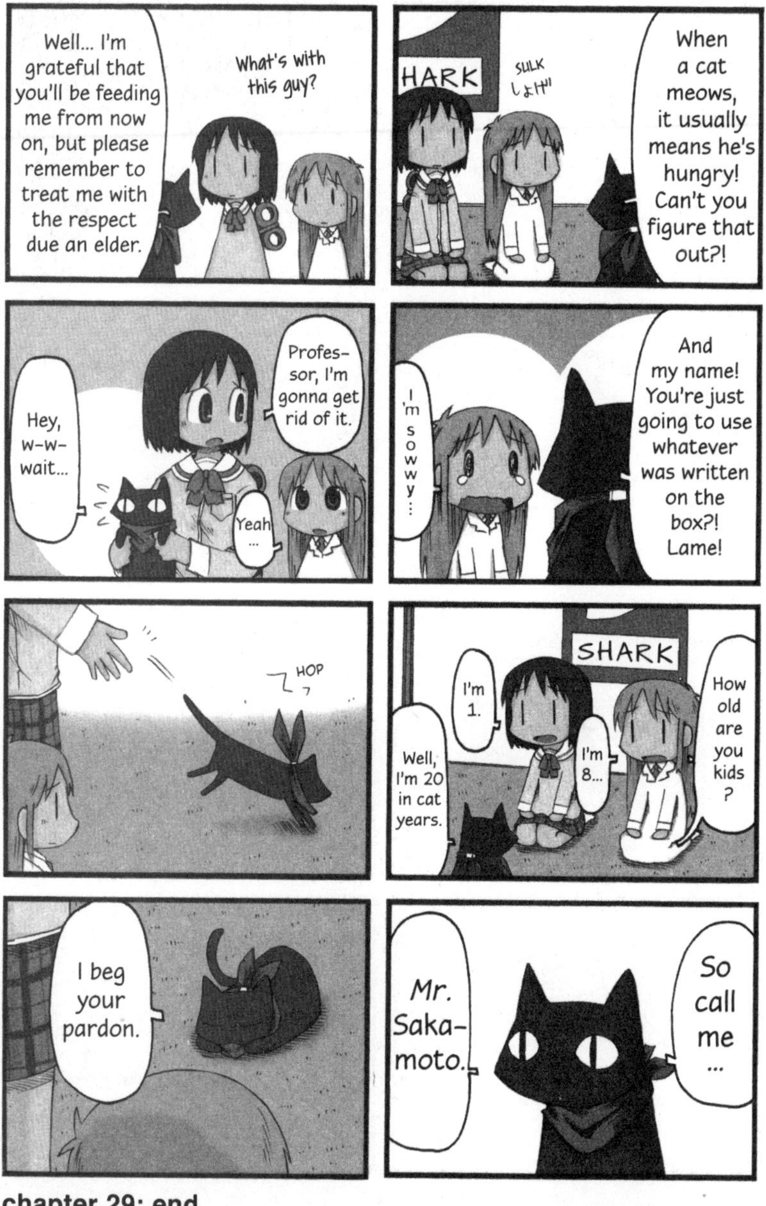
When a cat meows, it usually means he's hungry! Can't you figure that out?!
SULK
しょげ
HARK
And my name! You're just going to use whatever was written on the box?! Lame!
I'm sowwy...
How old are you kids?
SHARK
I'm 8...
I'm 1.
Well, I'm 20 in cat years.
So call me...
Mr. Saka-moto.
Well... I'm grateful that you'll be feeding me from now on, but please remember to treat me with the respect due an elder.
What's with this guy?
Profes-sor, I'm gonna get rid of it.
Yeah...
Hey, w-w-wait...
HOP
I beg your pardon.

chapter 29: end

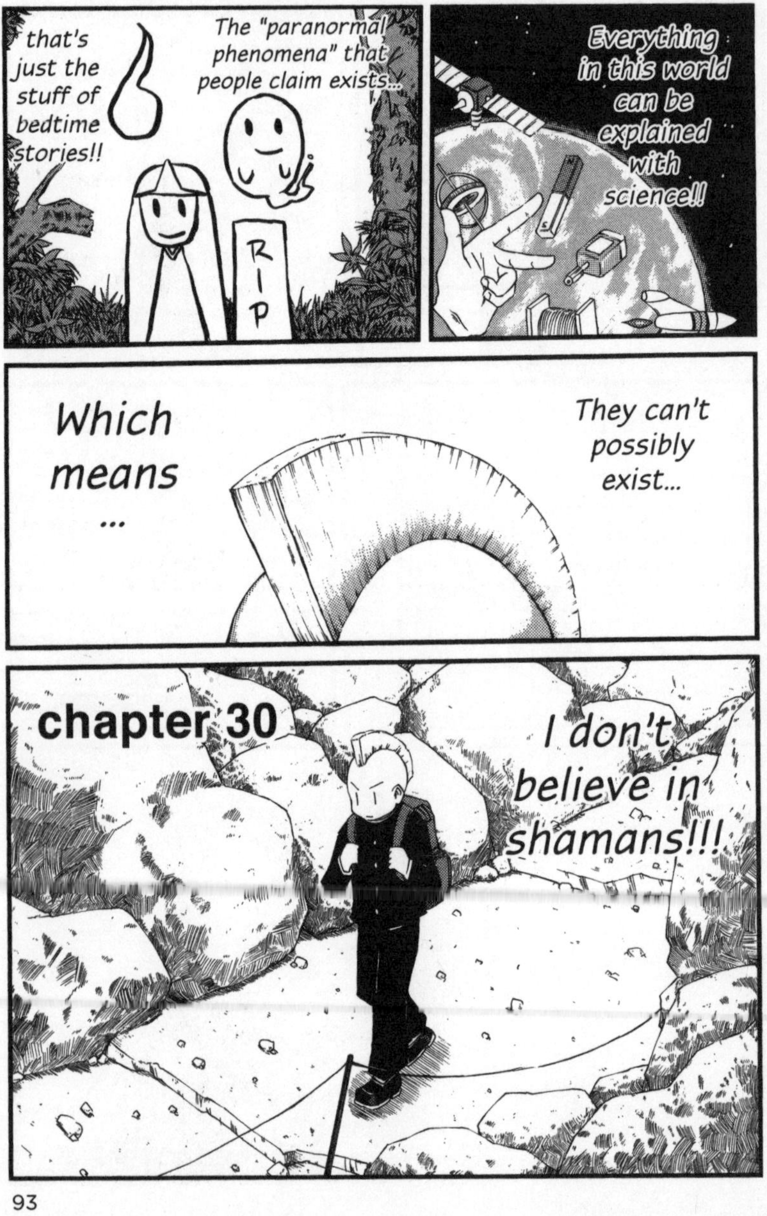
Everything in this world can be explained with science!!
The "paranormal phenomena" that people claim exists...
that's just the stuff of bedtime stories!!
RIP
Which means ...
They can't possibly exist...
I don't believe in shamans!!!
chapter 30

*Mt. Osore in Aomori Prefecture. Rumored to be the gate to hell.

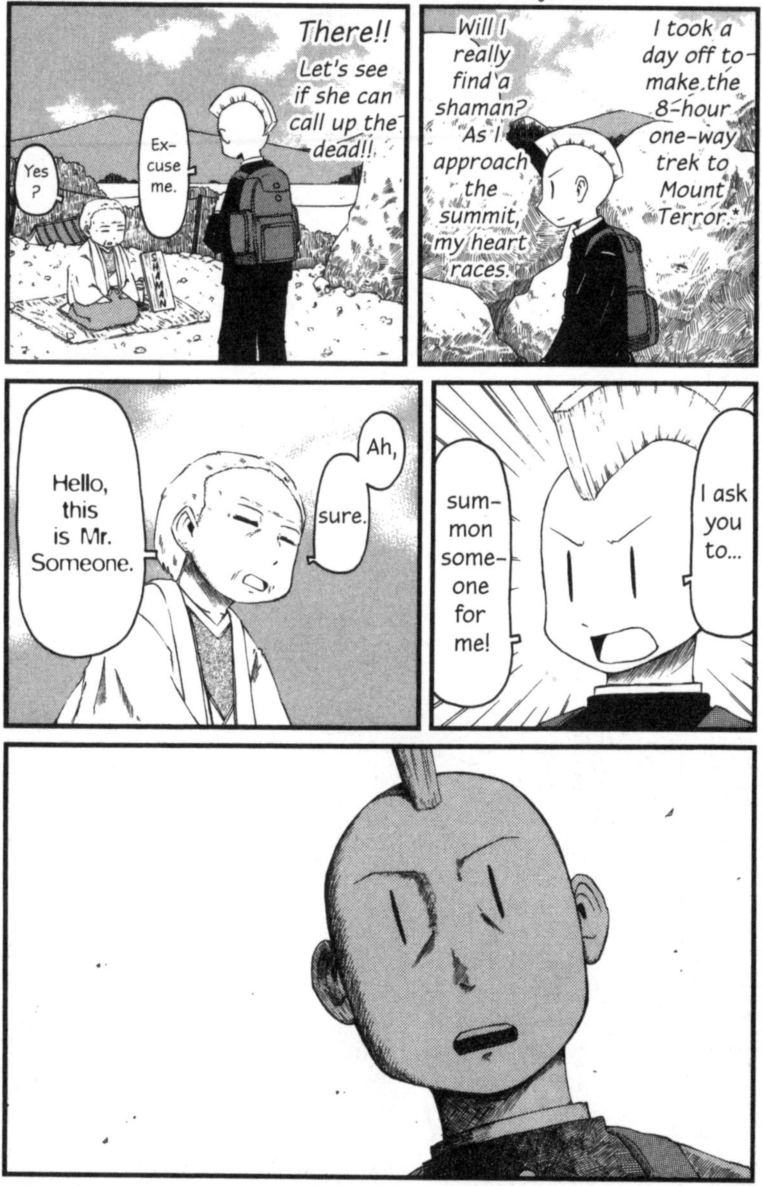
I took a day off to make the 8-hour one-way trek to Mount Terror.*
Will I really find a shaman? As I approach the summit, my heart races.
There!! Let's see if she can call up the dead!!
Excuse me.
Yes?
SHAMAN
I ask you to...
summon someone for me!
Ah,
sure.
Hello, this is Mr. Someone.

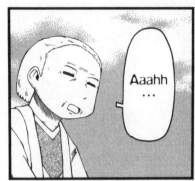

Aaahh
…

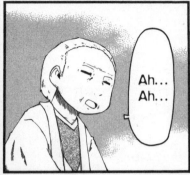

Ah…
Ah…

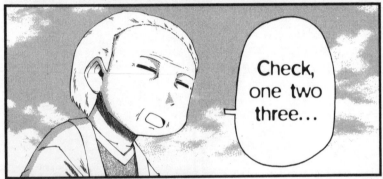

Check,
one two
three…

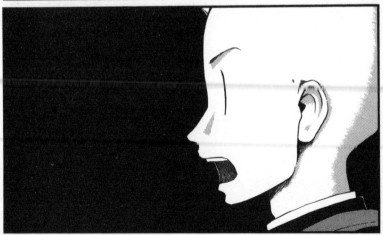

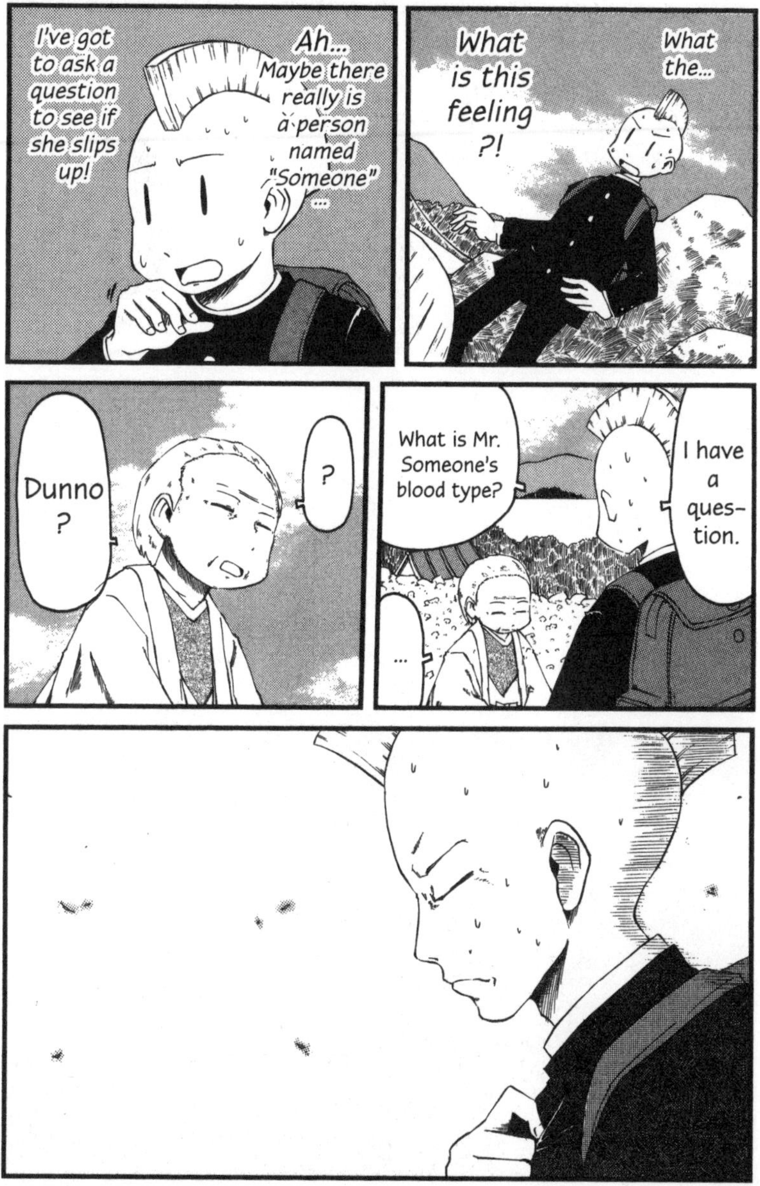
What the...
What is this feeling?!
Ah... Maybe there really is a person named "Someone"...
I've got to ask a question to see if she slips up!
I have a question.
What is Mr. Someone's blood type?
...
?
Dunno?

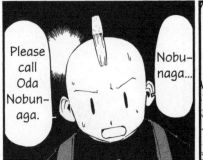

Maybe... Maybe I should pick someone more recognizable...
Pardon me...
GRIP
Nobunaga...
Please call Oda Nobunaga.
Give me
a break.

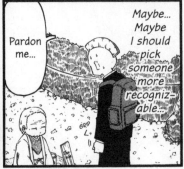

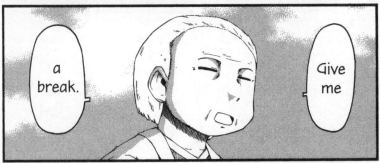

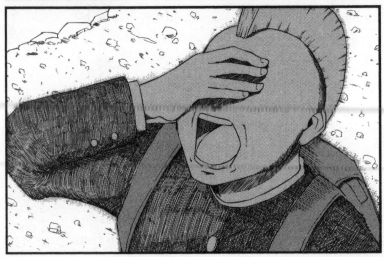

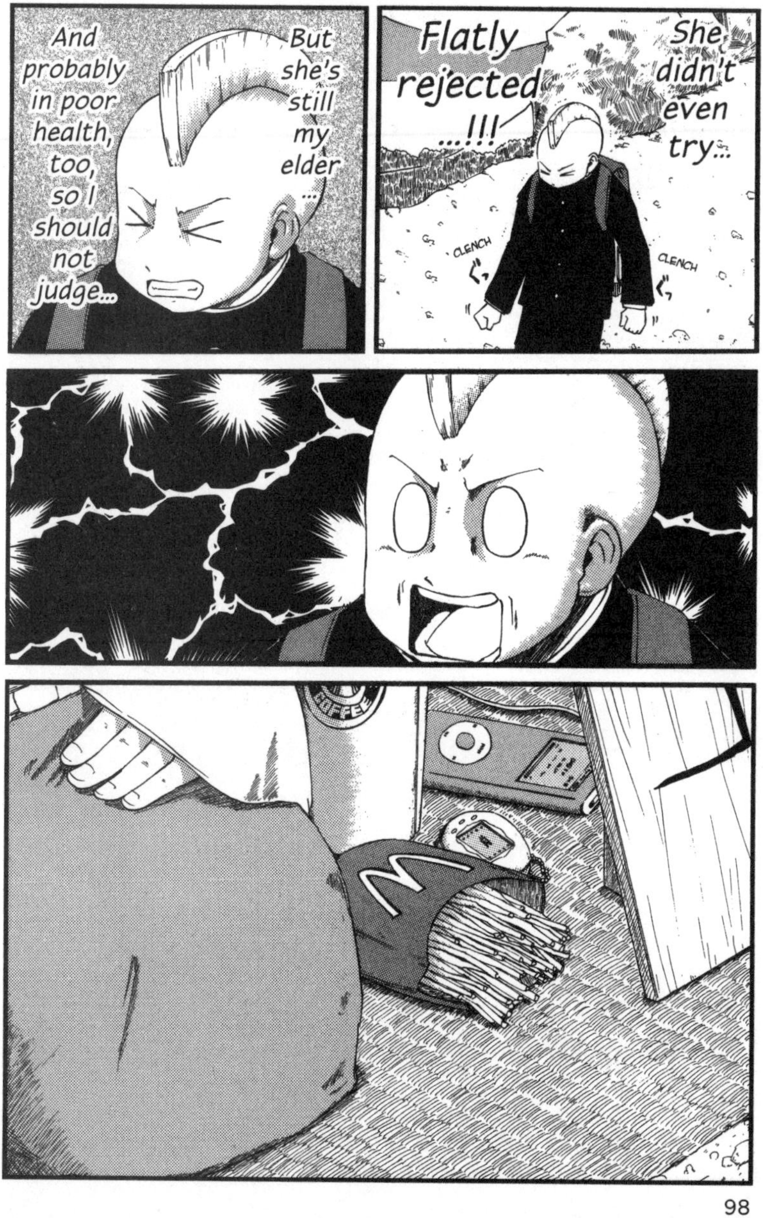
She didn't even try...
Flatly rejected ...!!!
CLENCH
CLENCH
But she's still my elder ...
And probably in poor health, too, so I should not judge...

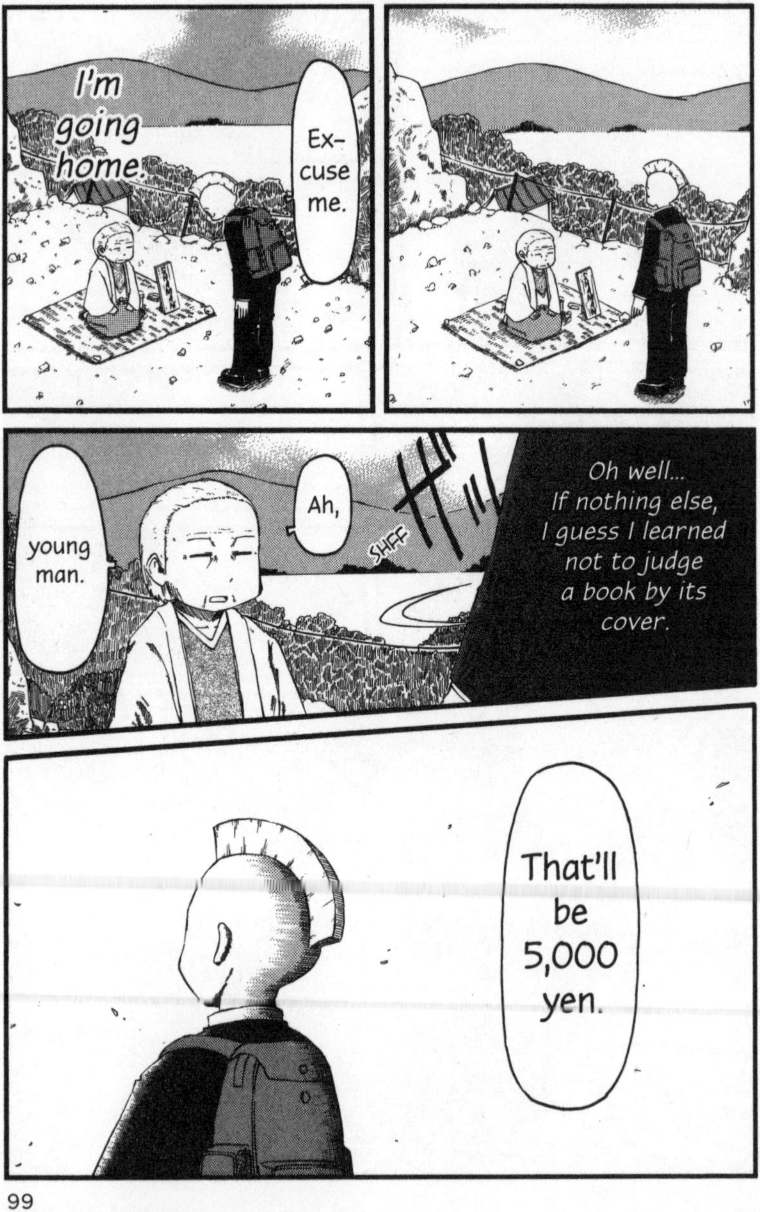
Ex–cuse me.
I'm going home.
Oh well... If nothing else, I guess I learned not to judge a book by its cover.
SHFF
Ah,
young man.
That'll be 5,000 yen.

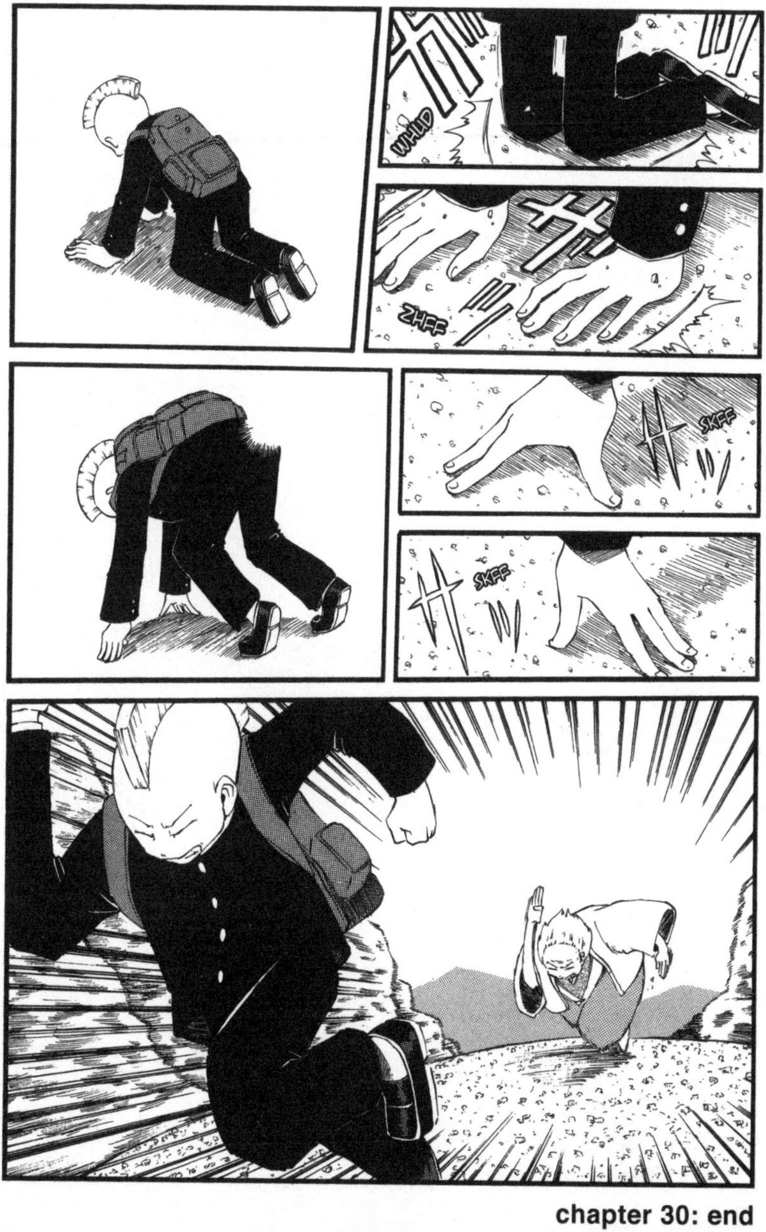
WHUD
ZHFF
SKFF
SKFF

chapter 30: end

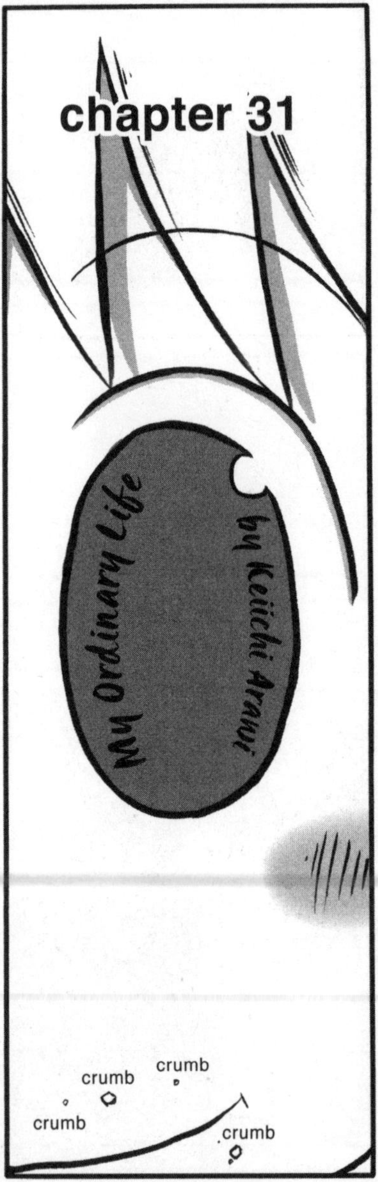
chapter 31
My Ordinary Life
by Keiichi Arawi
crumb
crumb
crumb
crumb

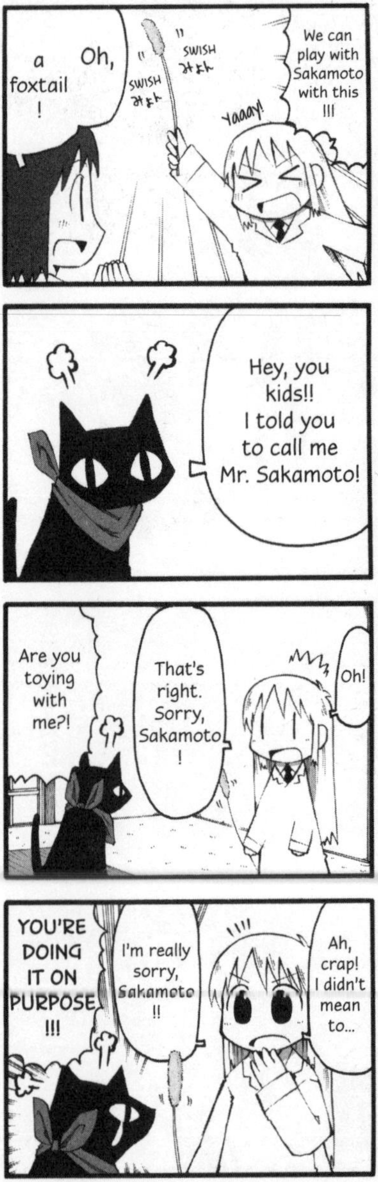
We can play with Sakamoto with this !!!
Yaaay!
SWISH みょん
SWISH みょん
Oh, a foxtail !
Hey, you kids!! I told you to call me Mr. Sakamoto!
Oh!
That's right. Sorry, Sakamoto !
Are you toying with me?!
Ah, crap! I didn't mean to...
I'm really sorry, Sakamoto !!
YOU'RE DOING IT ON PURPOSE !!!

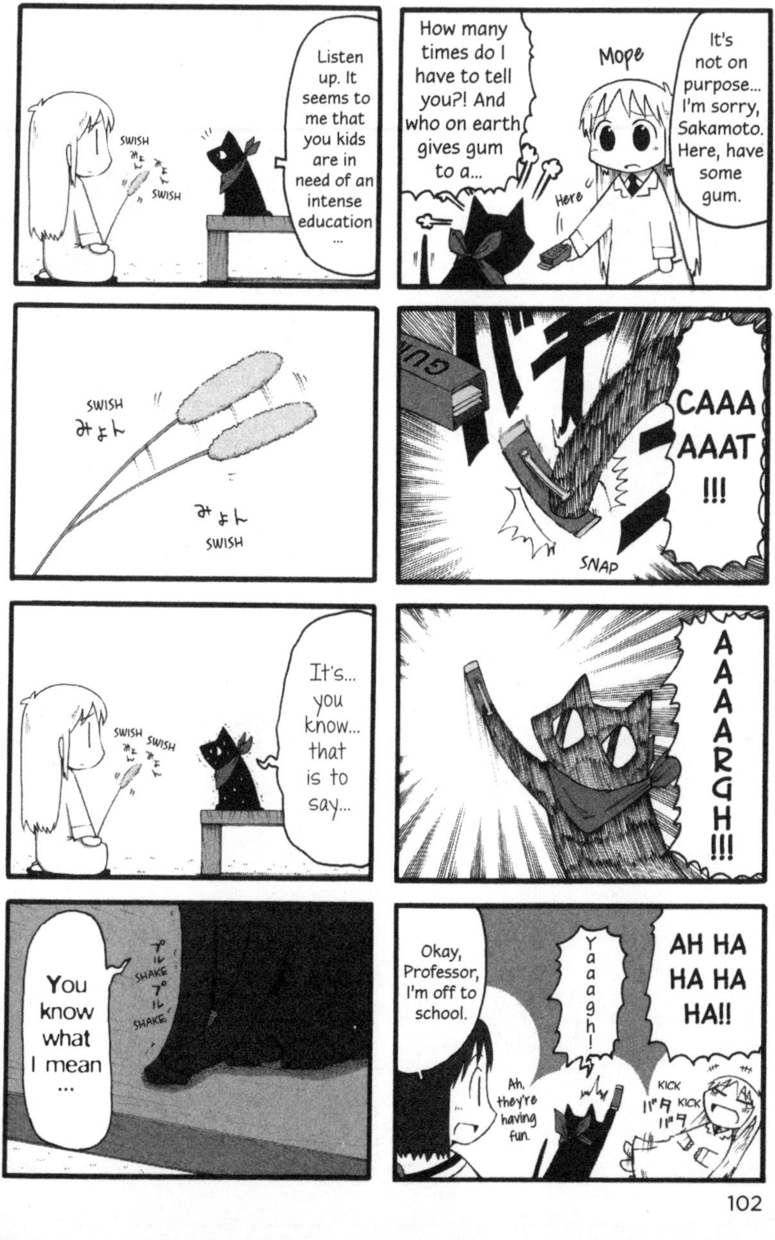
It's not on purpose... I'm sorry, Sakamoto. Here, have some gum.
Mope
How many times do I have to tell you?! And who on earth gives gum to a...
Here
Listen up. It seems to me that you kids are in need of an intense education ...
SWISH
SWISH
CAAAAAAT!!!
SNAP
SWISH
みょん
みょん
SWISH
AAAAARGH!!!
It's... you know... that is to say...
SWISH SWISH
AH HA HA HA HA!!
Yaaagh!
Okay, Professor, I'm off to school.
KICK
KICK
Ah, they're having fun.
SHAKE
SHAKE
You know what I mean ...

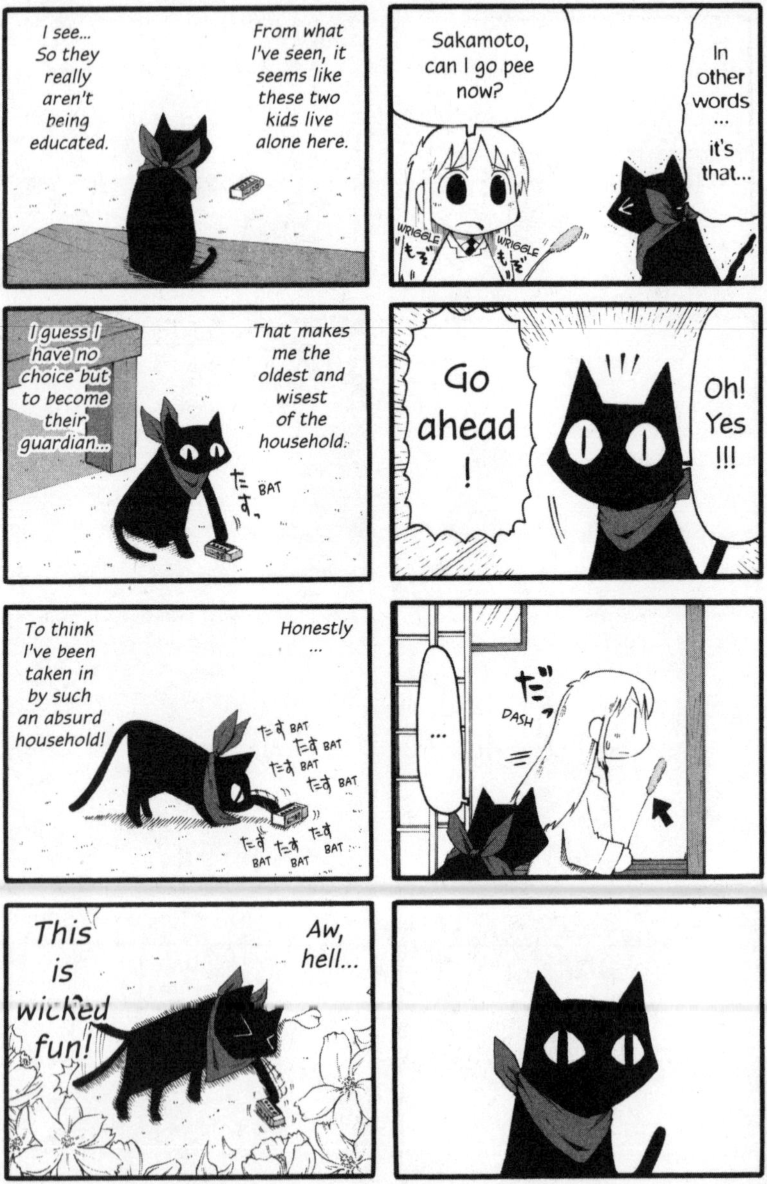

In other words ... it's that...
Sakamoto, can I go pee now?
もぞ WRIGGLE
もぞ WRIGGLE
From what I've seen, it seems like these two kids live alone here.
I see... So they really aren't being educated.
Oh! Yes !!!
Go ahead !
That makes me the oldest and wisest of the household.
I guess I have no choice but to become their guardian...
たす BAT
...
だっ DASH
Honestly ...
To think I've been taken in by such an absurd household!
たす BAT
たす BAT
たす BAT
たす BAT
たす BAT
たす BAT
たす BAT
Aw, hell...
This is wicked fun!

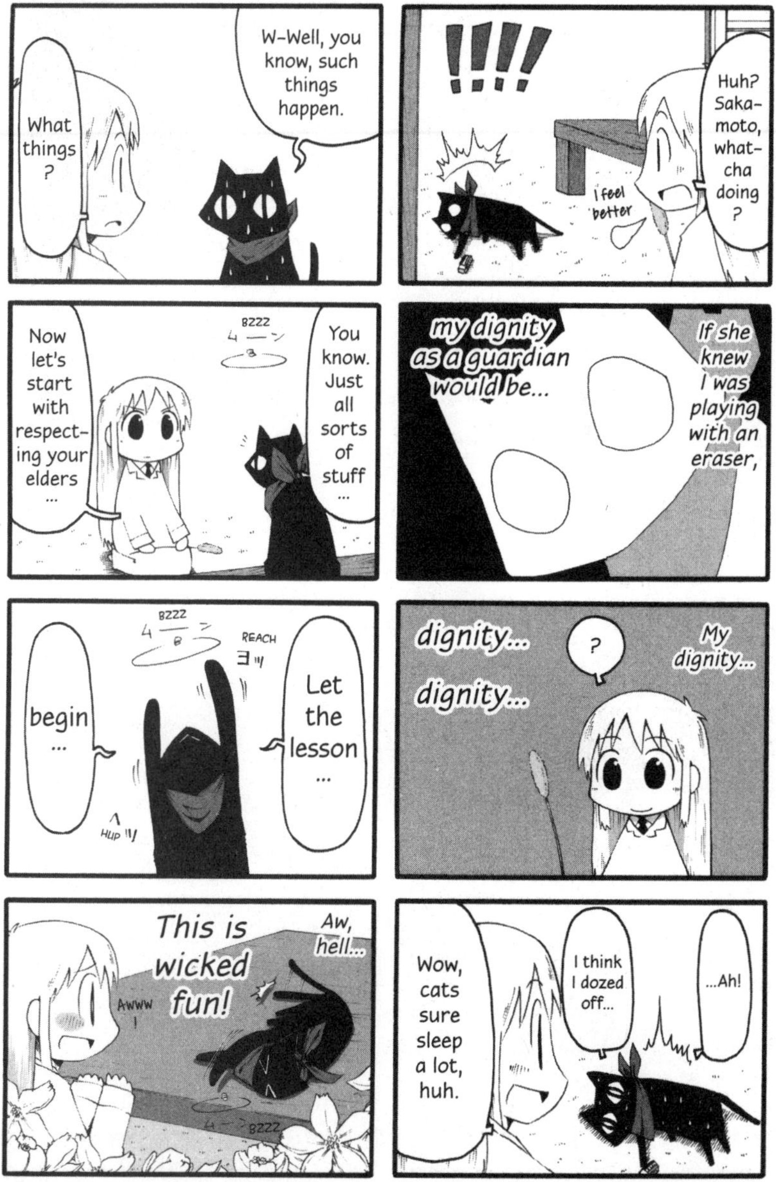
Huh? Sakamoto, whatcha doing?
!!!!
I feel better
W-Well, you know, such things happen.
What things?
If she knew I was playing with an eraser,
my dignity as a guardian would be...
You know. Just all sorts of stuff...
BZZZ
Now let's start with respecting your elders...
My dignity...
?
dignity...
dignity...
Let the lesson...
REACH
BZZZ
begin...
HUP
...Ah!
I think I dozed off...
Wow, cats sure sleep a lot, huh.
Aw, hell...
This is wicked fun!
Awww!
BZZZ

chapter 31: end

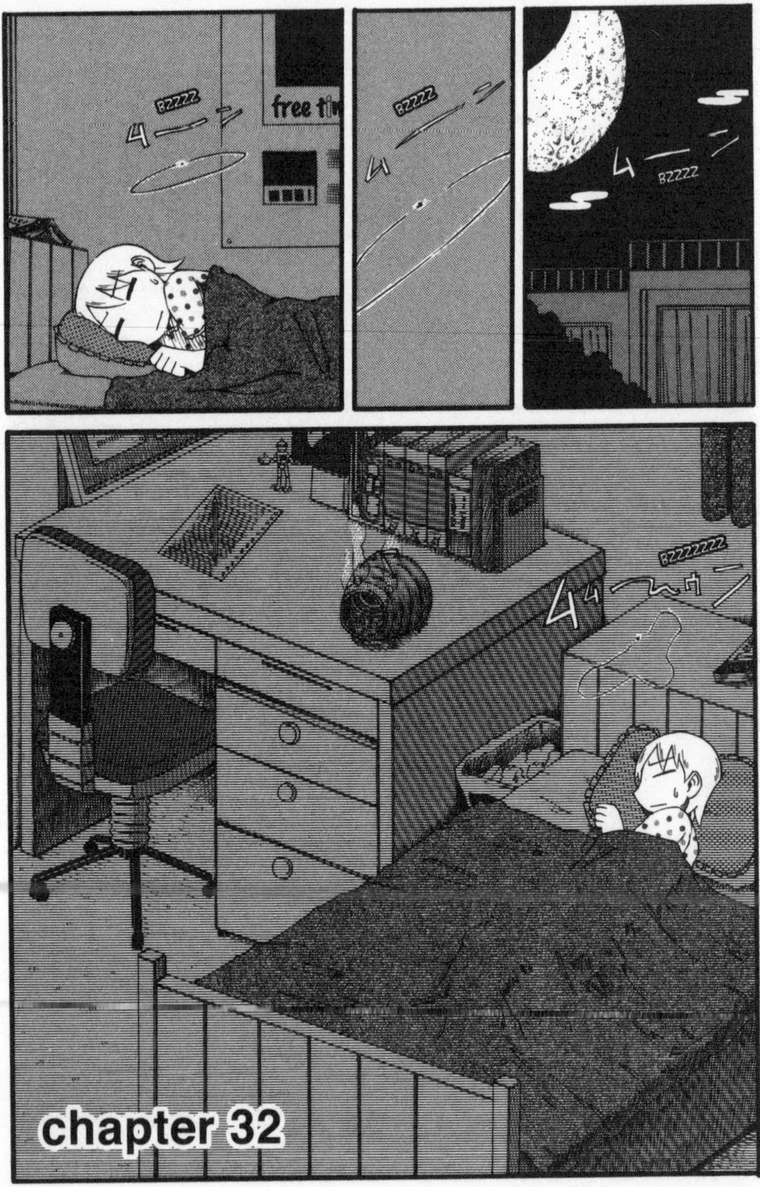
BZZZZ
BZZZZ
BZZZZ
BZZZZZZZ
chapter 32

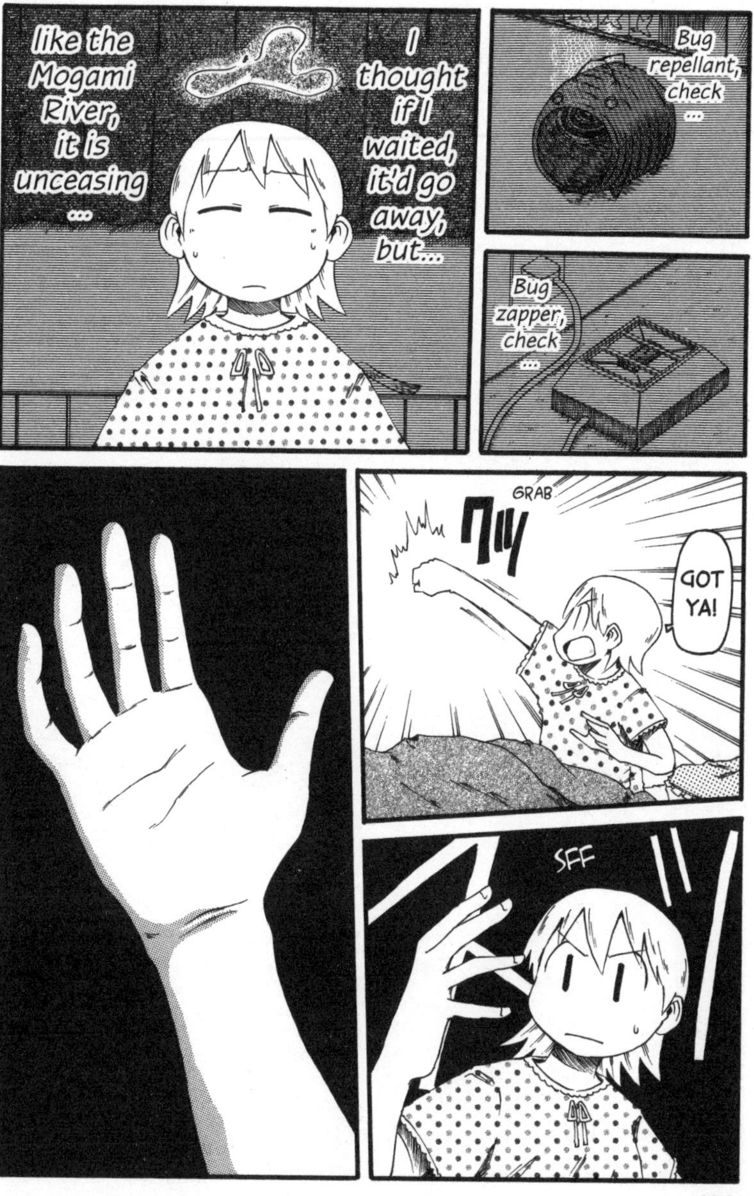
Bug repellant, check ...
Bug zapper, check ...
I thought if I waited, it'd go away, but...
like the Mogami River, it is unceasing ...
GRAB
GOT YA!
SFF

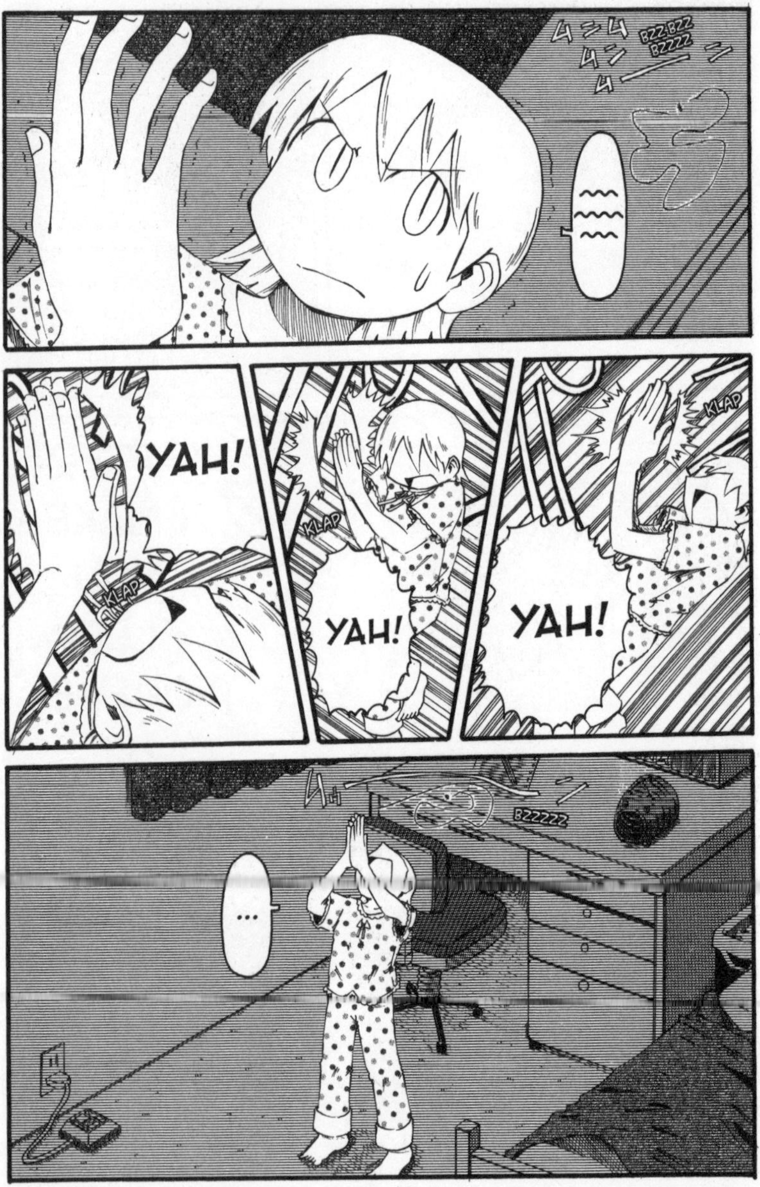
BZZ-BZZ
BZZZZ
KLAP
YAH!
KLAP
YAH!
YAH!
KLAP
BZZZZZ
...

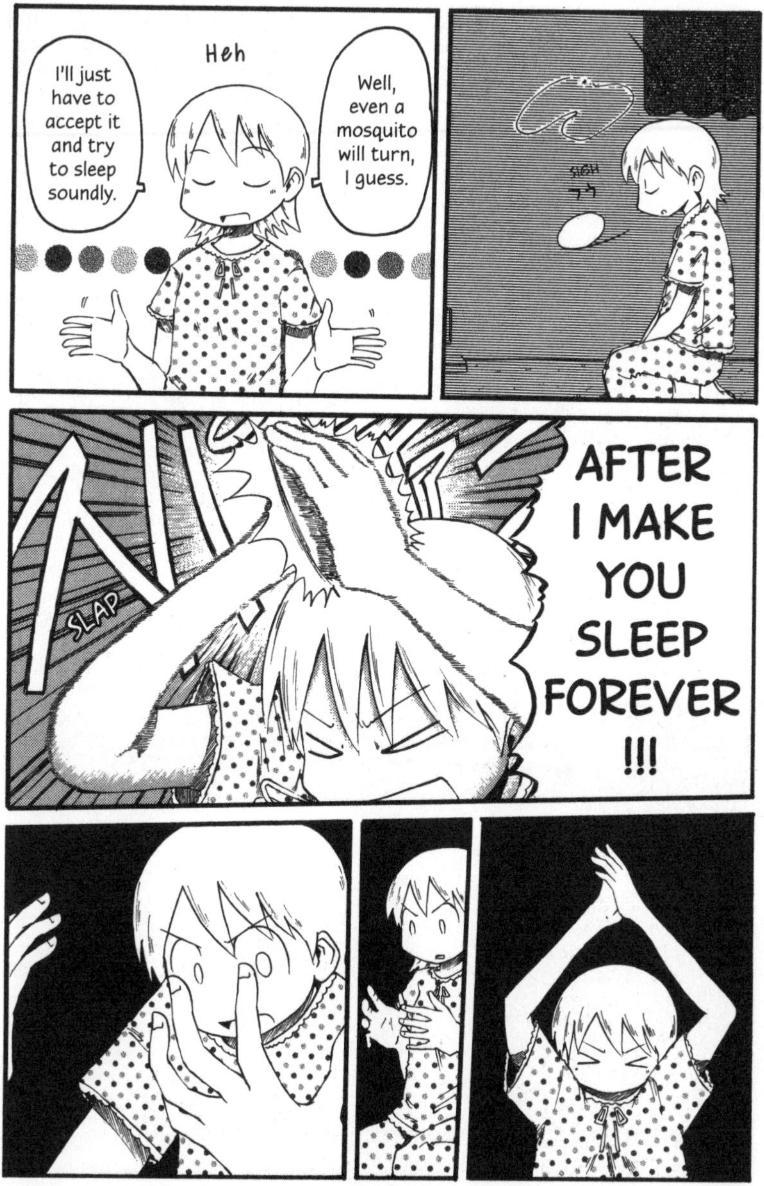
SIGH
Well, even a mosquito will turn, I guess.
Heh
I'll just have to accept it and try to sleep soundly.
AFTER I MAKE YOU SLEEP FOREVER !!!
SLAP

GOT YA !!!
Yay!!
sukk
IN THE CHEST !!!
SLAP
sukk
sukk

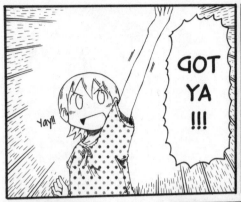

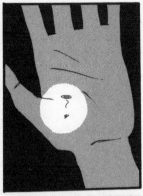

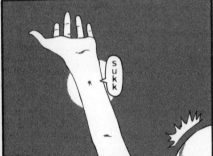

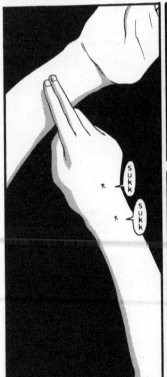

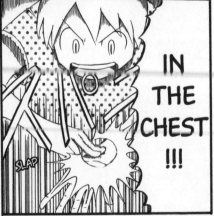

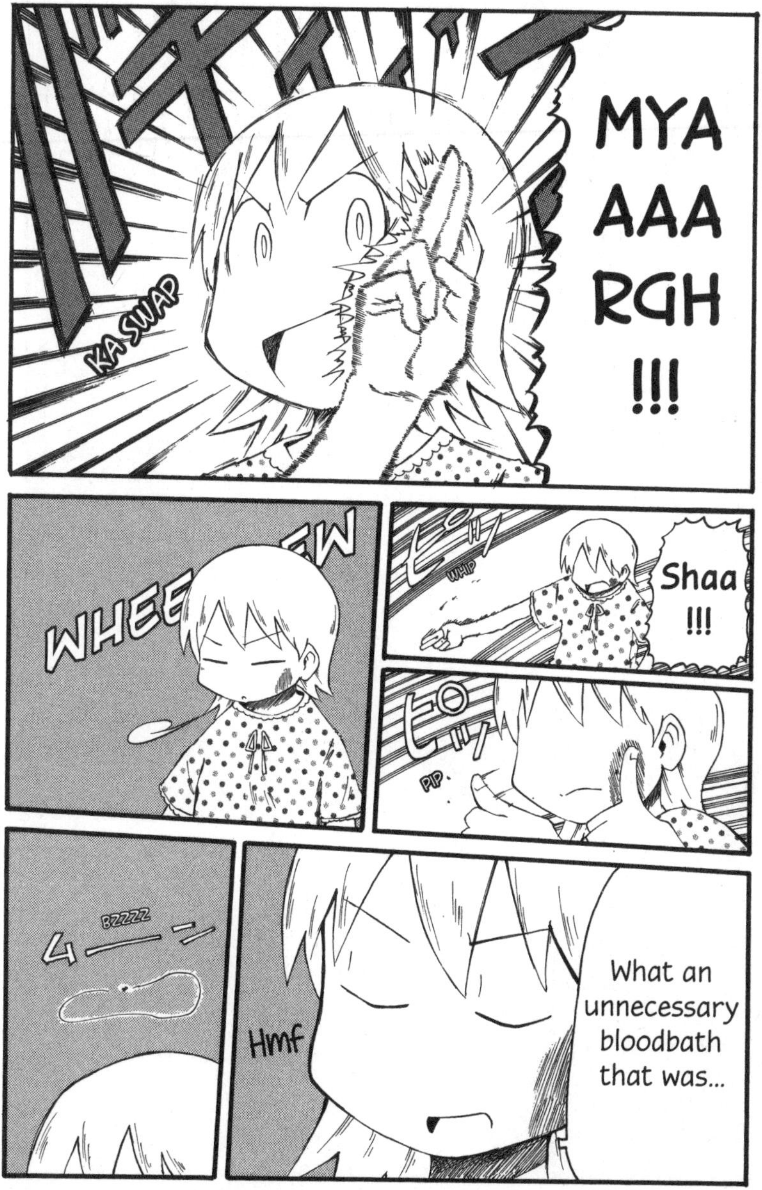
MYA AAA RGH !!!
KA SWAP
WHIP
Shaa !!!
PIP
WHEE
EW
What an unnecessary bloodbath that was...
Hmf
BZZZZ

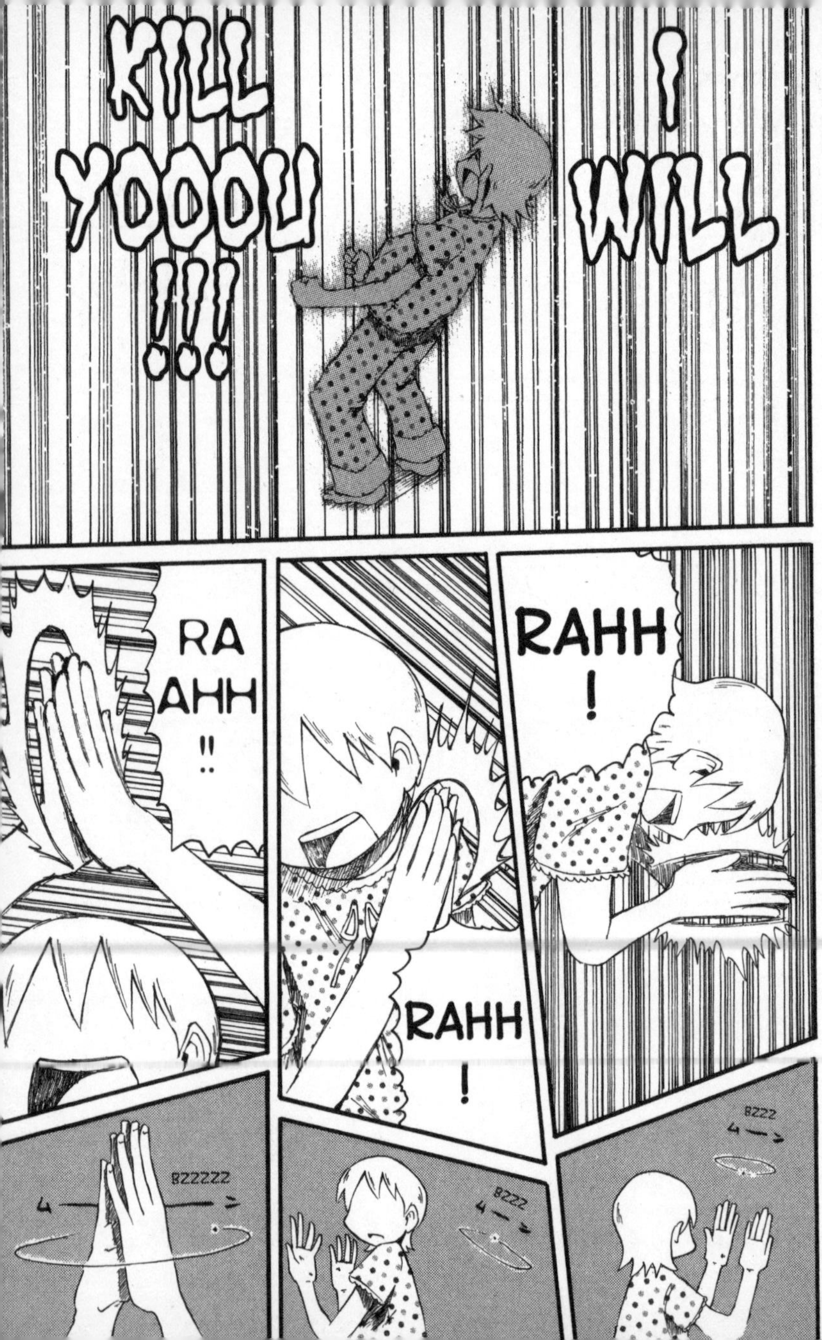
I WILL
KILL YOOOU!!!
RAHH!
RAHH!
RA AHH!!
BZZZ
BZZZ
BZZZZZ

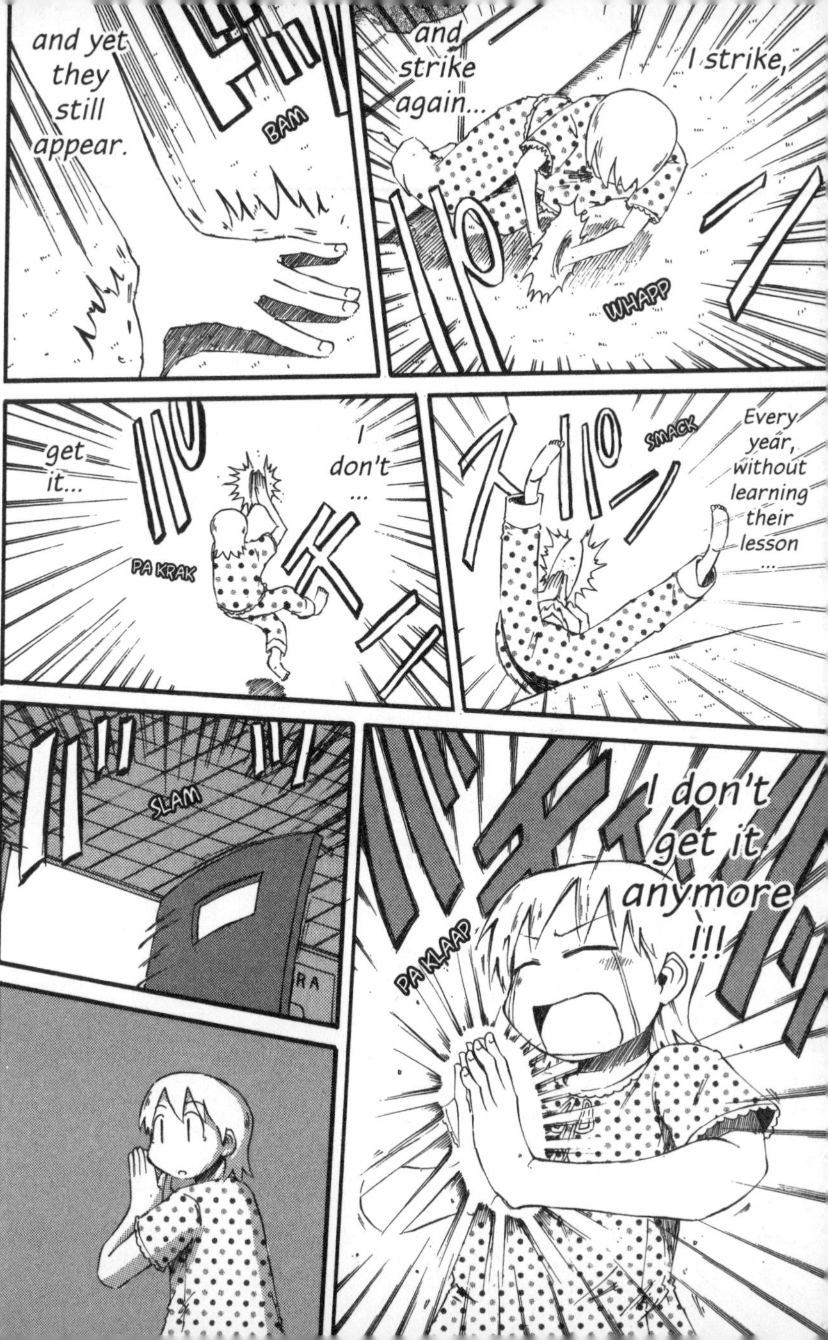
I strike,
and strike again...
WHAPP
and yet they still appear.
BAM
Every year, without learning their lesson ...
SMACK
I don't ...
get it...
PA KRAK
I don't get it anymore !!!
PA KLAAP
SLAM
RA

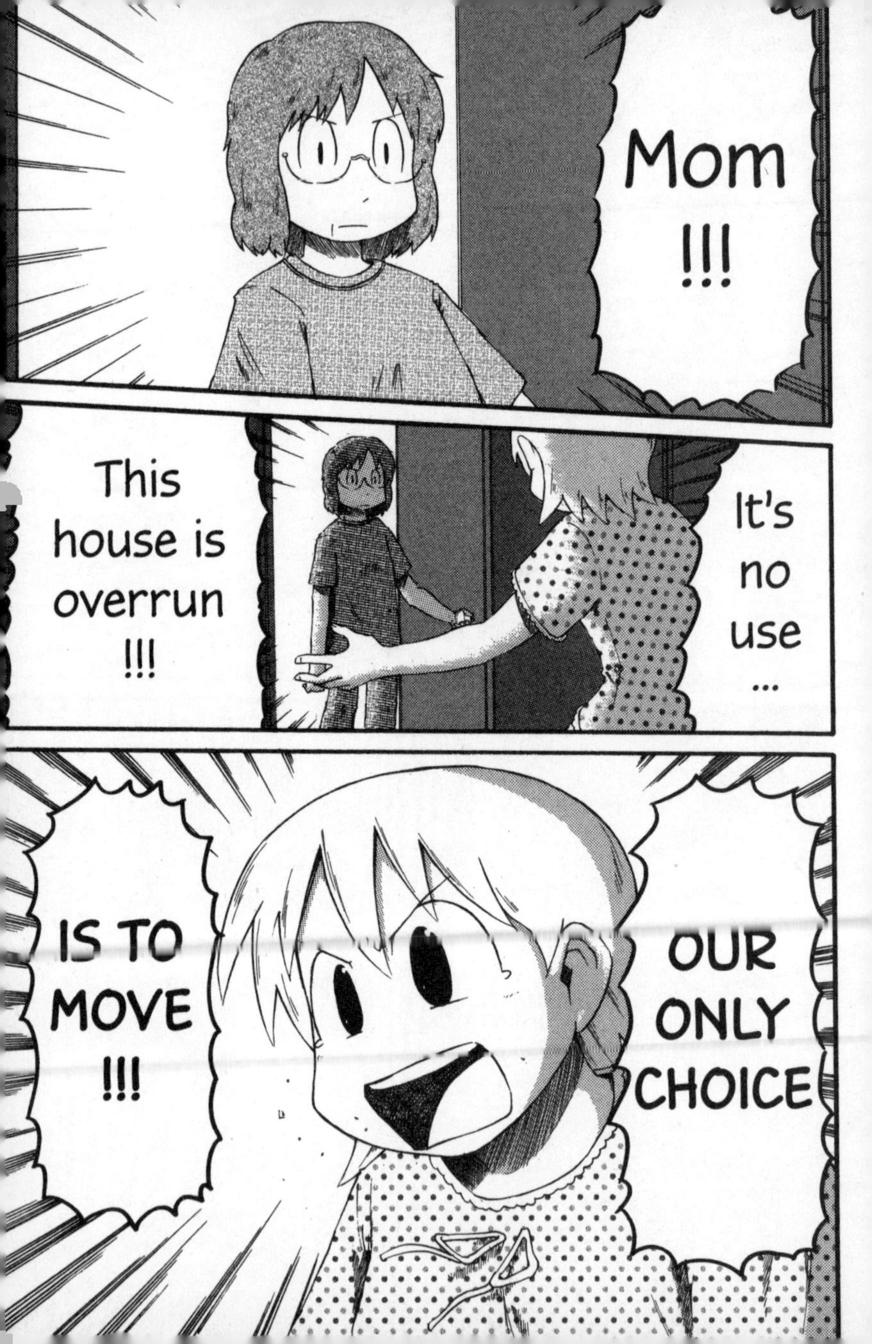
Mom !!!
It's no use ...
This house is overrun !!!
OUR ONLY CHOICE
IS TO MOVE !!!

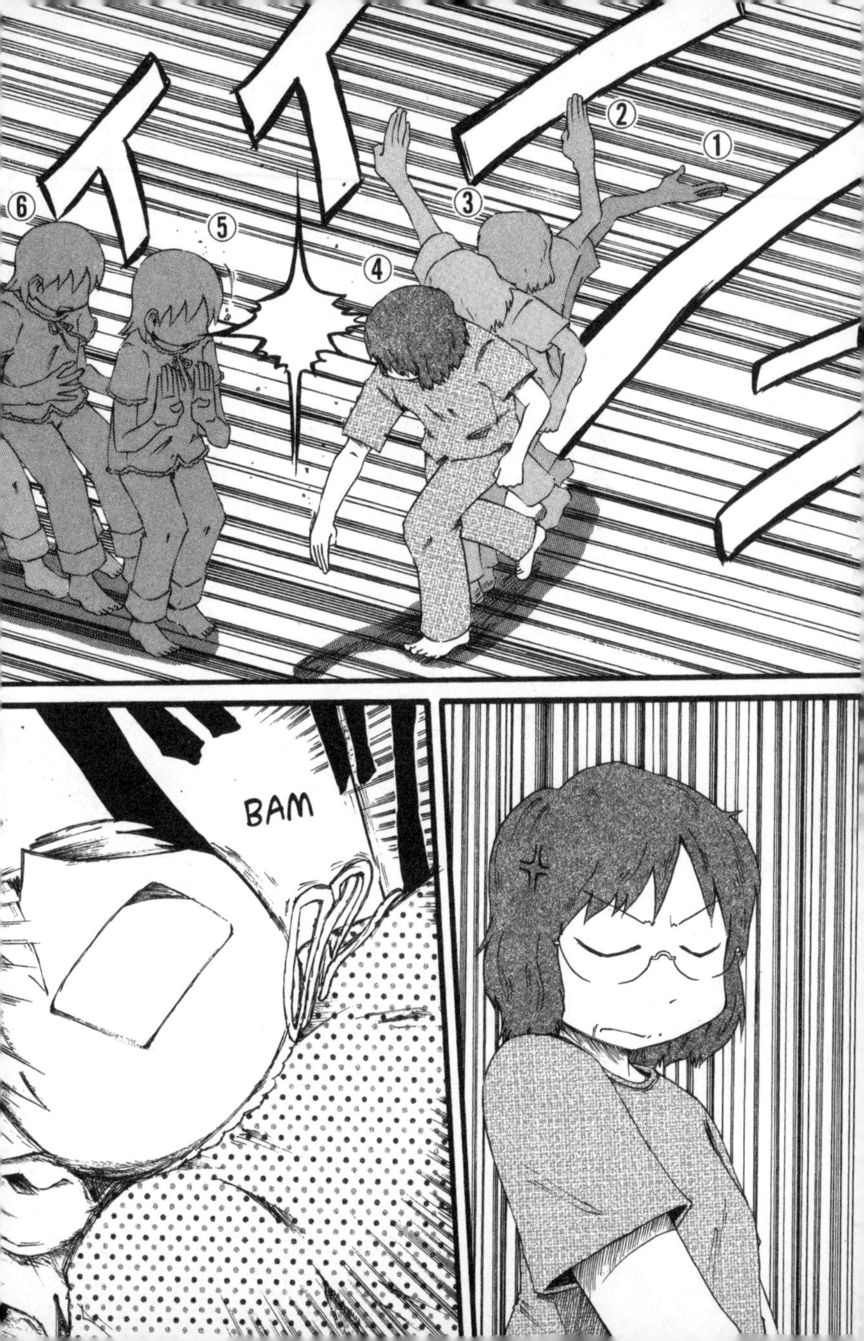
①
②
③
④
⑤
⑥
BAM

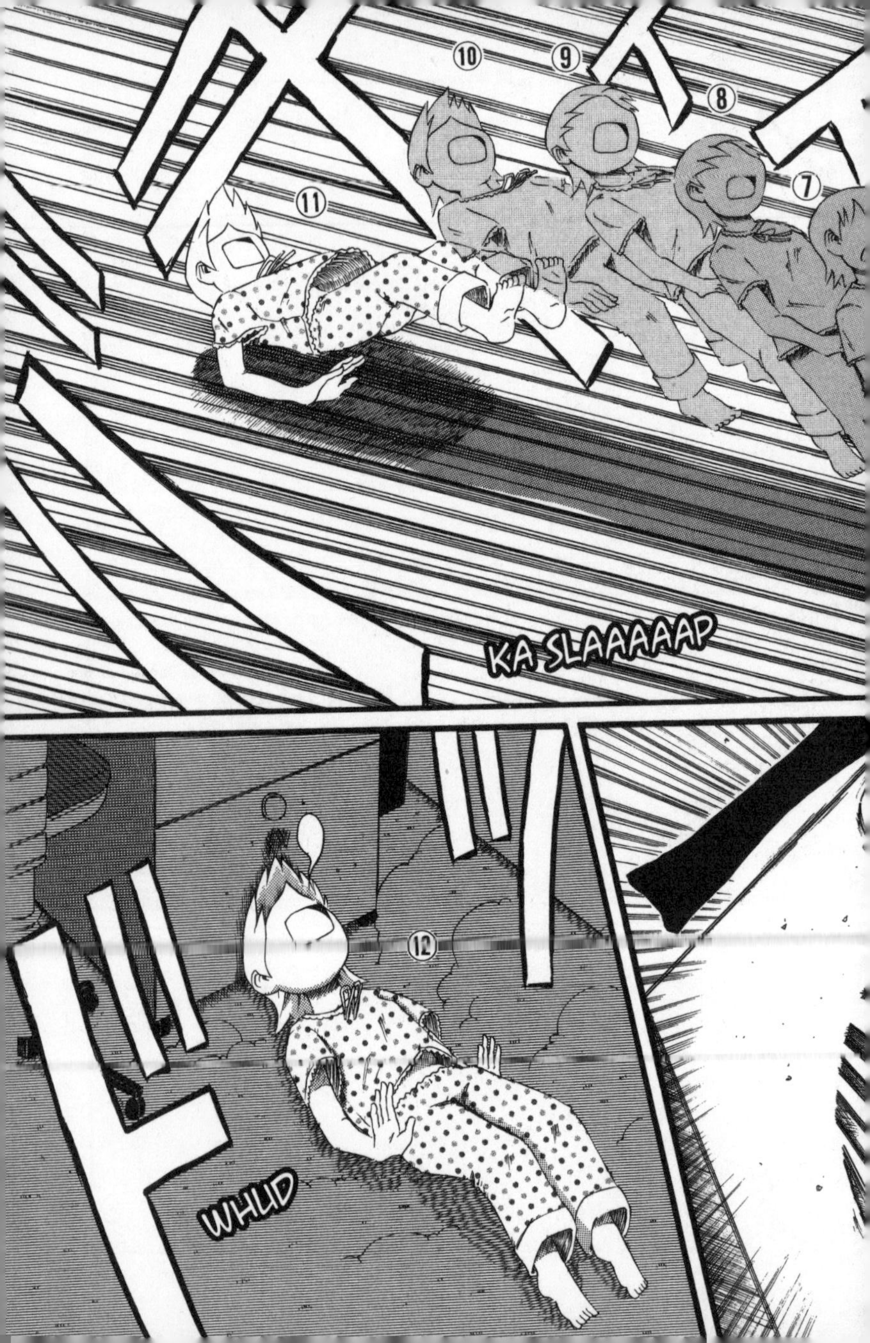
⑨
⑩
⑧
⑦
⑪
KA SLAAAAAP
⑫
WHUD

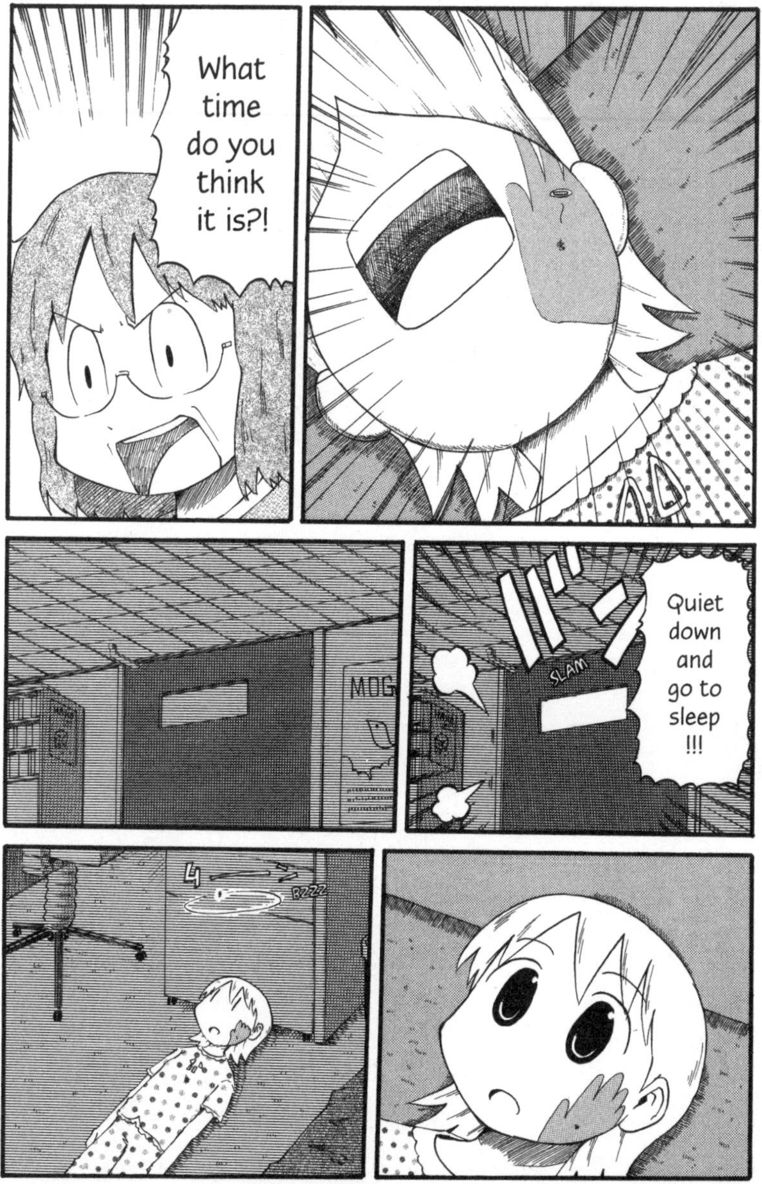
What time do you think it is?!
Quiet down and go to sleep!!!
SLAM
MOG
BZZZ

chapter 32: end

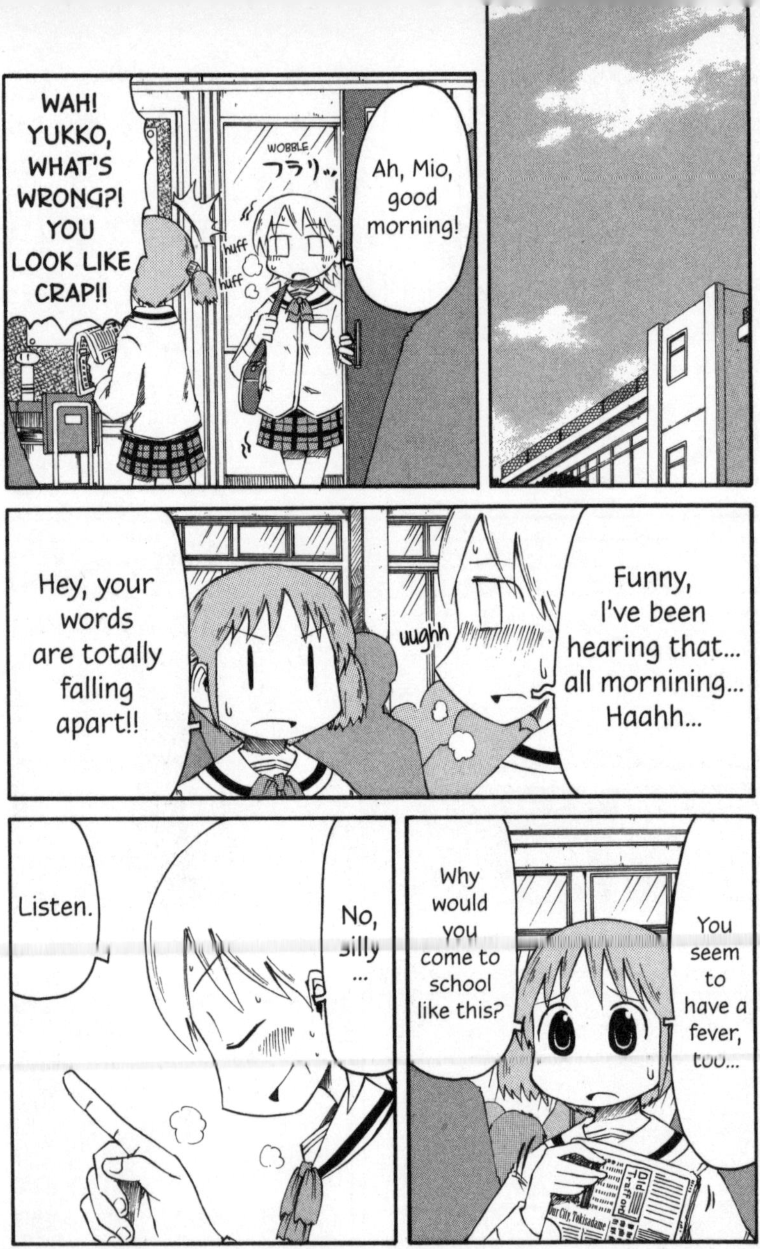
Ah, Mio, good morning!
WOBBLE
フラリッ
huff
huff
WAH! YUKKO, WHAT'S WRONG?! YOU LOOK LIKE CRAP!!
Funny, I've been hearing that... all mornining... Haahh...
uughh
Hey, your words are totally falling apart!!
You seem to have a fever, too...
Why would you come to school like this?
Old Trafford
Our City, Tokisadame
No, silly ...
Listen.

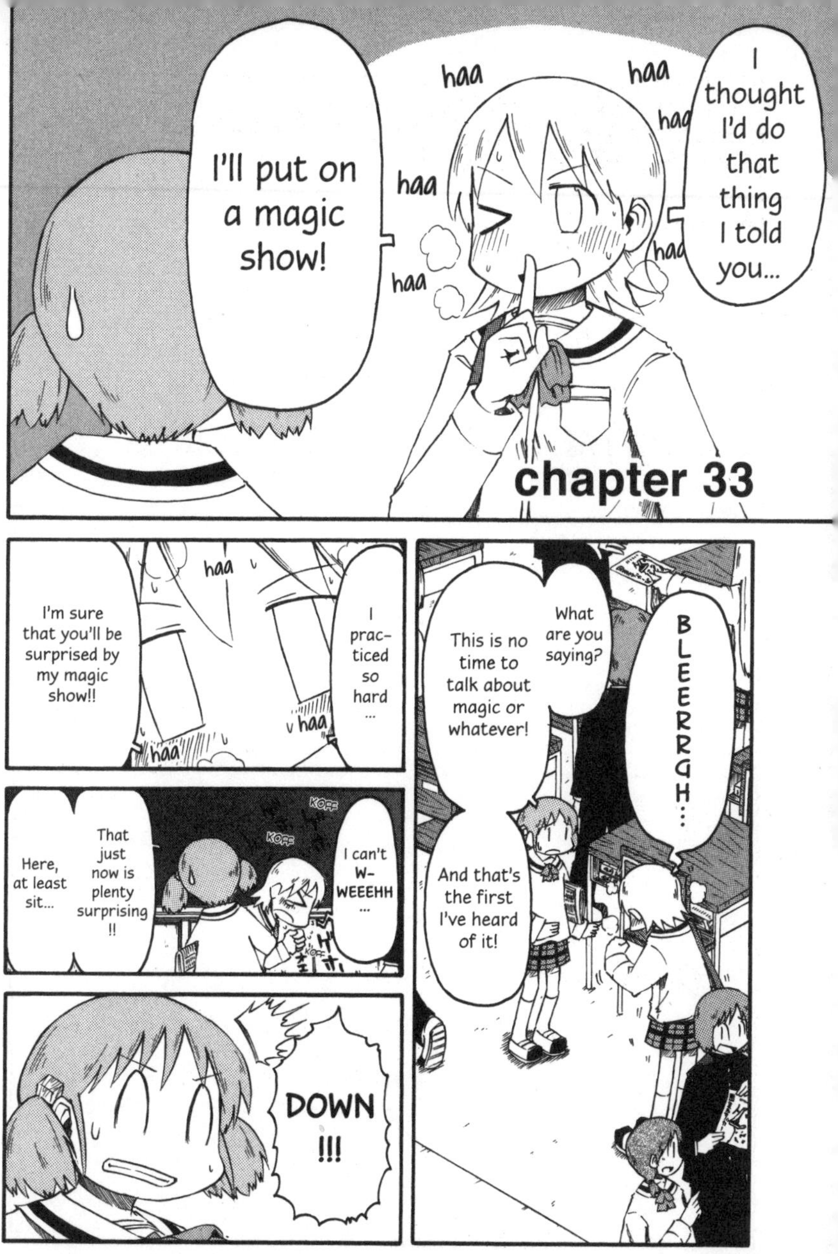
I thought I'd do that thing I told you...
haa haa haa haa haa haa
I'll put on a magic show!
chapter 33
BLEERRGH...
What are you saying?
This is no time to talk about magic or whatever!
And that's the first I've heard of it!
I practiced so hard ...
haa haa haa
I'm sure that you'll be surprised by my magic show!!
KOFF KOFF
I can't W-WEEEHH ...
That just now is plenty surprising !!
Here, at least sit...
DOWN !!!

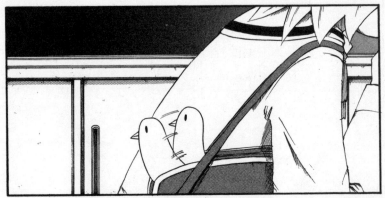

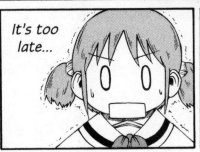

It's too late...

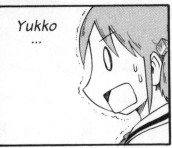

Yukko...

are
already
totally
showing
...

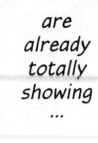

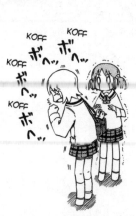

KOFF

KOFF

KOFF

KOFF

KOFF

Your
props...

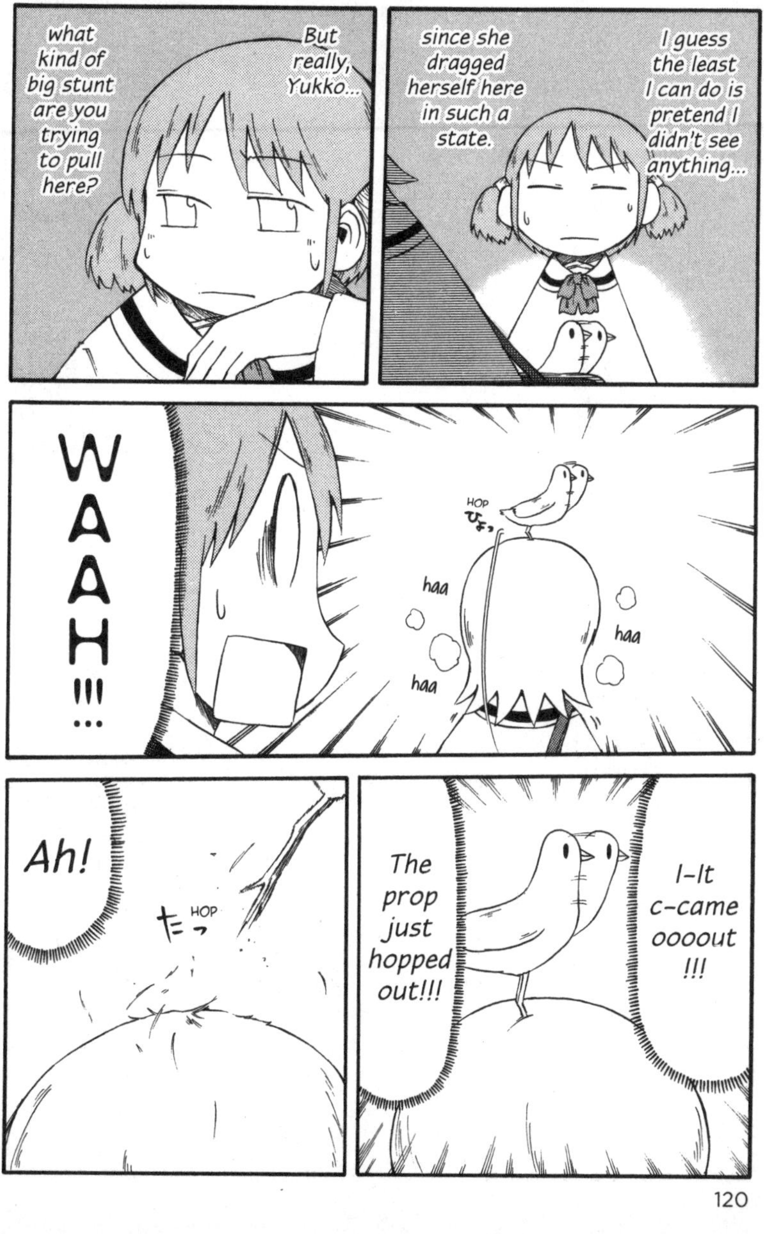
I guess the least I can do is pretend I didn't see anything...
since she dragged herself here in such a state.
But really, Yukko...
what kind of big stunt are you trying to pull here?
HOP
ぴょっ
haa
haa
haa
WAAAH!!!...
I-It c-came oooout!!!
The prop just hopped out!!!
Ah!
HOP
たっ

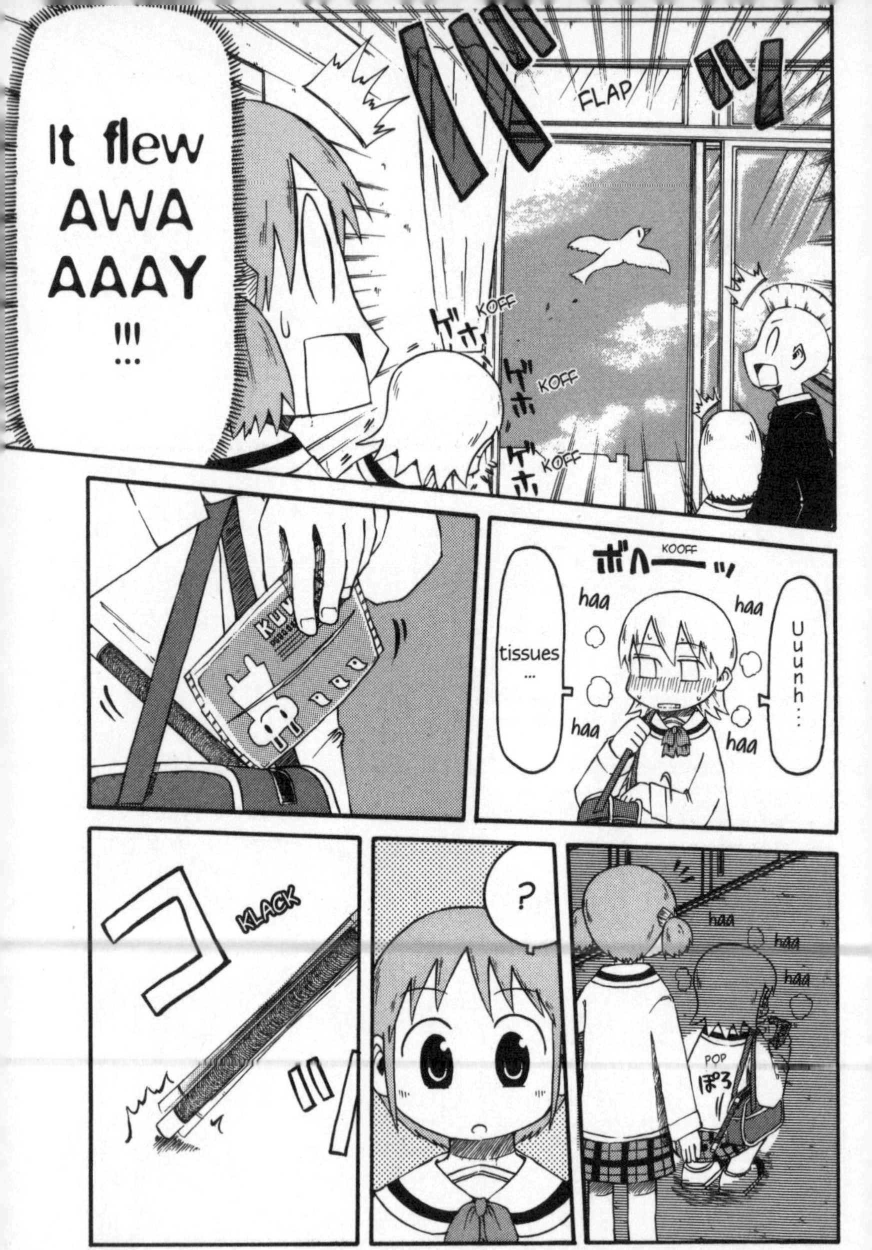

FLAP
It flew AWAAAAY!!!...
ゲホ KOFF
ゲホ KOFF
ゲホ KOFF
ボヘーッ KOOFF
haa
haa
Uuunh...
tissues...
haa
haa
haa
haa
haa
POP ぽろ
?
KLACK

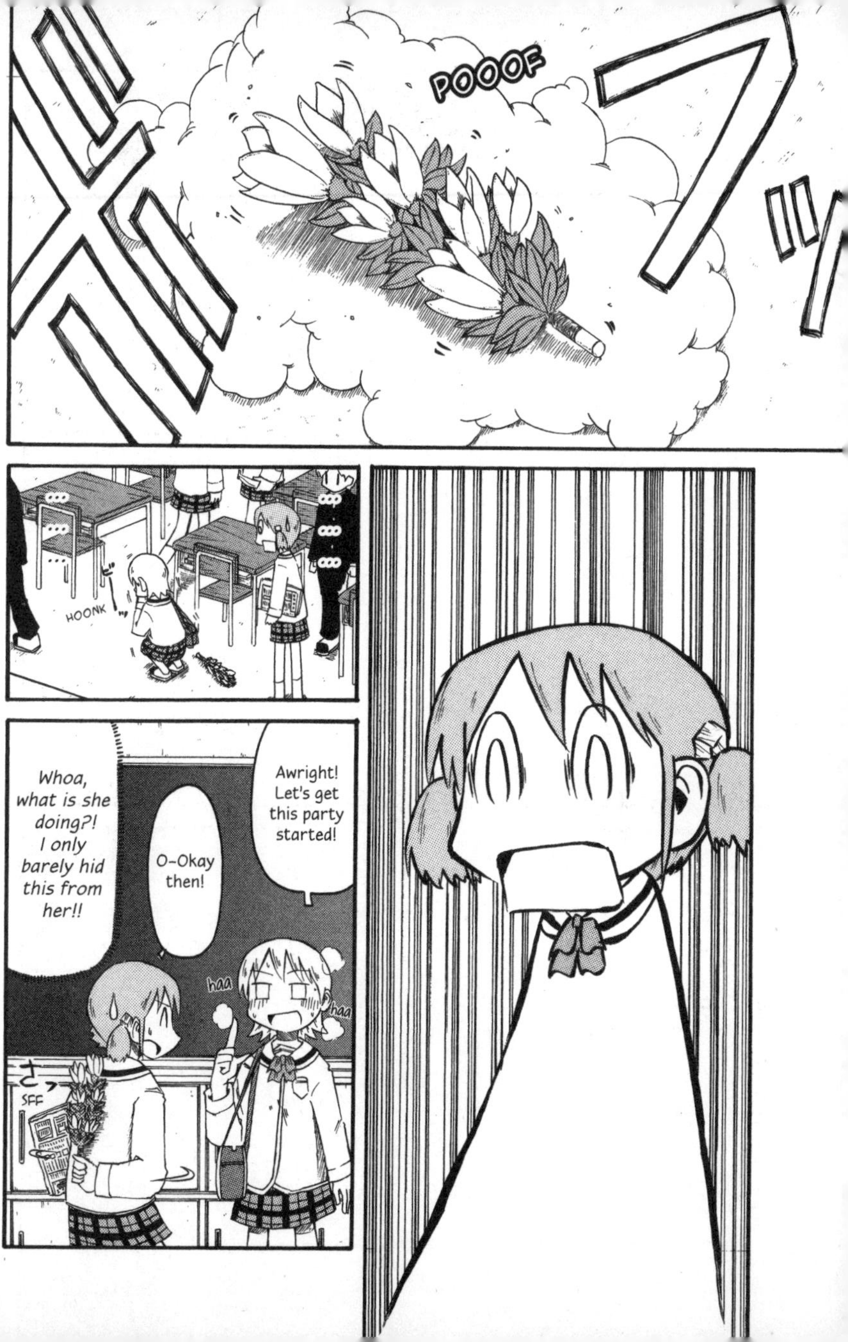
POOOF
HOONK
Awright! Let's get this party started!
O-Okay then!
Whoa, what is she doing?! I only barely hid this from her!!
haa
haa
SFF

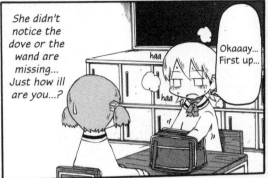

She didn't notice the dove or the wand are missing... Just how ill are you...?

haa

haa

Okaaay... First up...

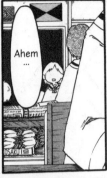

Ahem...

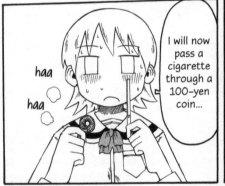

haa

haa

I will now pass a cigarette through a 100-yen coin...

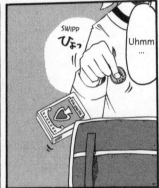

SWIPP

Uhmm...

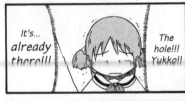

It's... already there!!!

The hole!!! Yukke!!

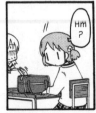

Hm?

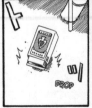

DROP

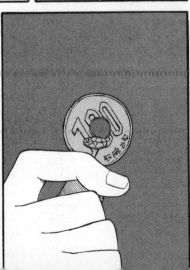

123

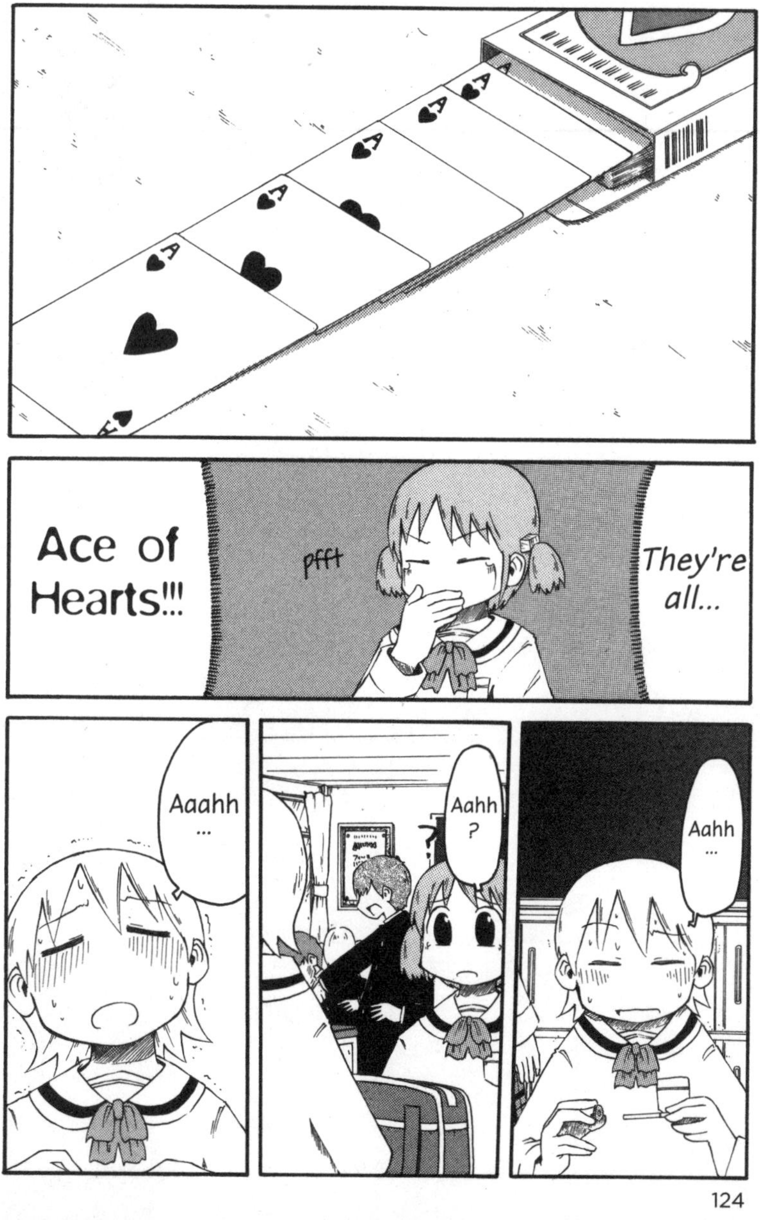
They're all...
pfft
Ace of Hearts!!!
Aahh ...
Aahh ?
Aaahh ...

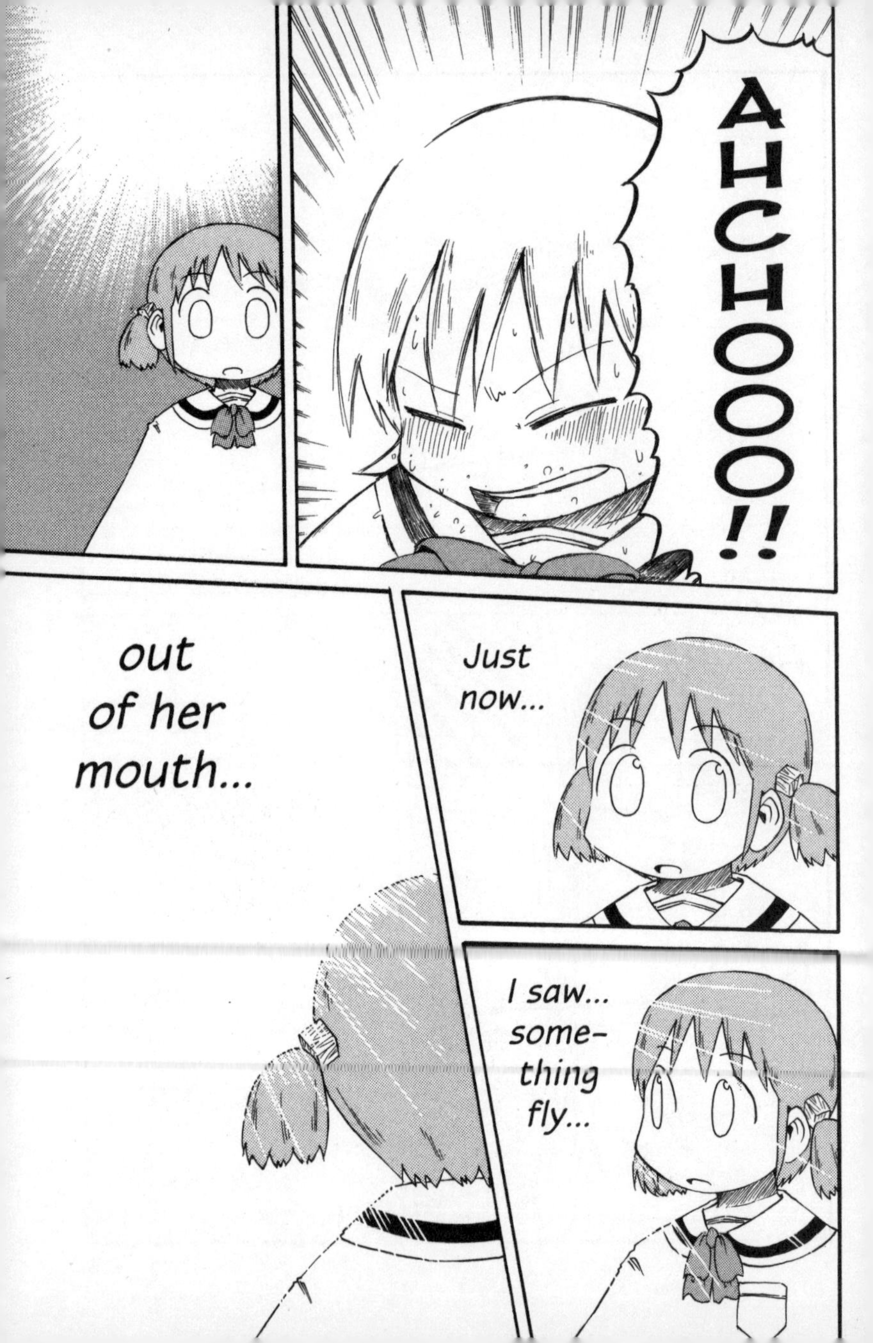
AHCHOOO!!
Just now...
I saw... some-thing fly...
out of her mouth...

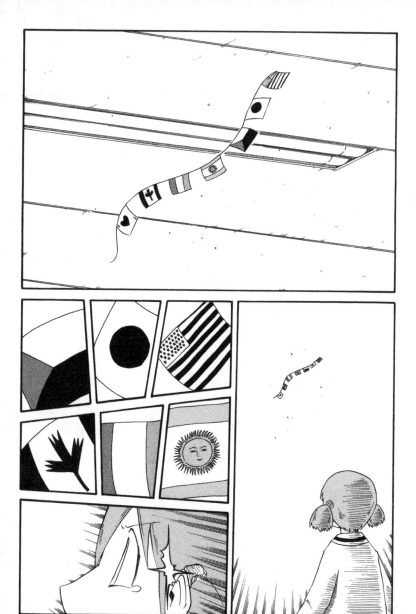

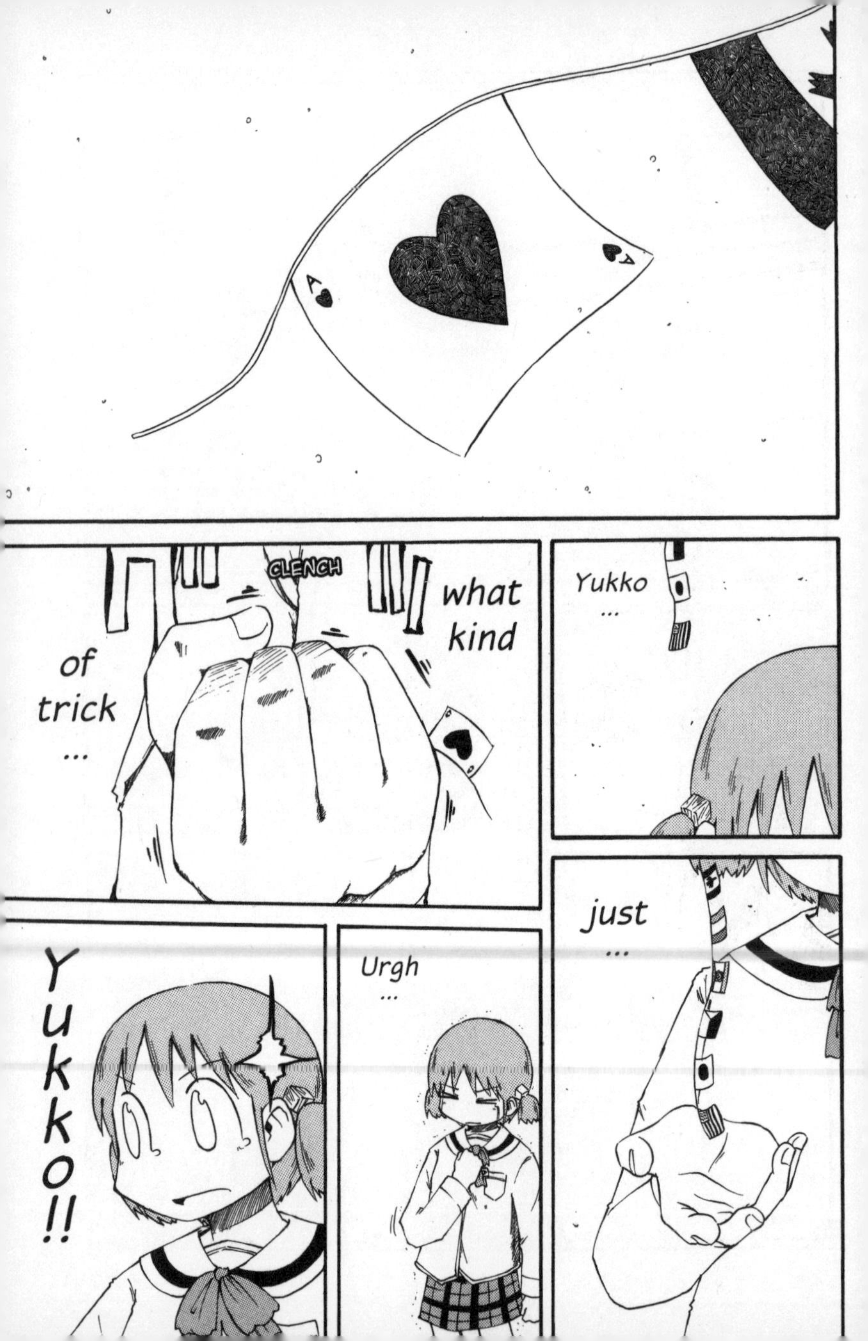
Yukko
...
CLENCH
what kind of trick
...
just
...
Urgh
...
Yukko!!

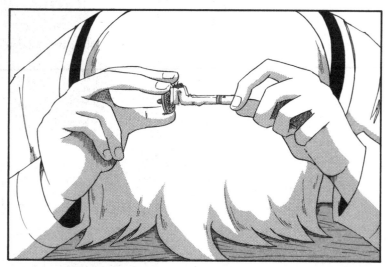

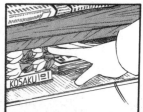

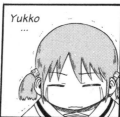

Yukko
...

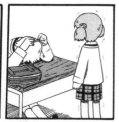

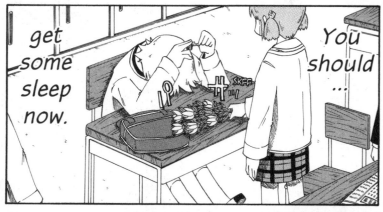

get
some
sleep
now.

You
should
...

chapter 33: end

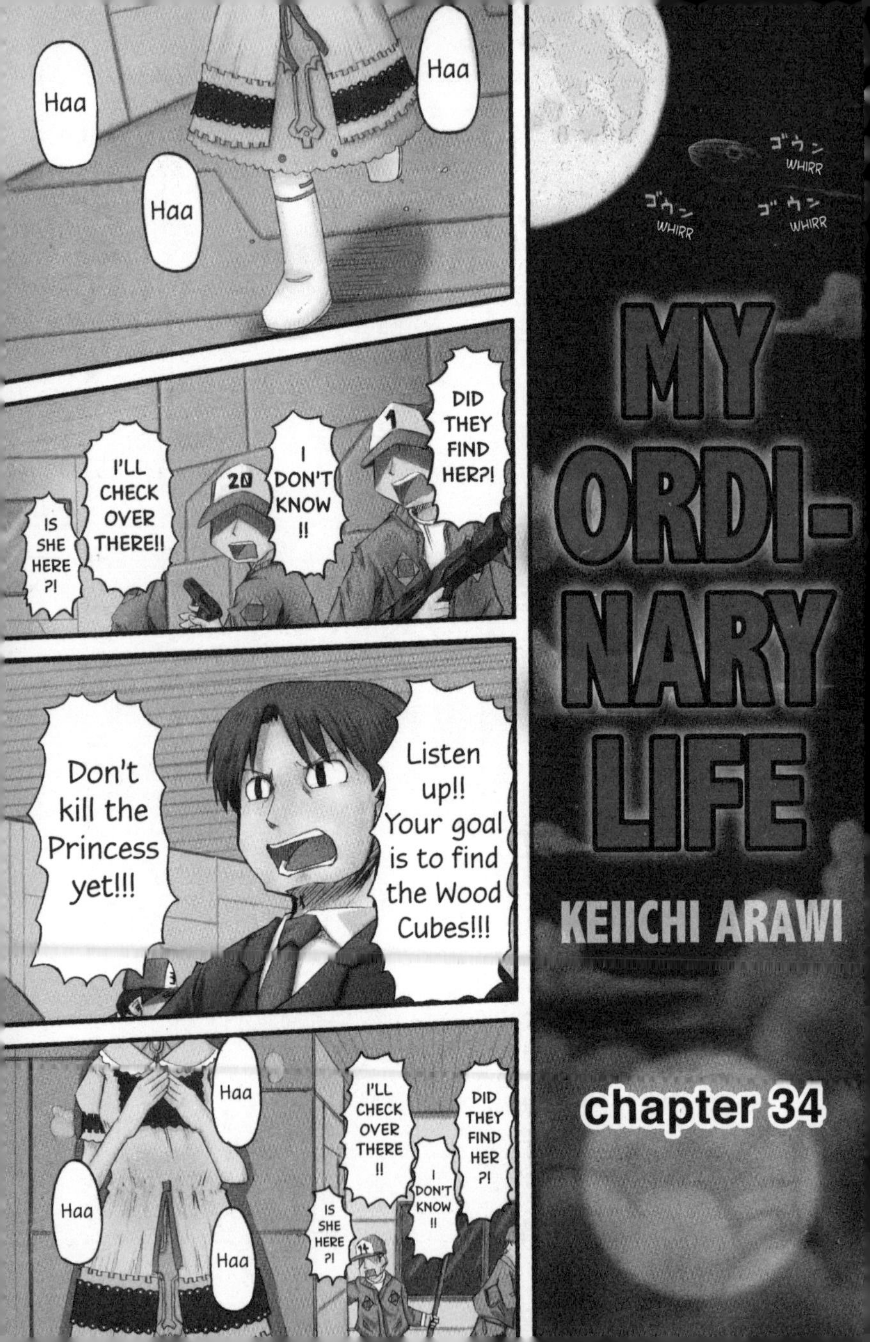
ゴウン
WHIRR
ゴウン
WHIRR
ゴウン
WHIRR
MY ORDINARY LIFE
KEIICHI ARAWI
chapter 34
Haa
Haa
Haa
DID THEY FIND HER?!
I DON'T KNOW!!
I'LL CHECK OVER THERE!!
IS SHE HERE?!
Listen up!! Your goal is to find the Wood Cubes!!!
Don't kill the Princess yet!!!
DID THEY FIND HER?!
I'LL CHECK OVER THERE!!
I DON'T KNOW!!
IS SHE HERE?!
Haa
Haa
Haa

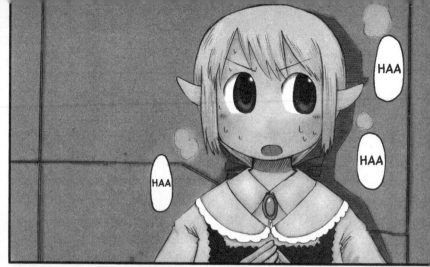

HAA

HAA

HAA

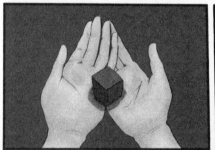

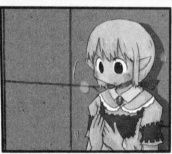

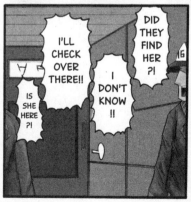

I'LL CHECK OVER THERE!!

DID THEY FIND HER ?!

I DON'T KNOW !!

IS SHE HERE ?!

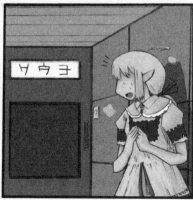

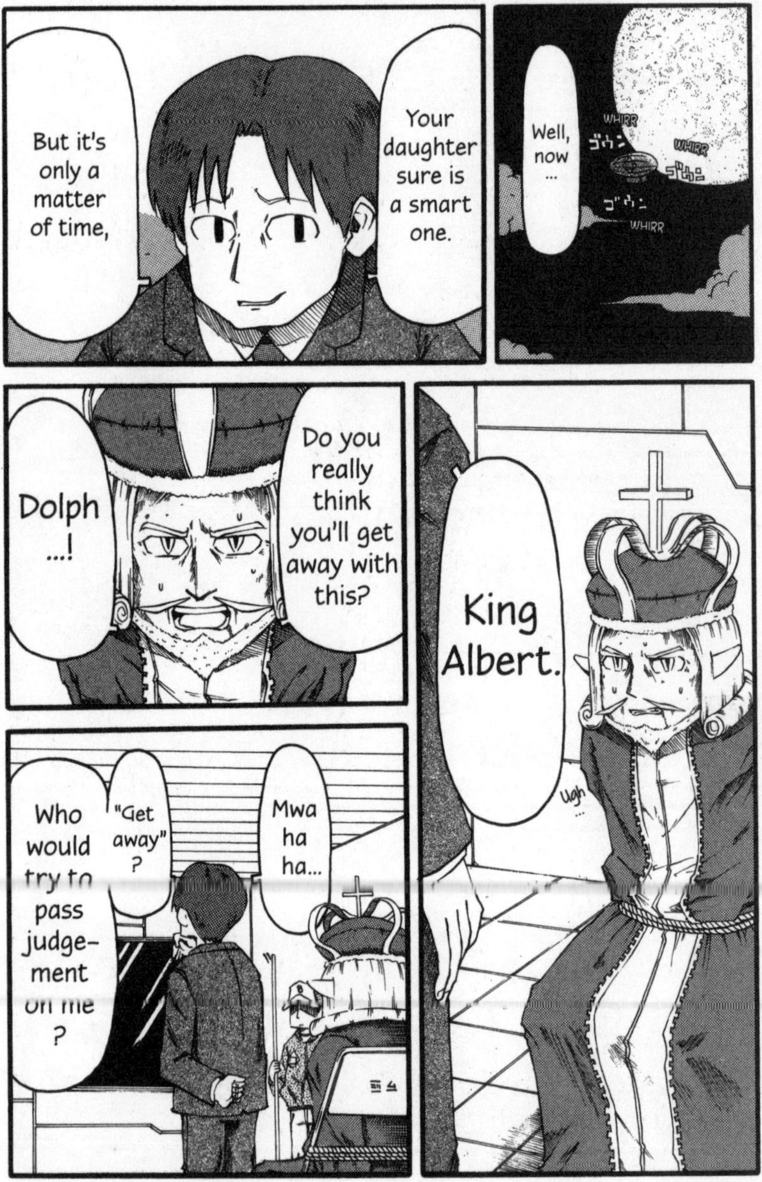

Well, now ...
WHIRR
ゴウン
WHIRR
WHIRR
Your daughter sure is a smart one.
But it's only a matter of time,
King Albert.
Ugh ...
Do you really think you'll get away with this?
Dolph ...!
Mwa ha ha...
"Get away" ?
Who would try to pass judge-ment on me ?

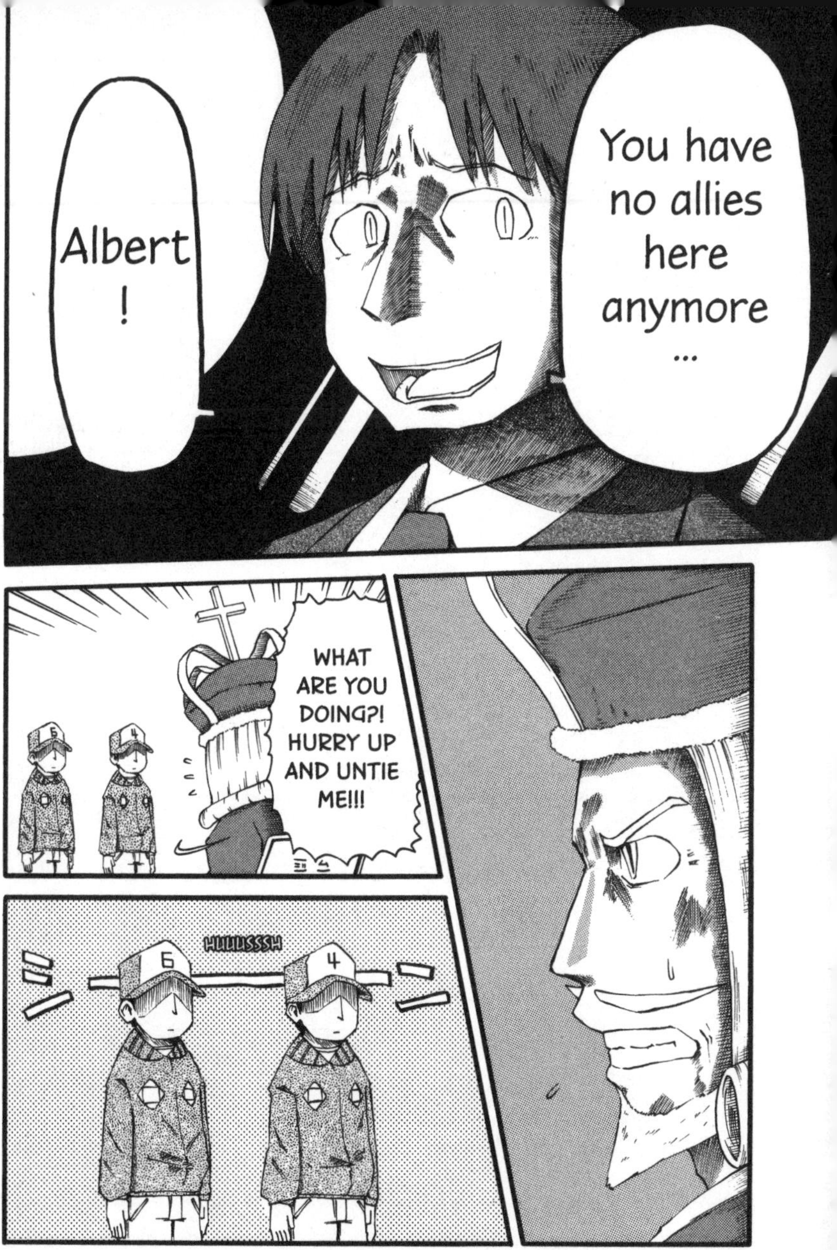
You have no allies here anymore ...
Albert !
WHAT ARE YOU DOING?! HURRY UP AND UNTIE ME!!!
HUUUSSSH

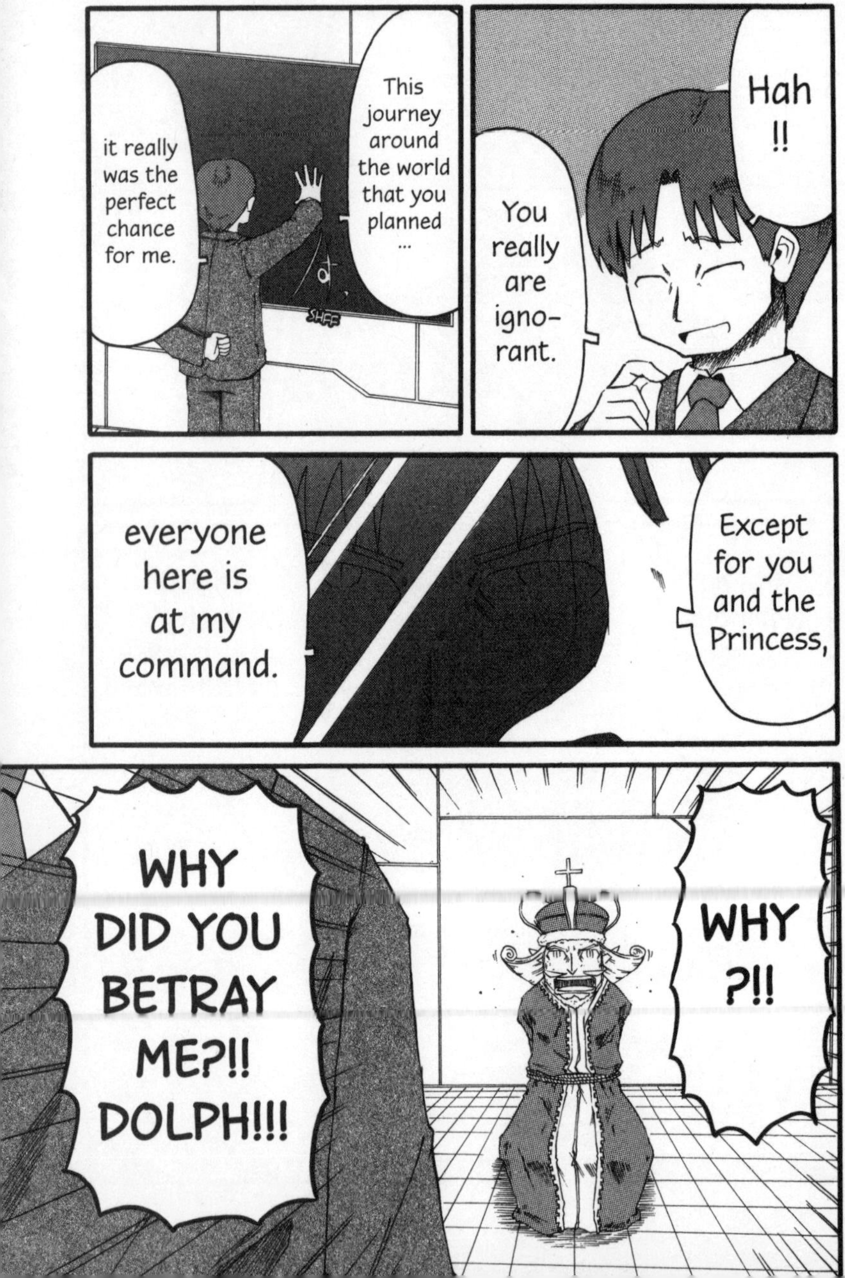
Hah !!
You really are igno- rant.
This journey around the world that you planned ...
it really was the perfect chance for me.
SHFF
Except for you and the Princess,
everyone here is at my command.
WHY ?!!
WHY DID YOU BETRAY ME?!! DOLPH!!!

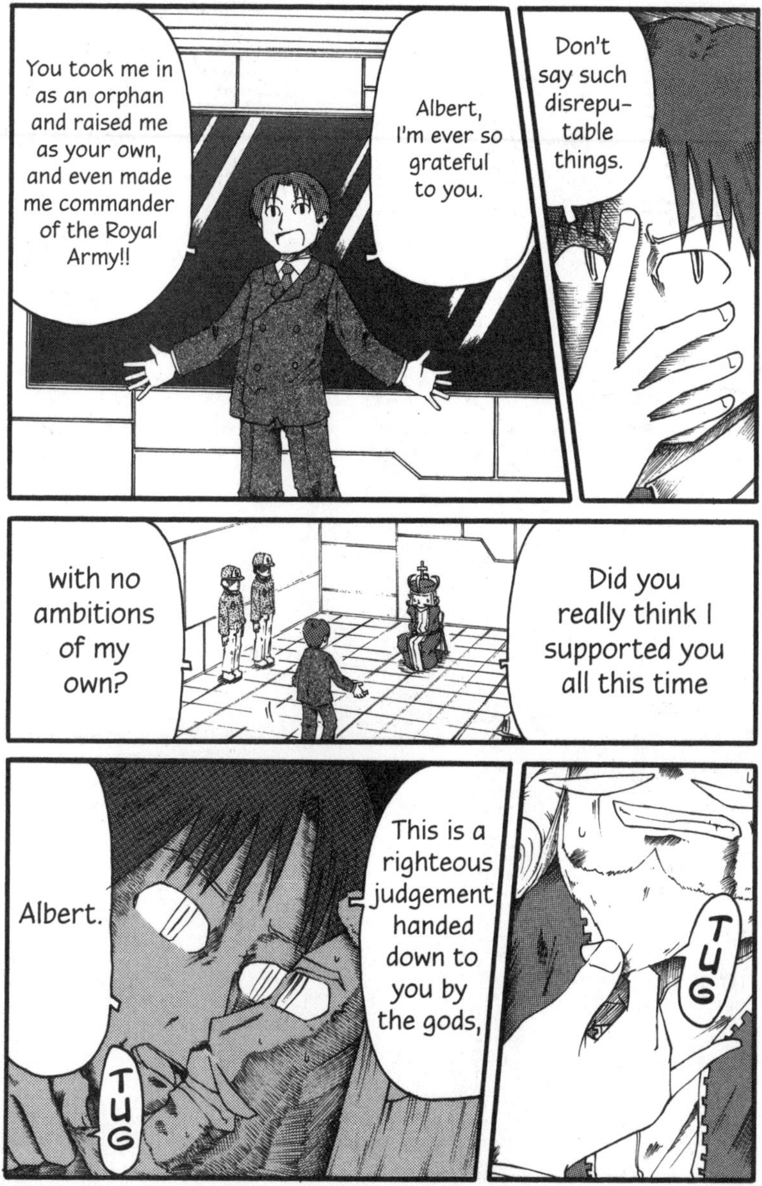
Don't say such disrepu- table things.
Albert, I'm ever so grateful to you.
You took me in as an orphan and raised me as your own, and even made me commander of the Royal Army!!
Did you really think I supported you all this time
with no ambitions of my own?
TUG
This is a righteous judgement handed down to you by the gods,
Albert.
TUG

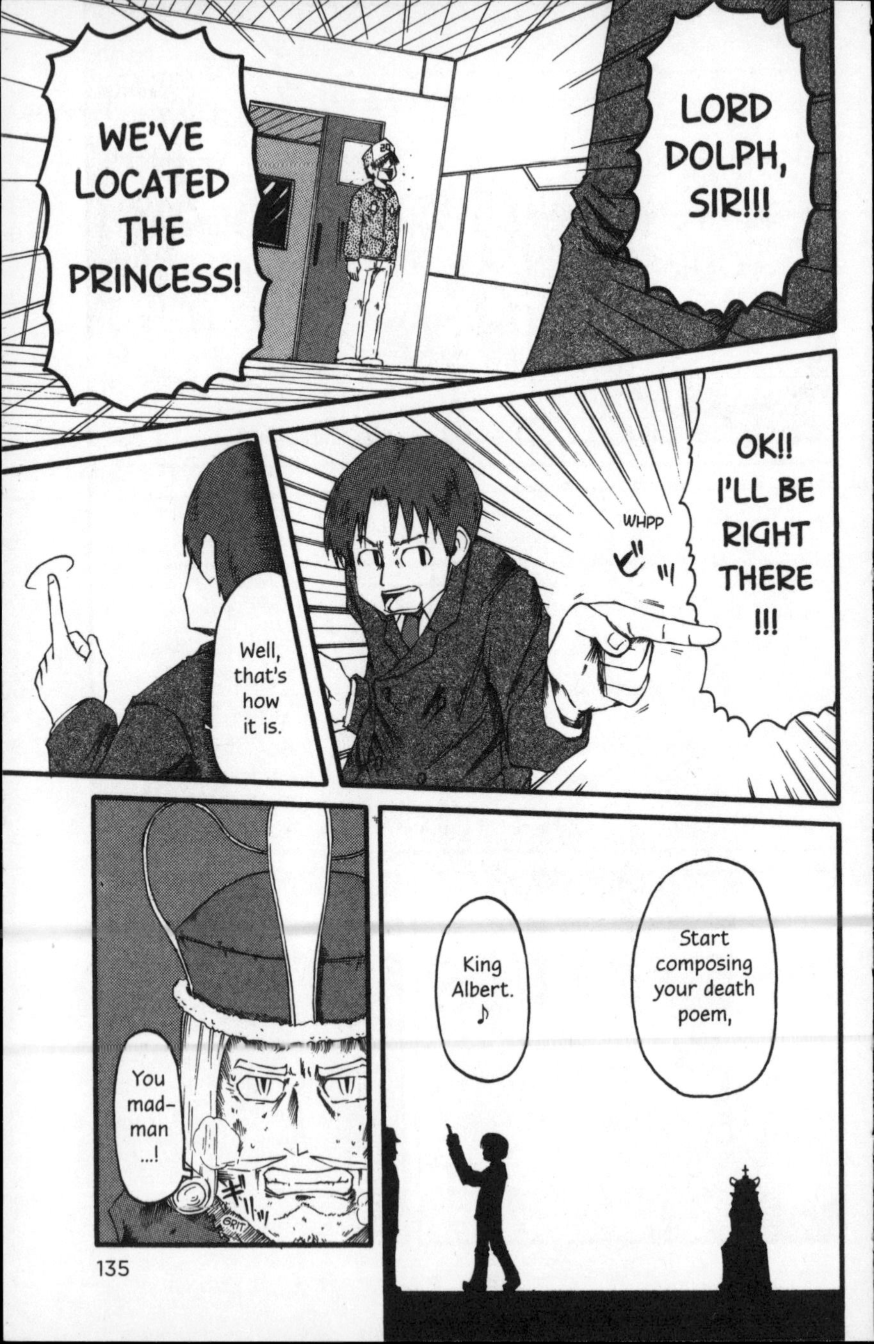
LORD DOLPH, SIR!!!
WE'VE LOCATED THE PRINCESS!
OK!! I'LL BE RIGHT THERE !!!
WHPP
Well, that's how it is.
Start composing your death poem,
King Albert. ♪
You mad-man ...!
GRIT

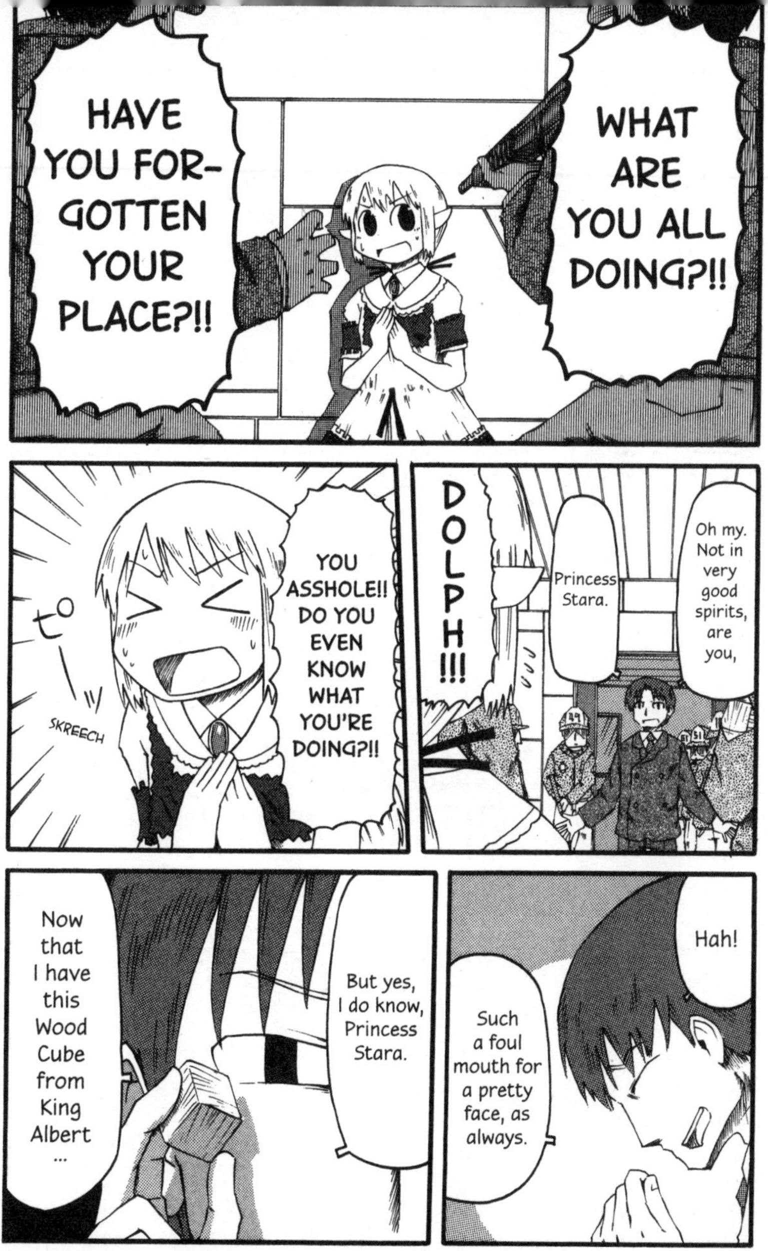
WHAT ARE YOU ALL DOING?!!
HAVE YOU FOR-GOTTEN YOUR PLACE?!!
Oh my. Not in very good spirits, are you,
Princess Stara.
DOLPH!!!
YOU ASSHOLE!! DO YOU EVEN KNOW WHAT YOU'RE DOING?!!
SKREECH
Hah!
Such a foul mouth for a pretty face, as always.
But yes, I do know, Princess Stara.
Now that I have this Wood Cube from King Albert ...

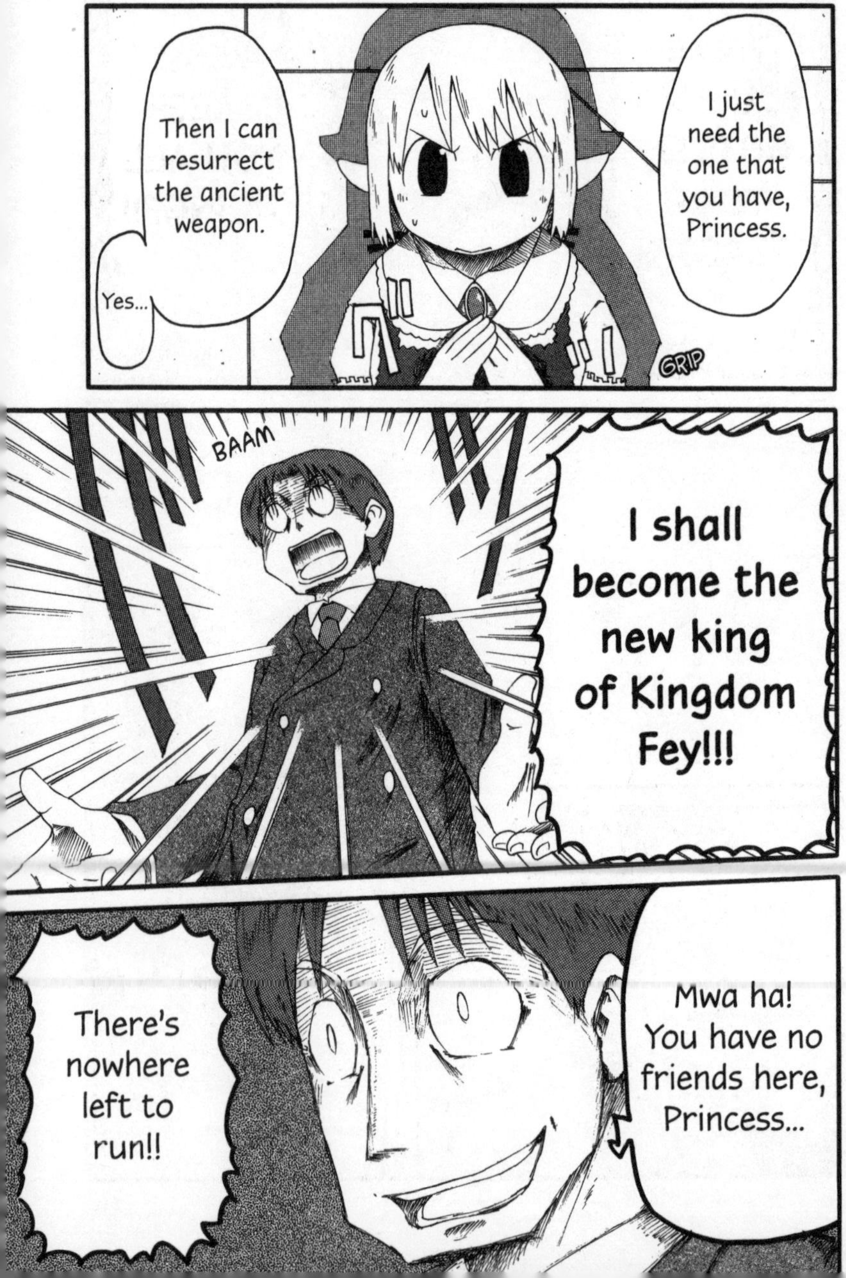
I just need the one that you have, Princess.
Then I can resurrect the ancient weapon.
Yes...
GRIP
I shall become the new king of Kingdom Fey!!!
BAAM
Mwa ha! You have no friends here, Princess...
There's nowhere left to run!!

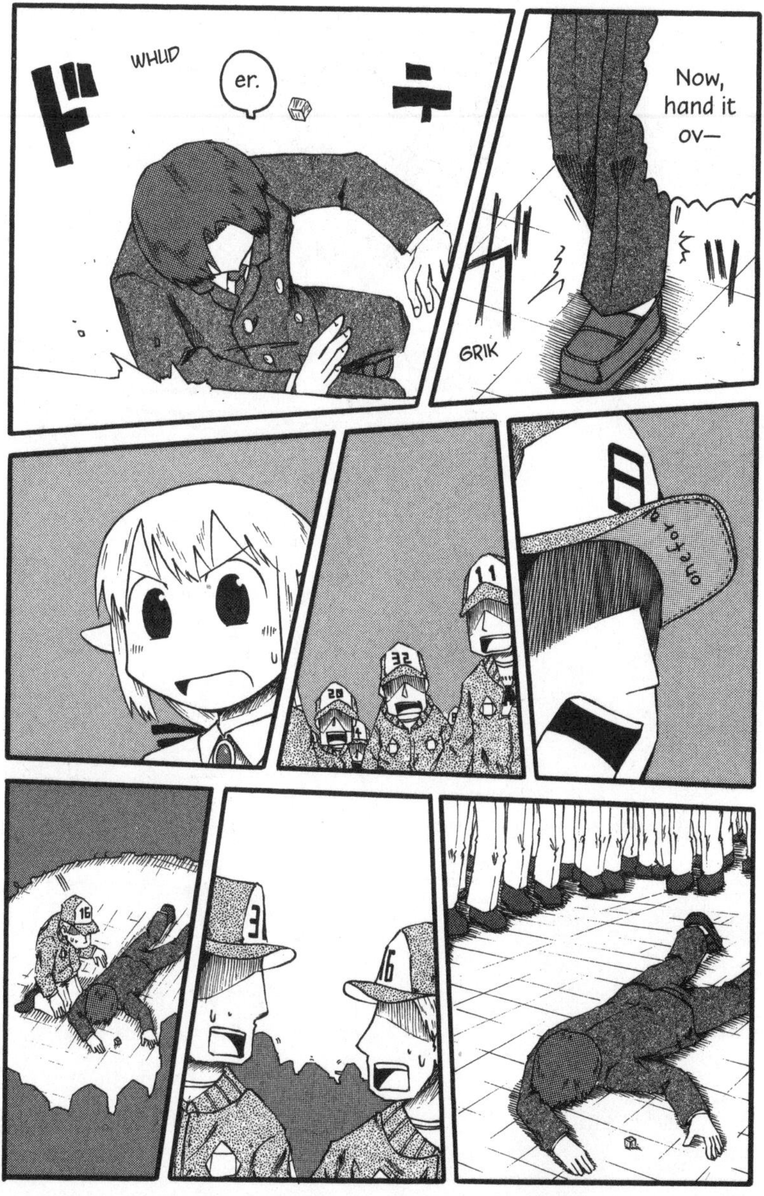
Now, hand it ov—
GRIK
er.
WHUD

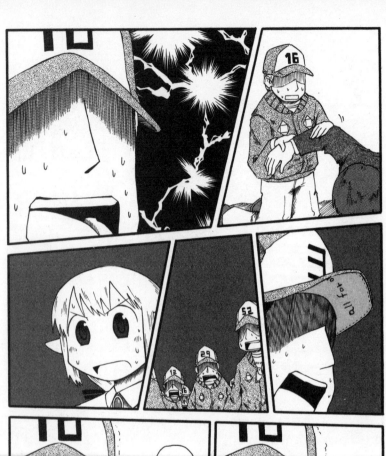

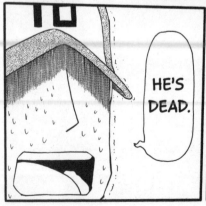

HE'S
DEAD.

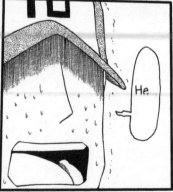

He...

139

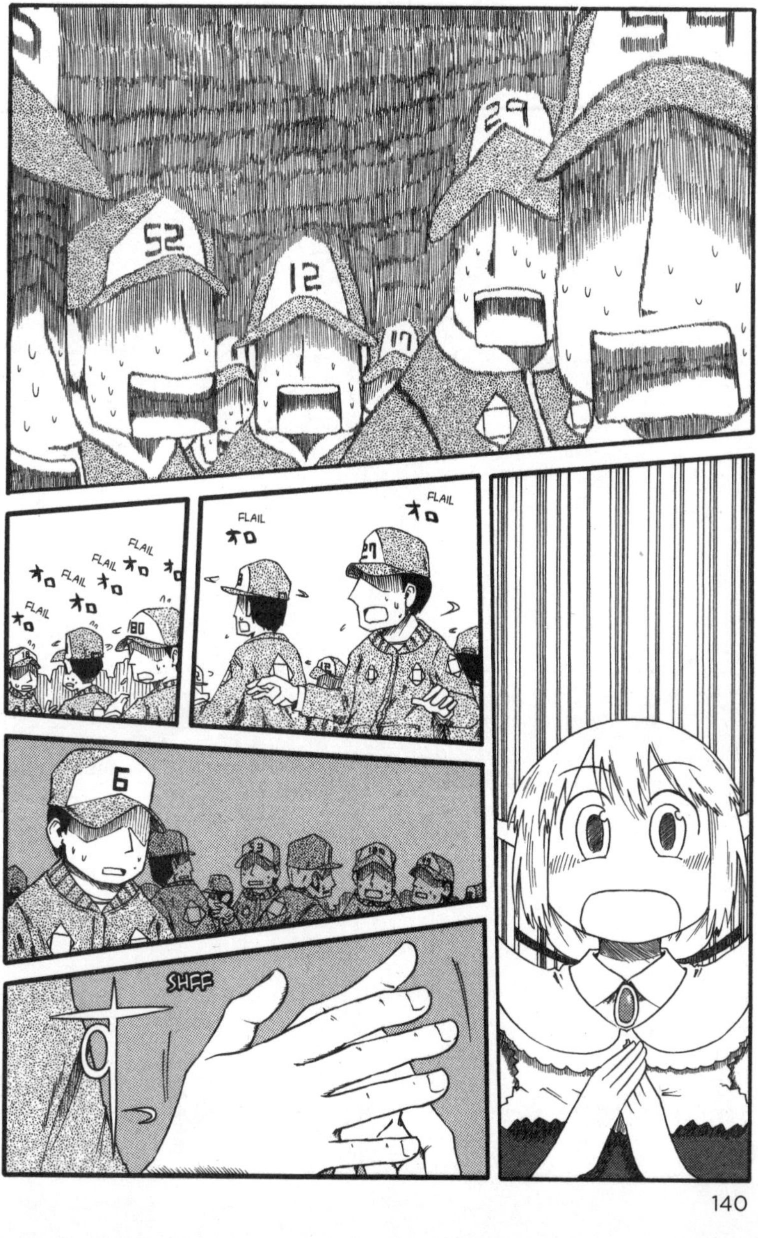
FLAIL
オロ
FLAIL
オロ
FLAIL
オロ
FLAIL
オロ
FLAIL
オロ
FLAIL
オロ
オロ
SHFF

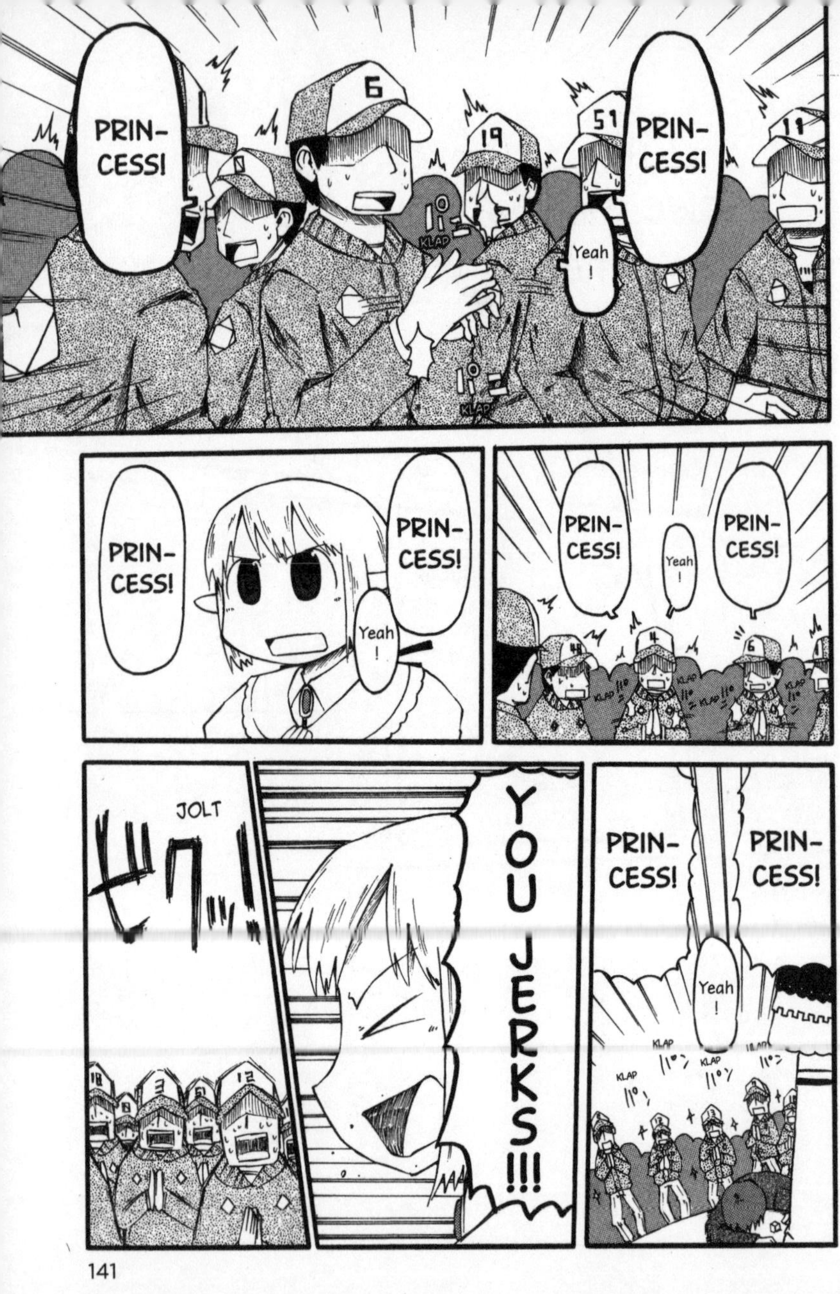
PRIN-CESS!
Yeah!
PRIN-CESS!
KLAP
KLAP
PRIN-CESS!
Yeah!
PRIN-CESS!
KLAP
KLAP
KLAP
KLAP
PRIN-CESS!
Yeah!
PRIN-CESS!
PRIN-CESS!
PRIN-CESS!
Yeah!
KLAP
KLAP
KLAP
KLAP
YOU JERKS!!!
JOLT

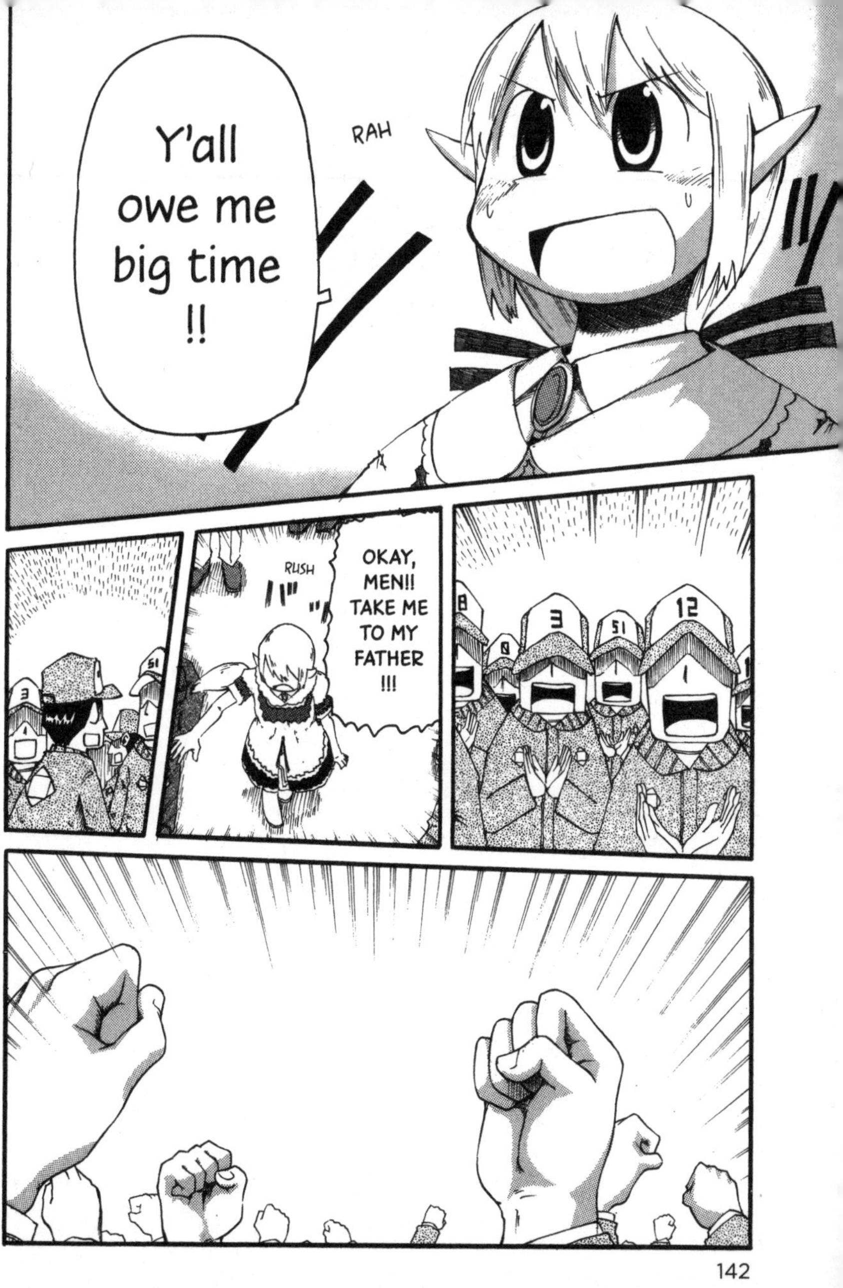
RAH
Y'all owe me big time !!
OKAY, MEN!! TAKE ME TO MY FATHER !!!
RUSH

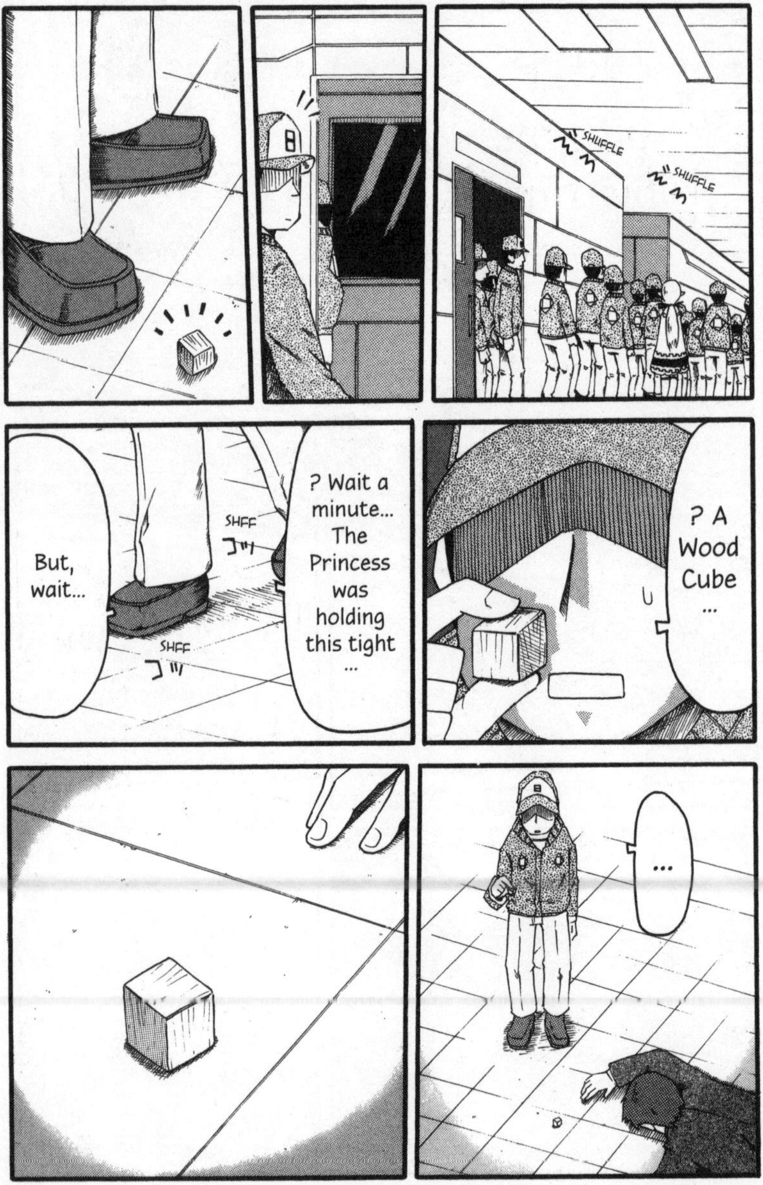
SHUFFLE
SHUFFLE
? A Wood Cube ...
? Wait a minute... The Princess was holding this tight ...
SHFF
SHFF
But, wait...
...

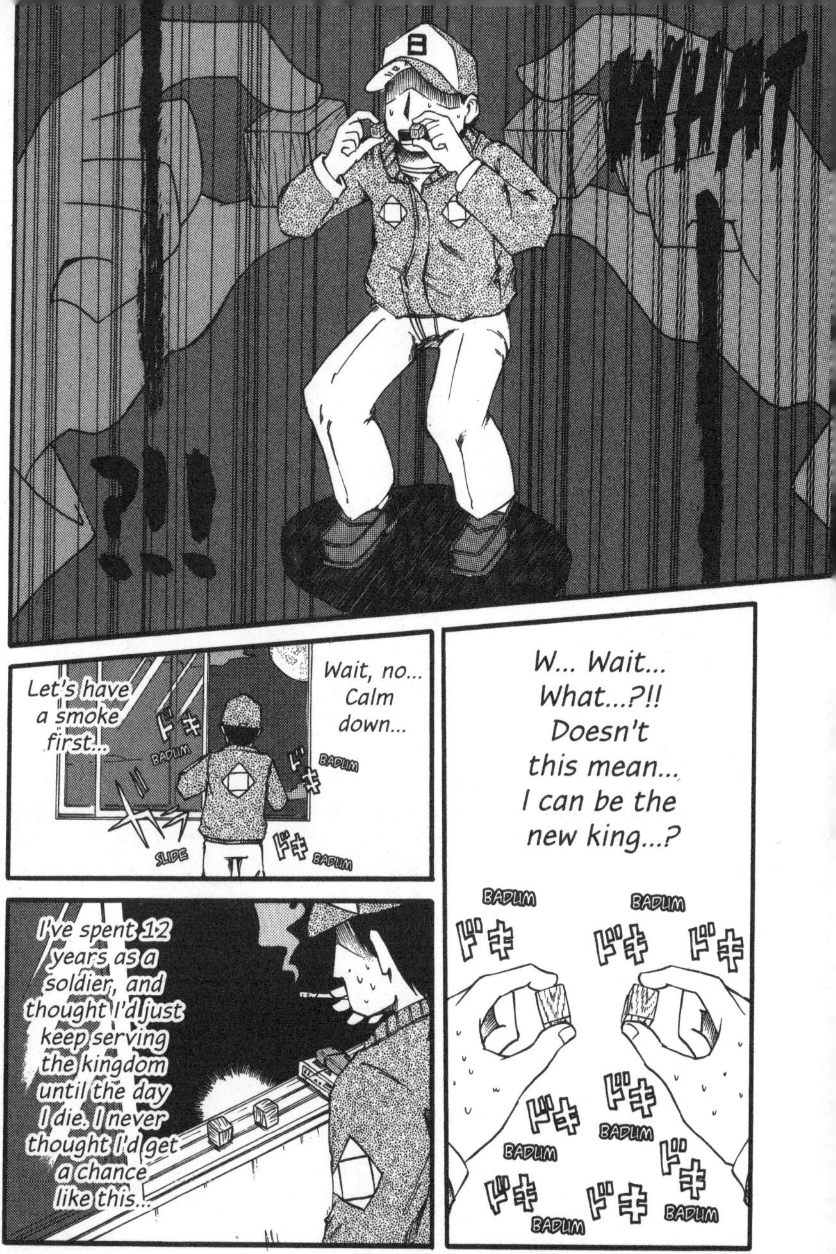
WHAT
?!!
W... Wait... What...?!! Doesn't this mean... I can be the new king...?
BADUM
ドキ
BADUM
ドキ
ドキ
ドキ
ドキ
BADUM
BADUM
ドキ
ドキ
ドキ
BADUM
BADUM
Wait, no... Calm down...
Let's have a smoke first...
ドキ
BADUM
ドキ
BADUM
ドキ
BADUM
ガラ
SLIDE
I've spent 12 years as a soldier, and thought I'd just keep serving the kingdom until the day I die. I never thought I'd get a chance like this...

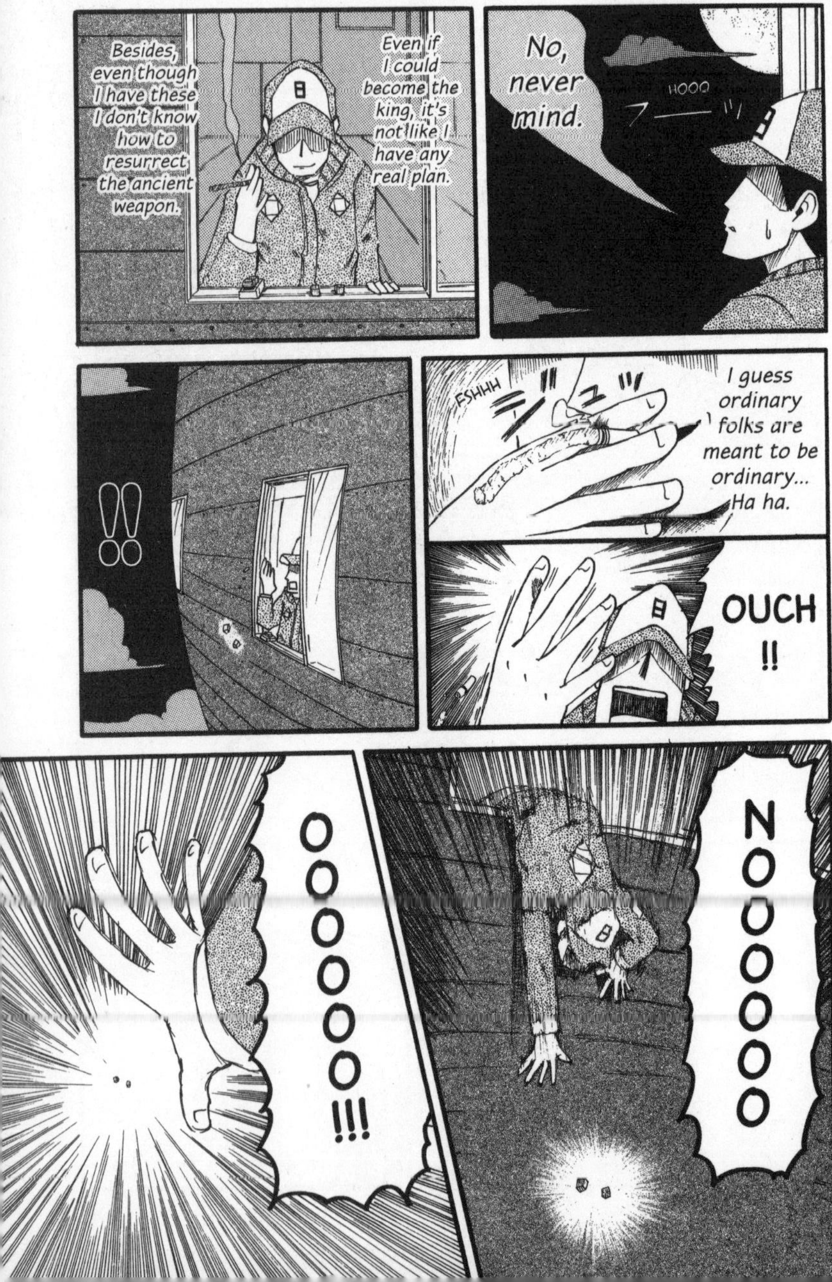
HOOO
No, never mind.
Even if I could become the king, it's not like I have any real plan.
Besides, even though I have these I don't know how to resurrect the ancient weapon.
FSHHH
I guess ordinary folks are meant to be ordinary... Ha ha.
OUCH!!
!!
NOOOOOOO
OOOOOOO!!!

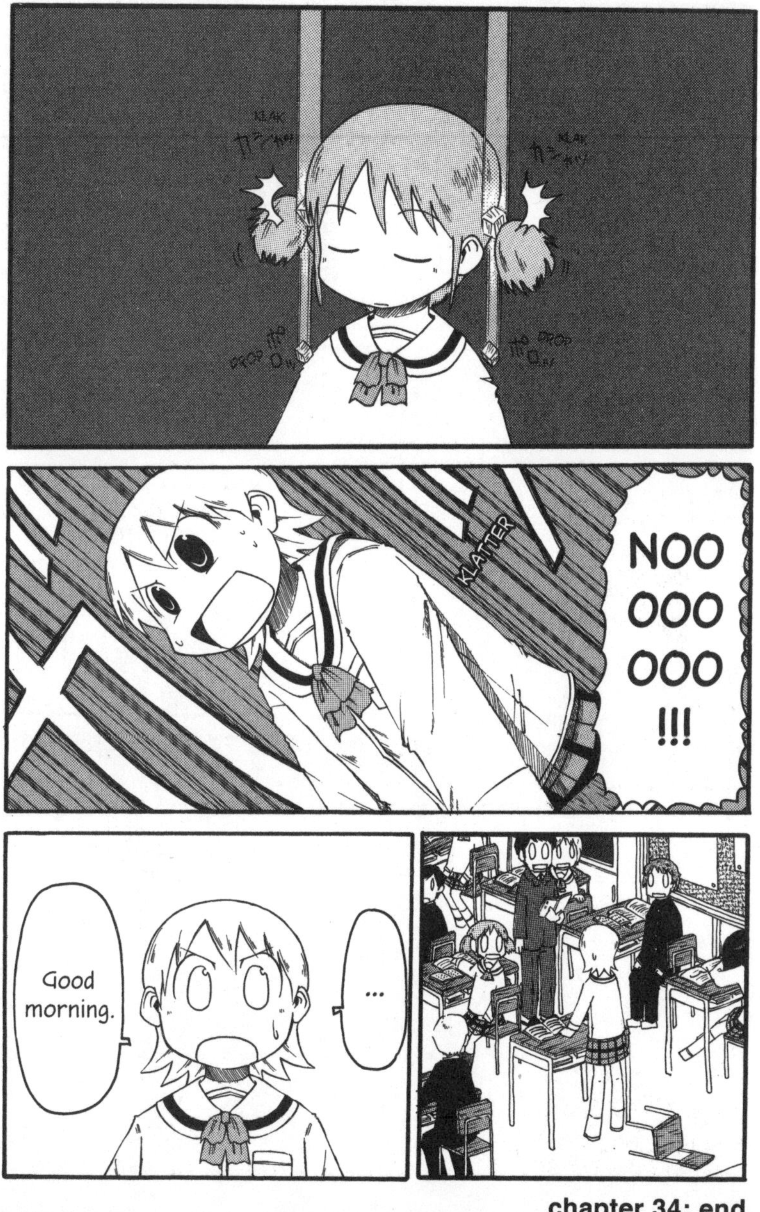
KLAK
KLAK
DROP
DROP
NOO OOO OOO !!!
KLATTER
...
Good morning.

chapter 34: end

chapter 34.5

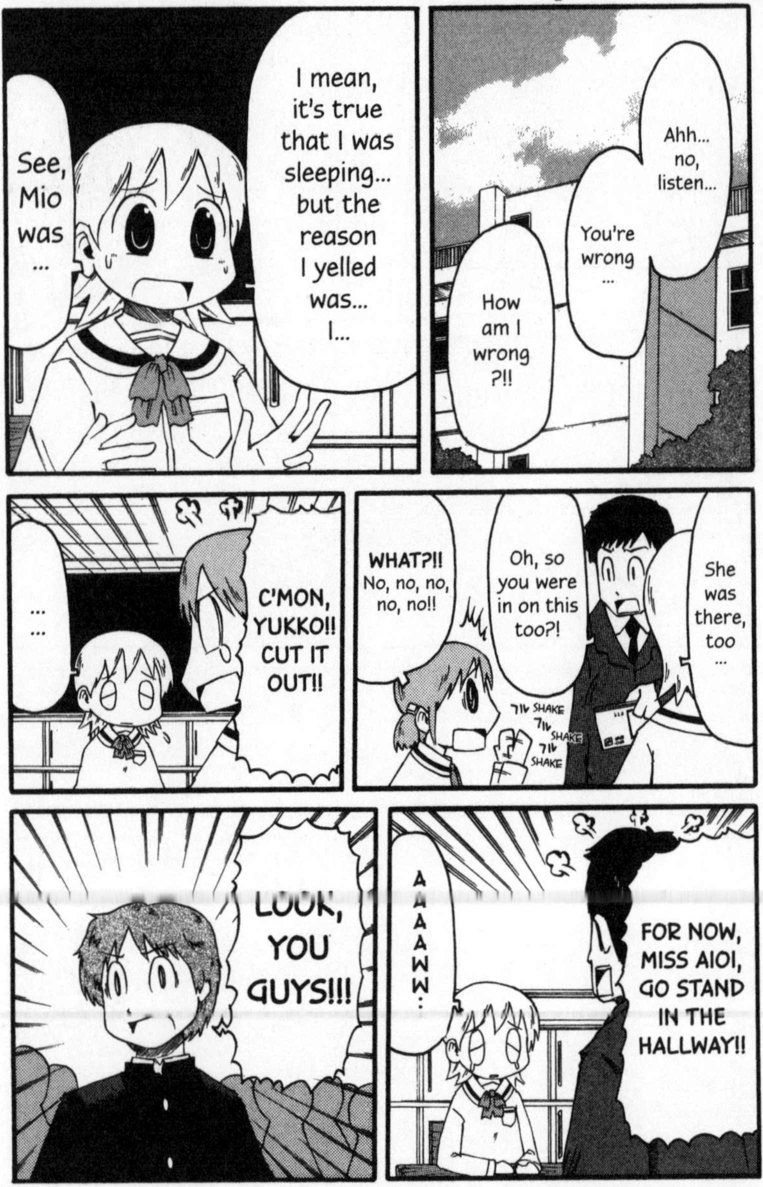
Ahh... no, listen...
You're wrong ...
How am I wrong ?!!
I mean, it's true that I was sleeping... but the reason I yelled was... I...
See, Mio was ...
She was there, too ...
Oh, so you were in on this too?!
WHAT?!! No, no, no, no, no!!
SHAKE SHAKE SHAKE
C'MON, YUKKO!! CUT IT OUT!!
... ...
FOR NOW, MISS AIOI, GO STAND IN THE HALLWAY!!
AAAAWW..
LOOK, YOU GUYS!!!

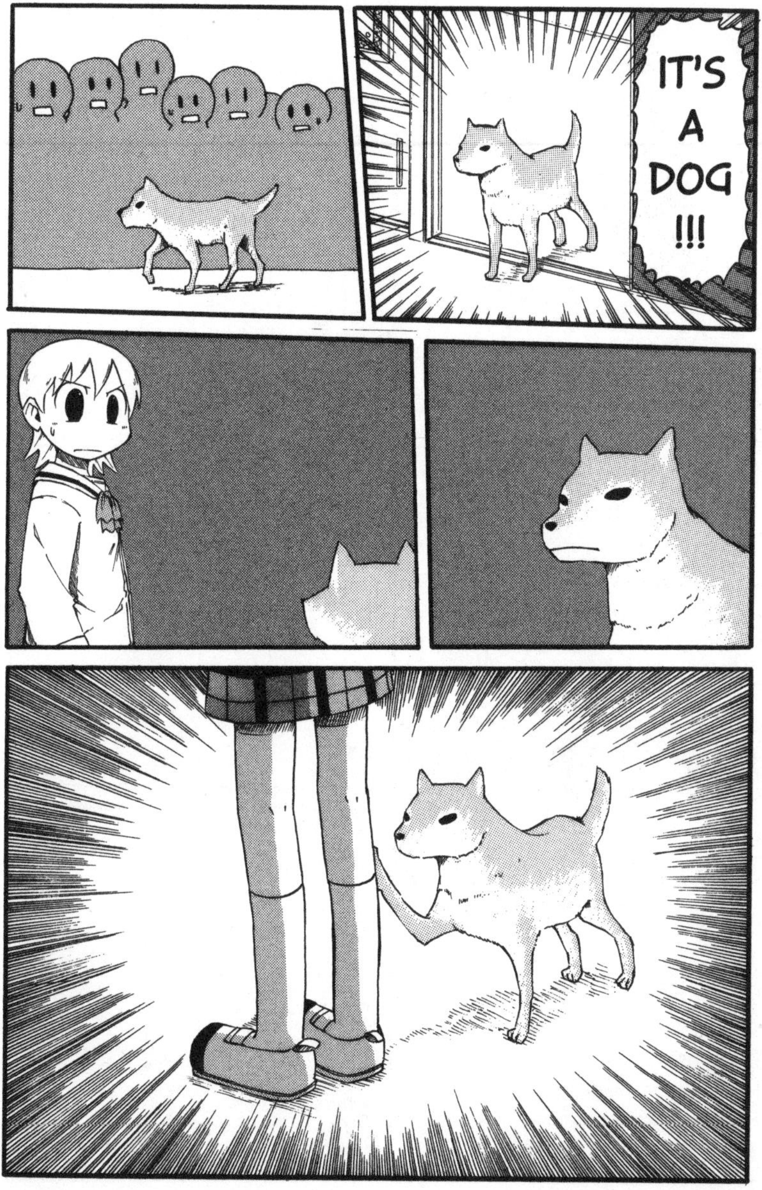
IT'S A DOG !!!

chapter 34.5: end

ordinary shorts

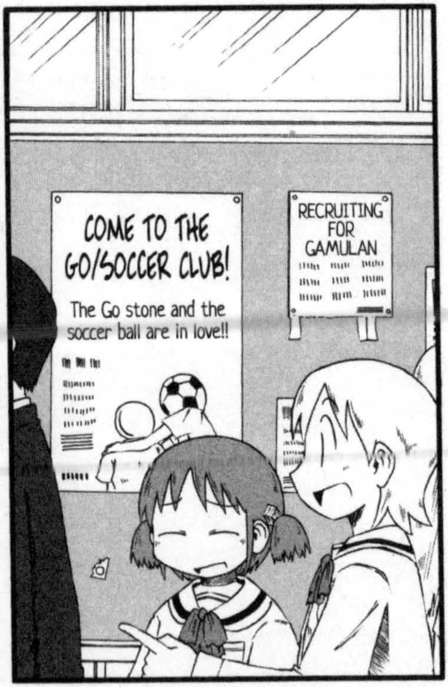
RECRUITING FOR GAMULAN
COME TO THE GO/SOCCER CLUB!
The Go stone and the soccer ball are in love!!

go/soccer club

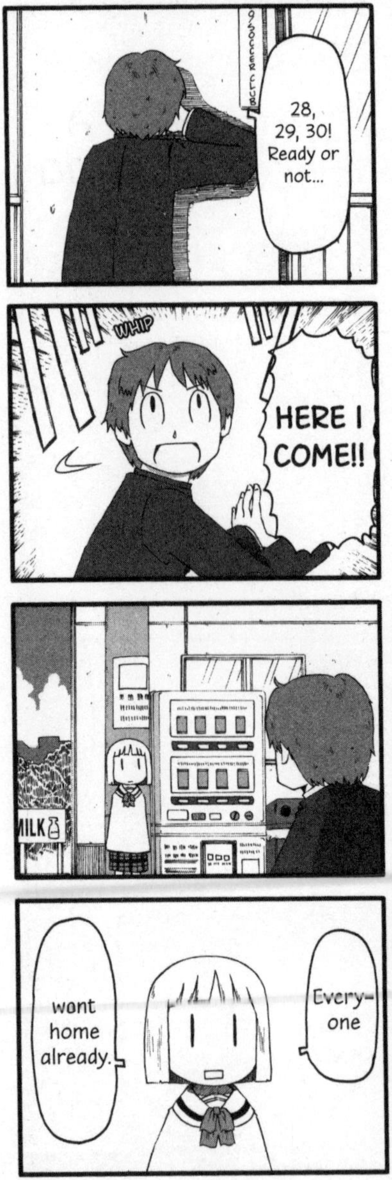
9/SOCCER CLUB
28, 29, 30! Ready or not...
WHIP
HERE I COME!!
MILK
Every-one
went home already.

guidance counselor

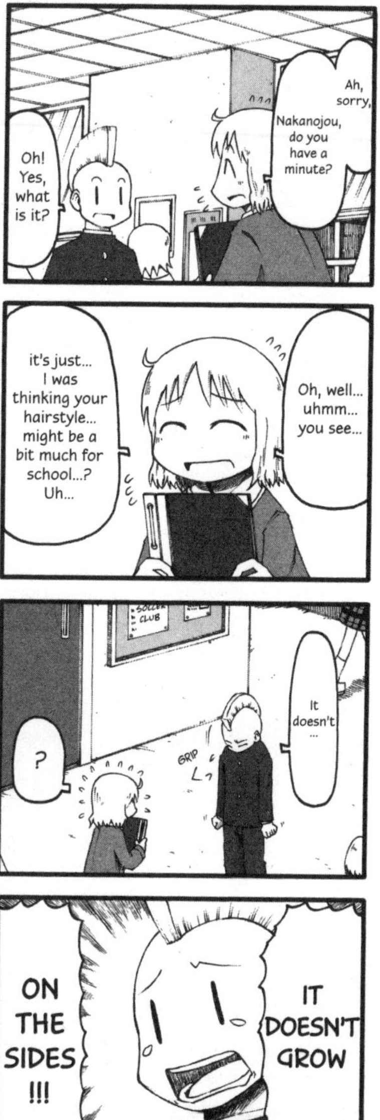

Ah, sorry, Nakanojou, do you have a minute?
Oh! Yes, what is it?
Oh, well... uhmm... you see...
it's just... I was thinking your hairstyle... might be a bit much for school...? Uh...
It doesn't...
GRIP
?
IT DOESN'T GROW
ON THE SIDES!!!

buddy

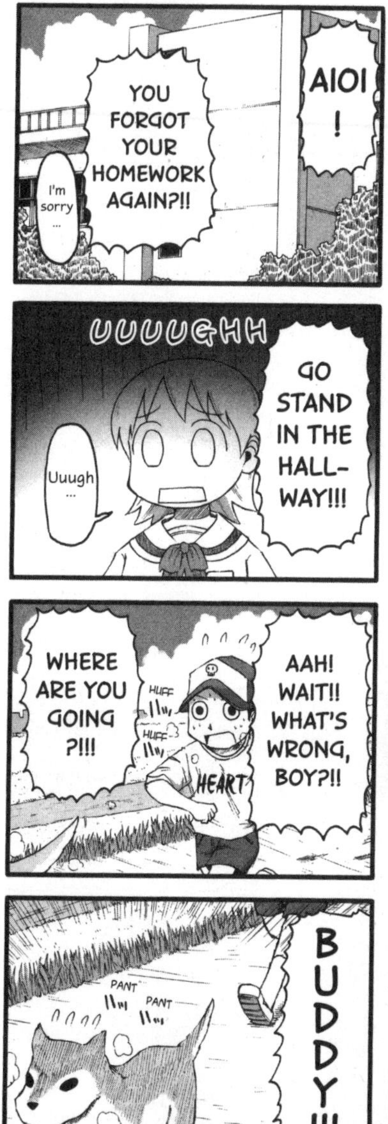

AIOI!
YOU FORGOT YOUR HOMEWORK AGAIN?!!
I'm sorry...
GO STAND IN THE HALLWAY!!!
UUUUGHH
Uuugh...
AAH! WAIT!! WHAT'S WRONG, BOY?!!
HUFF
HUFF
HEART
WHERE ARE YOU GOING?!!!
BUDDY!!!
PANT
PANT

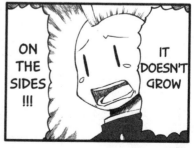

go/soccer club 2

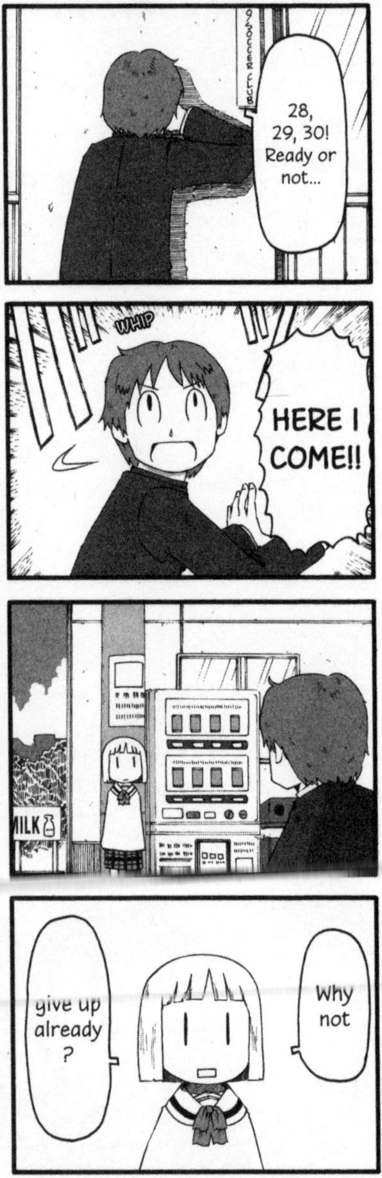
9/SOCCER CLUB
28, 29, 30! Ready or not...
WHIP
HERE I COME!!
MILK
Why not
give up already ?

hallway

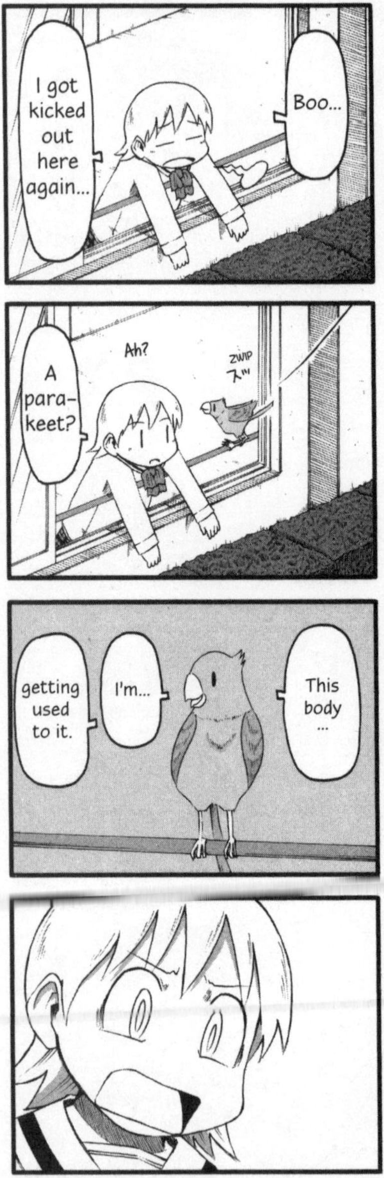
Boo...
I got kicked out here again...
ZWIP
Ah?
A parakeet?
This body ...
I'm...
getting used to it.

sasahara

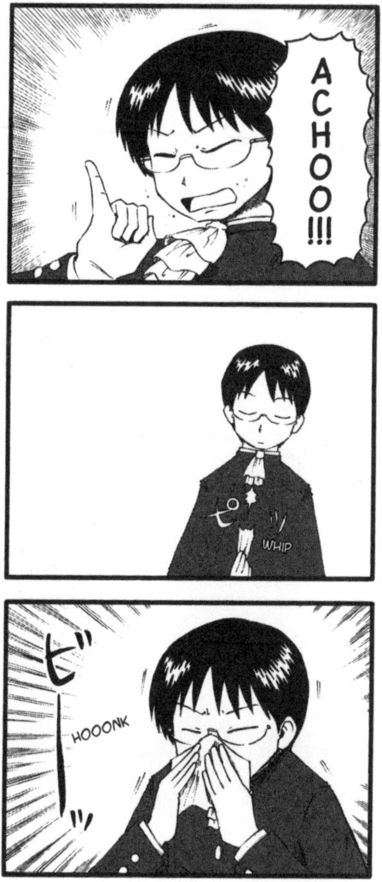
ACHOO!!!
WHIP
HOOONK
No way!!
tissues?!
WHIP

go/soccer club 3

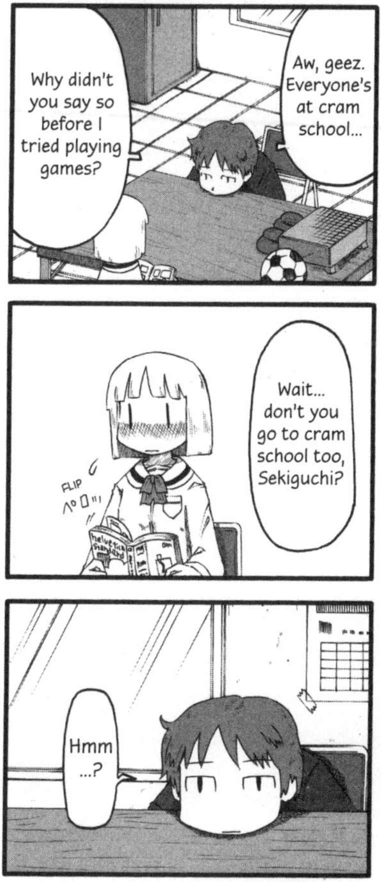
Aw, geez. Everyone's at cram school...
Why didn't you say so before I tried playing games?
Wait... don't you go to cram school too, Sekiguchi?
FLIP
Hmm ...?
No way!!
JERK

ordinary shorts: end

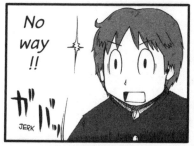

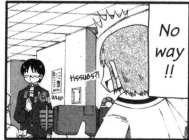

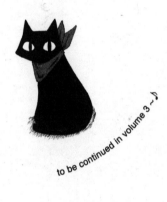

to be continued in volume 3 ~ ♪

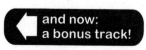and now:
a bonus track!

**the following pages are an early
prototype for nichijou.**

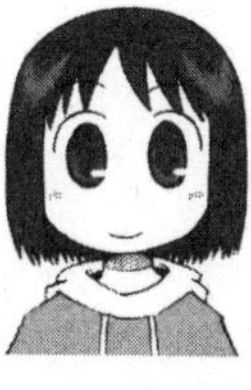

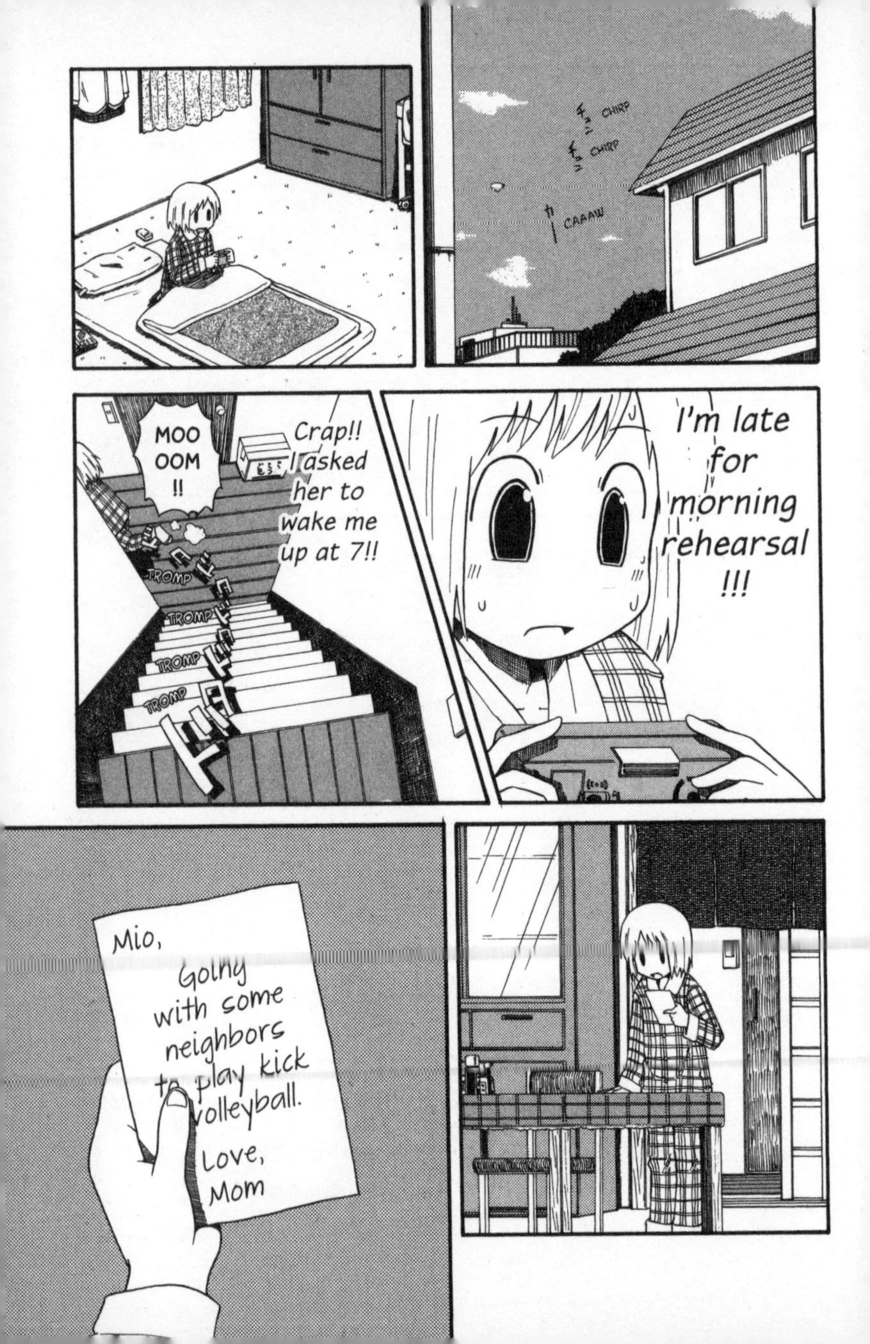
CHIRP
CHIRP
CAAAW
I'm late for morning rehearsal !!!
Crap!! I asked her to wake me up at 7!!
MOO OOM !!
TROMP
TROMP
TROMP
TROMP
Mio,
Going with some neighbors to play kick volleyball.
Love, Mom

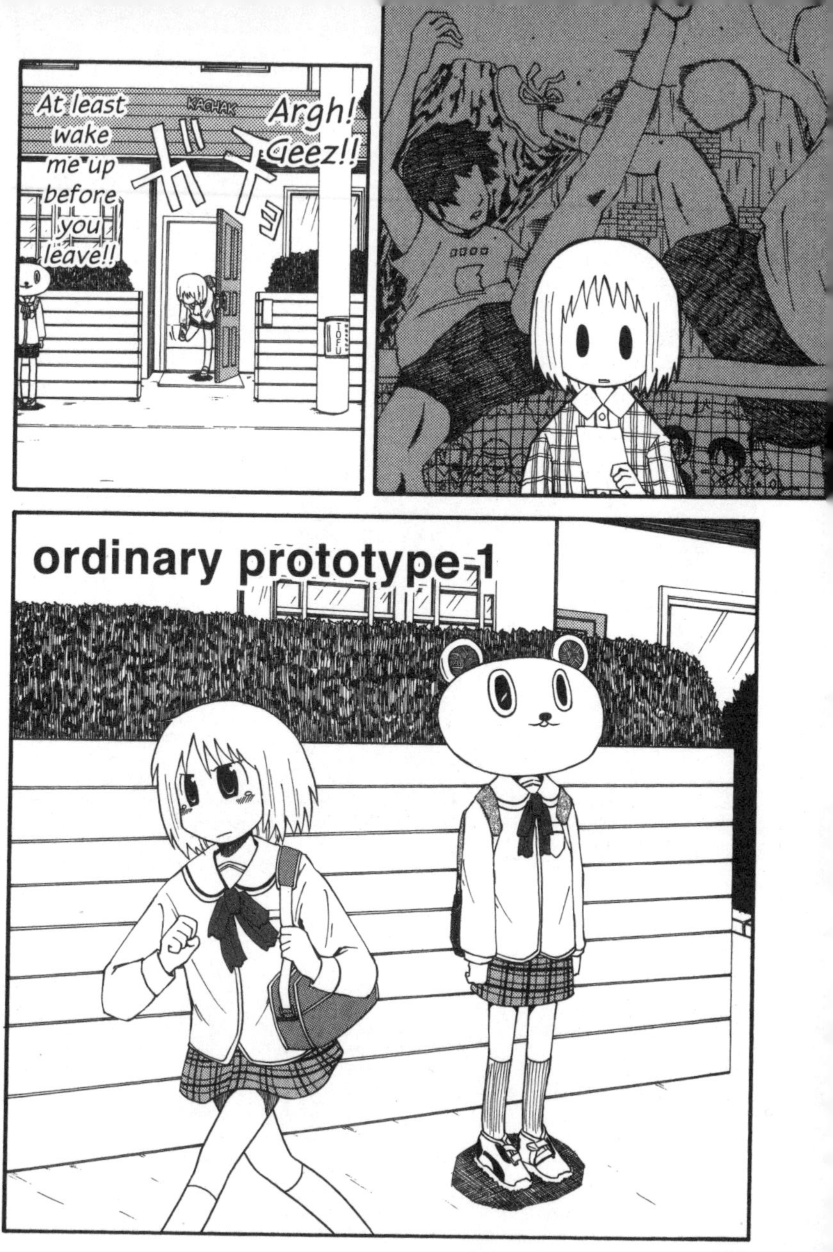
Argh! Geez!!
KACHAK
At least wake me up before you leave!!
TOFU
ordinary prototype 1

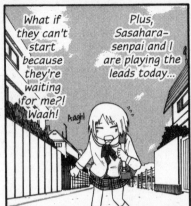

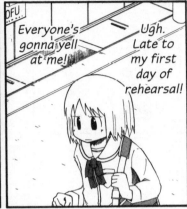

Ugh. Late to my first day of rehearsal!
Everyone's gonna yell at me!
Plus, Sasahara-senpai and I are playing the leads today...
What if they can't start because they're waiting for me?! Waah!
Aagh!
Well... Sasahara-senpai and me as the leads...
TOFU
Hang on.
I think ...

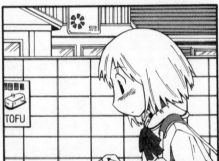

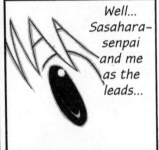

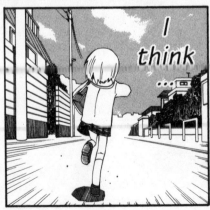

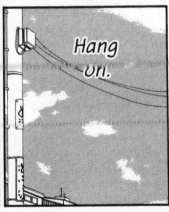

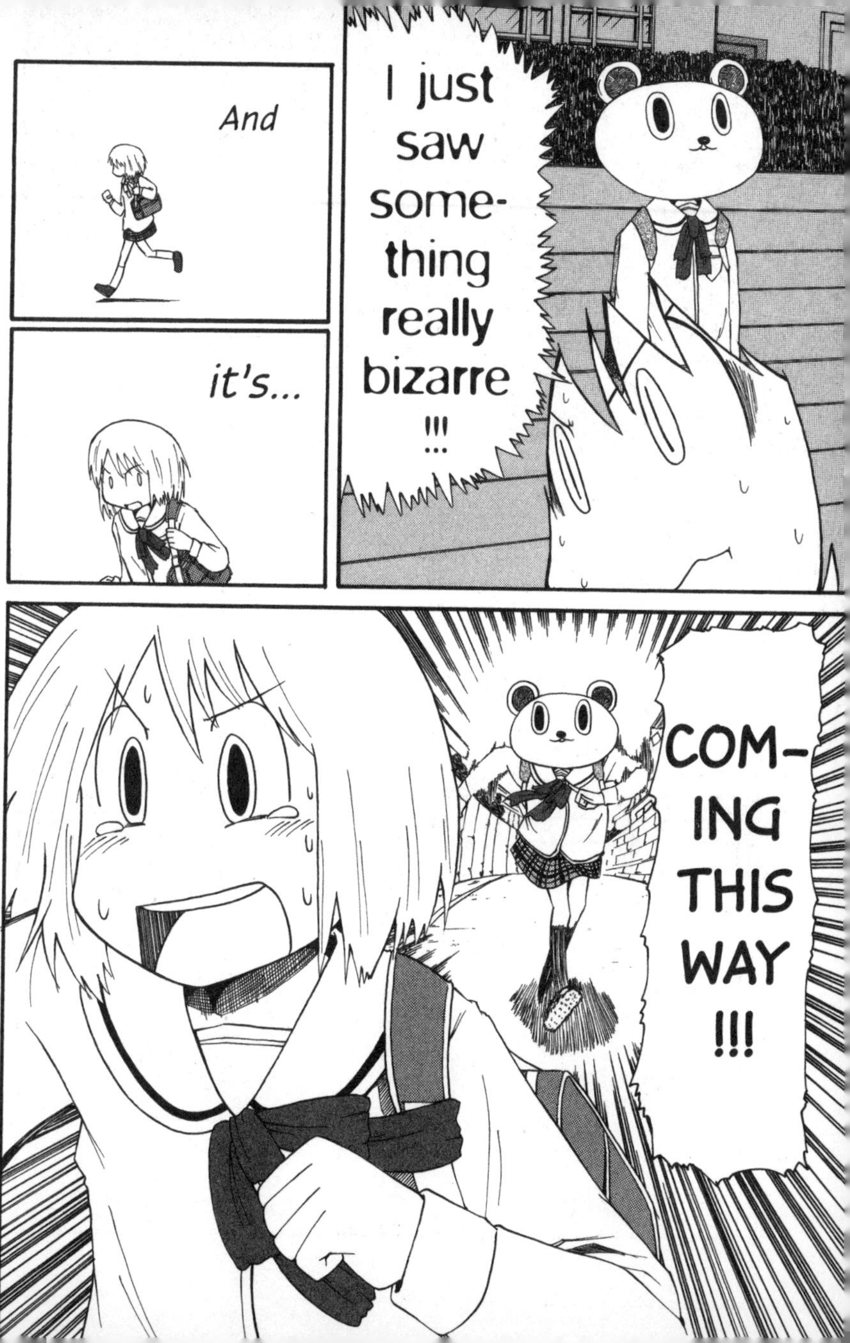
I just saw some-thing really bizarre !!!
And
it's...
COM-ING THIS WAY !!!

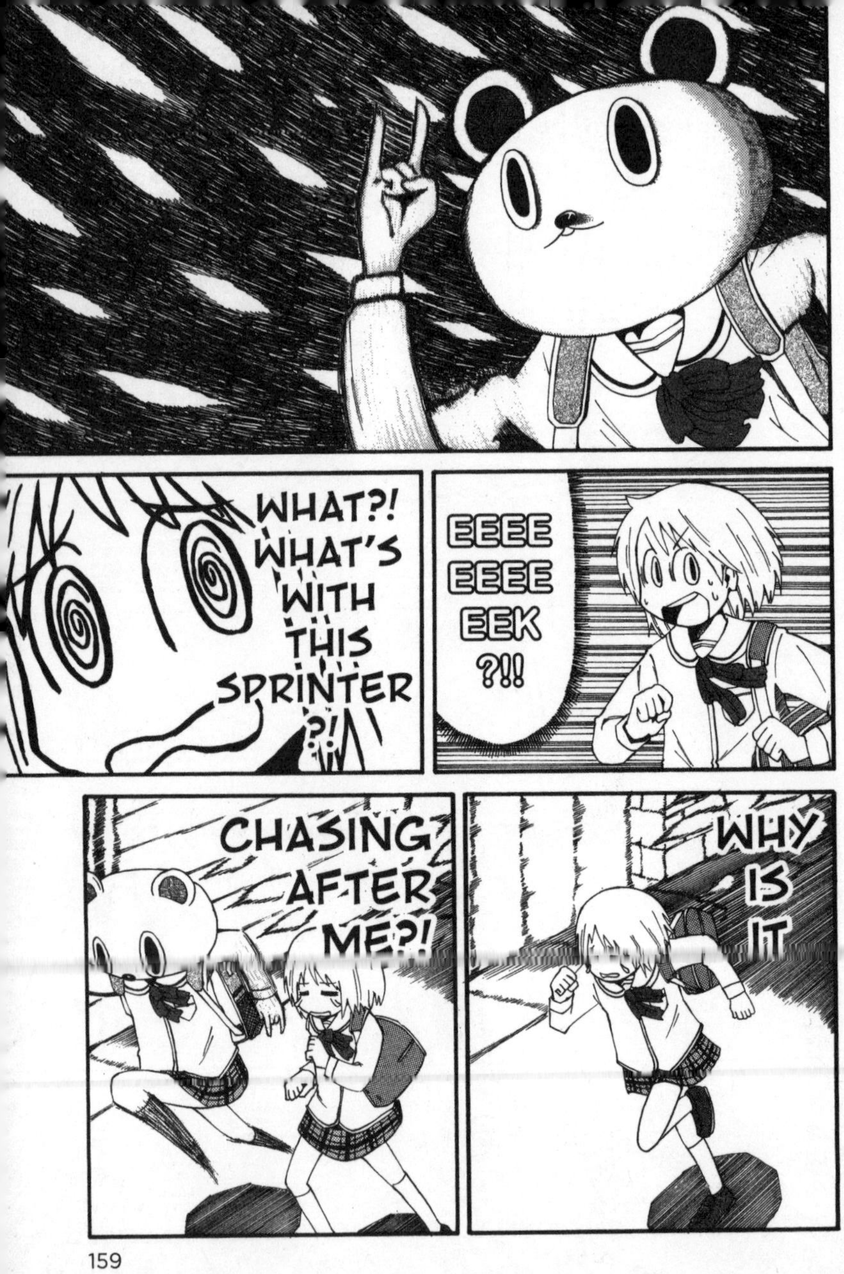
EEEE EEEE EEK ?!!
WHAT?! WHAT'S WITH THIS SPRINTER ?!
WHY IS IT
CHASING AFTER ME?!

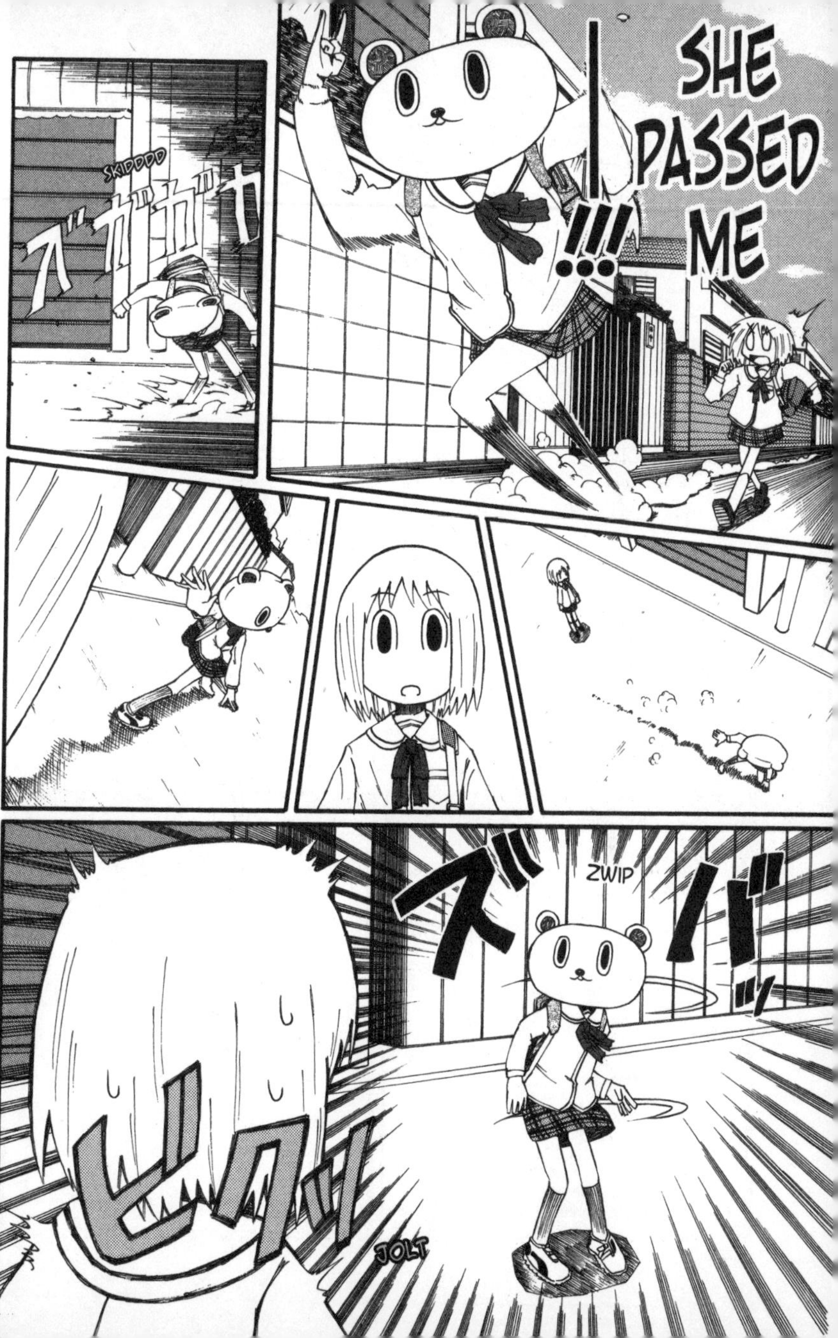
SHE PASSED ME
!!!
SKIDDDD
ZWIP
ズバッ
ビクッ
JOLT

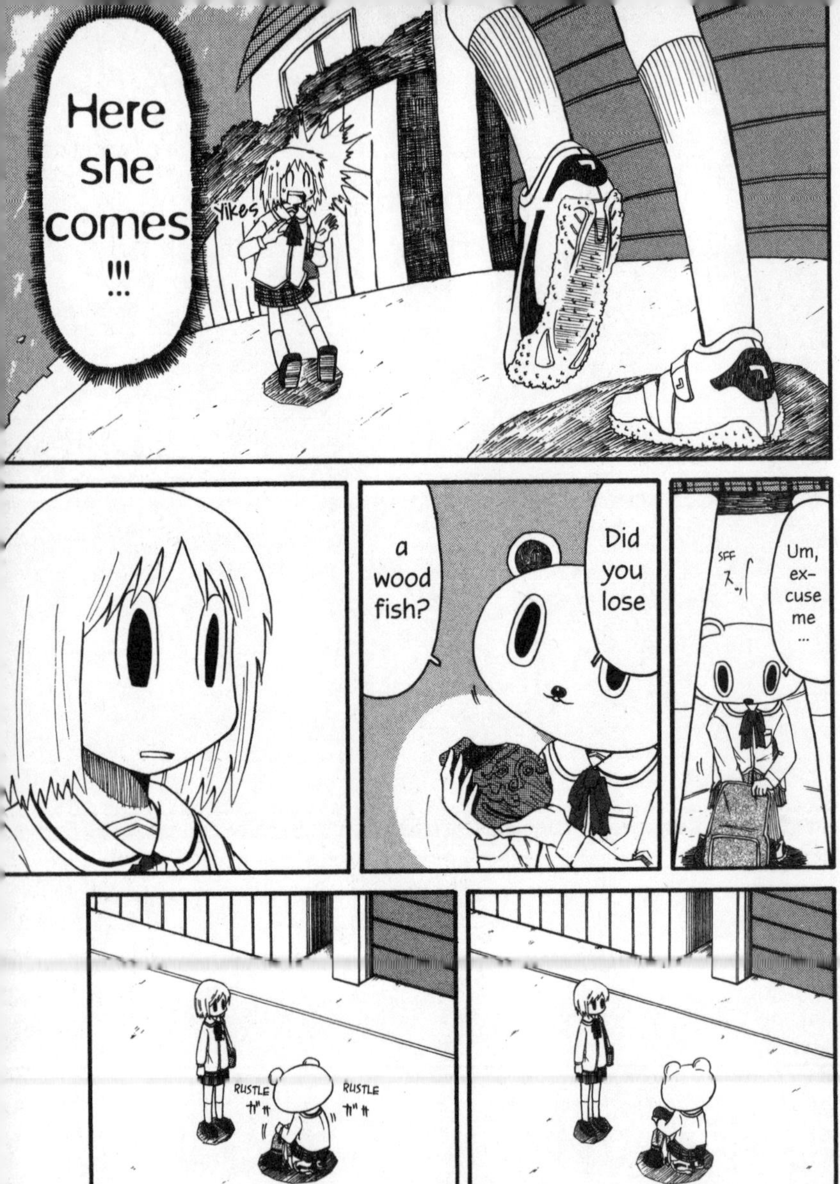
Here she comes!!!
Yikes
Um, ex-cuse me ...
SFF
Did you lose
a wood fish?
RUSTLE
RUSTLE

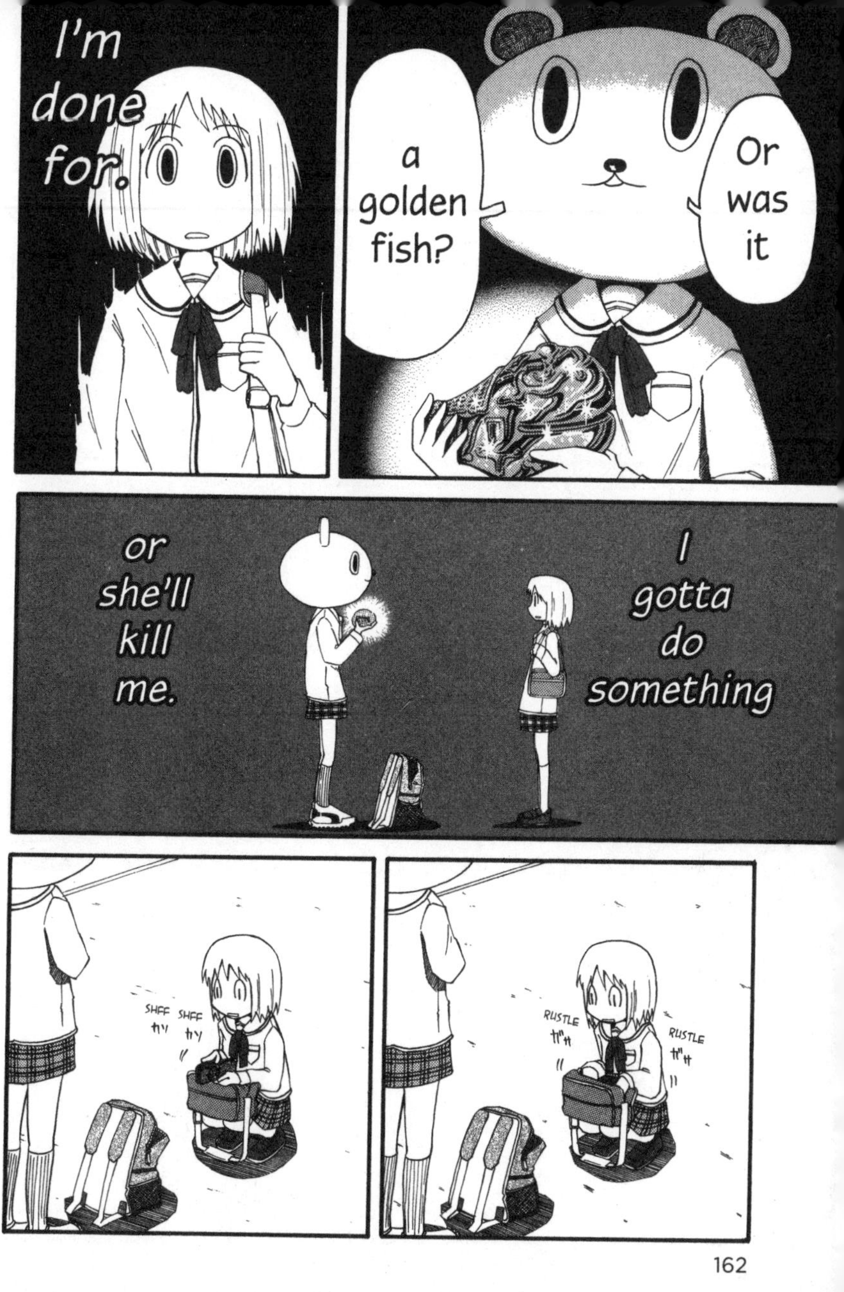
Or was it
a golden fish?
I'm done for.
I gotta do something
or she'll kill me.
RUSTLE
RUSTLE
SHFF
SHFF

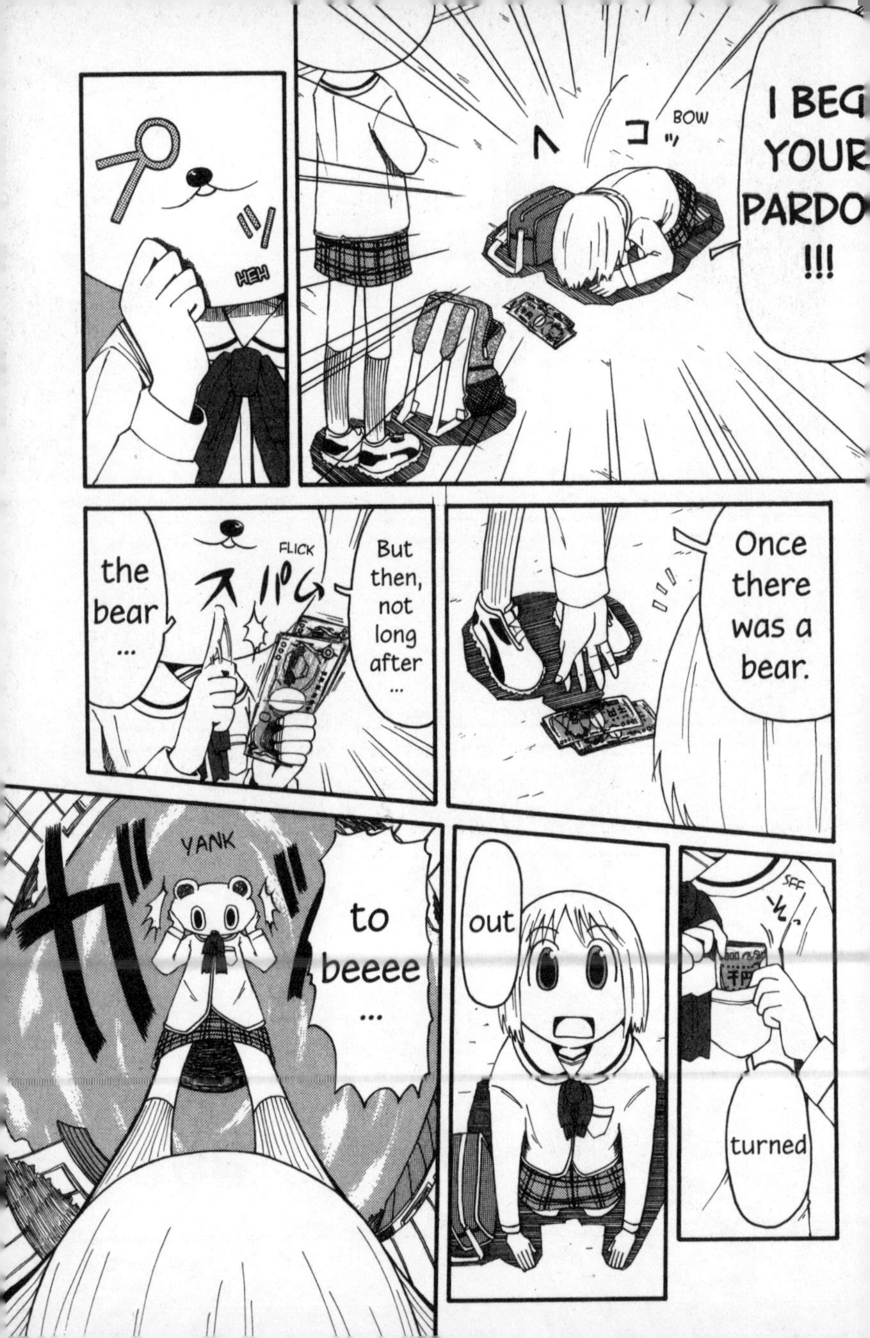
I BEG YOUR PARDO !!!
BOW
HEH
Once there was a bear.
But then, not long after ...
FLICK
the bear ...
SFF
turned
out
YANK
to beeee ...

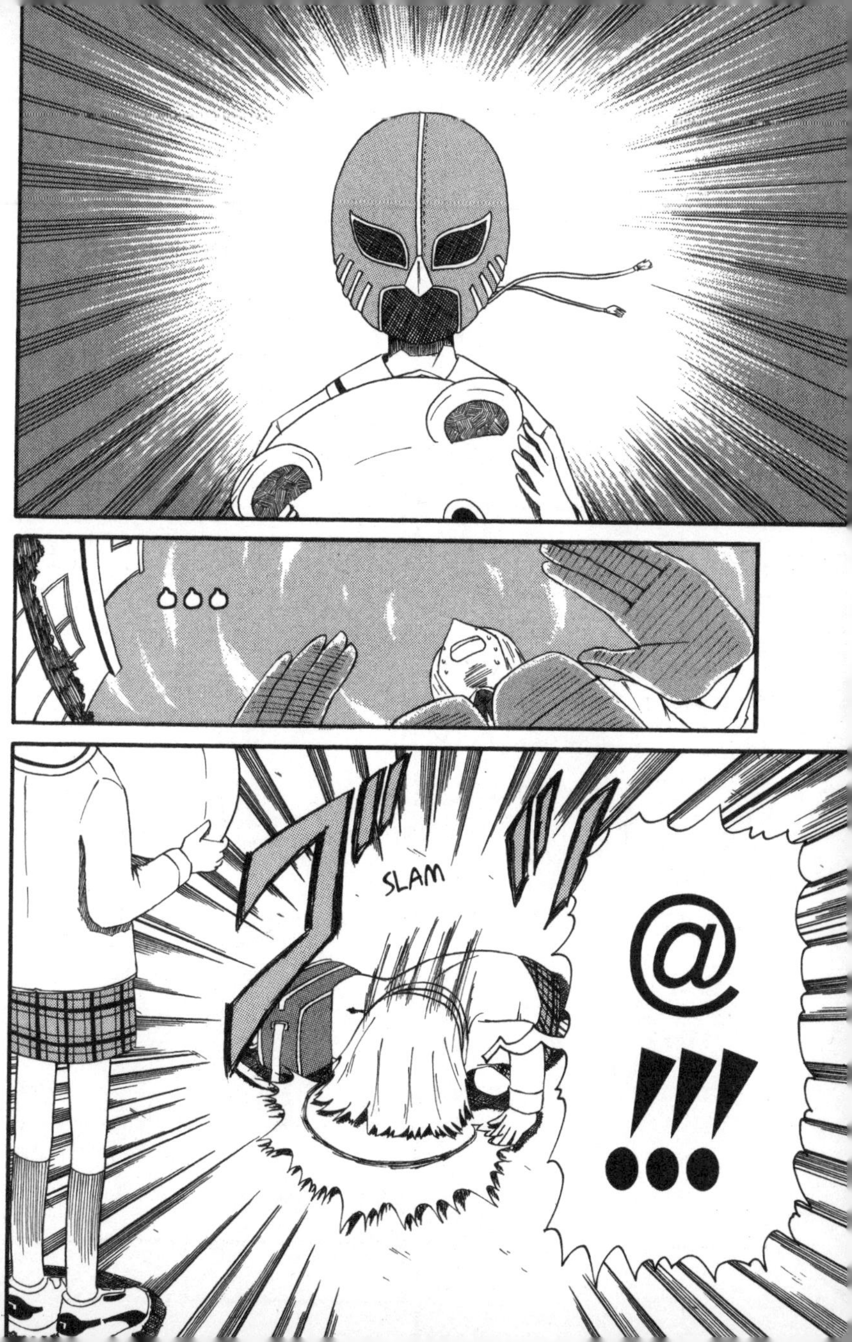
SLAM
@ !!!

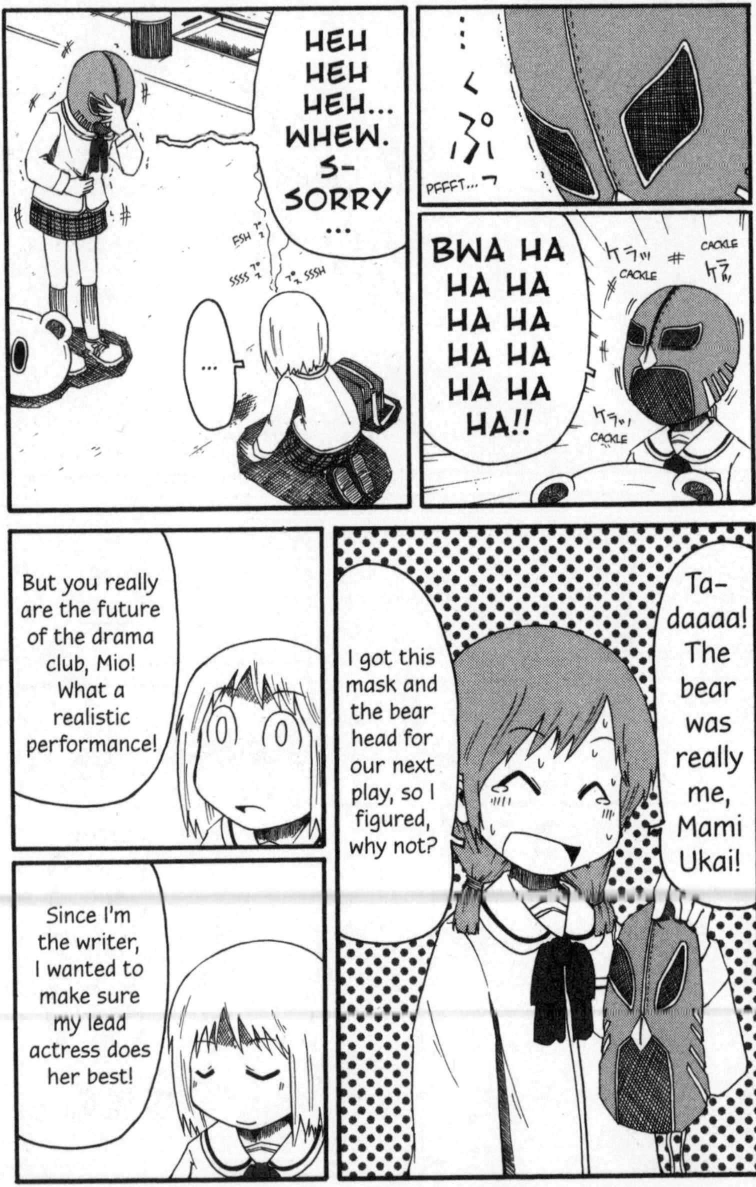

...
PFFFT...
BWA HA HA HA HA HA HA HA HA HA HA!!
CACKLE
CACKLE
CACKLE
HEH HEH HEH... WHEW. S-SORRY...
FSH
SSSS
SSSH
...
Ta-daaaa! The bear was really me, Mami Ukai!
I got this mask and the bear head for our next play, so I figured, why not?
But you really are the future of the drama club, Mio! What a realistic performance!
Since I'm the writer, I wanted to make sure my lead actress does her best!

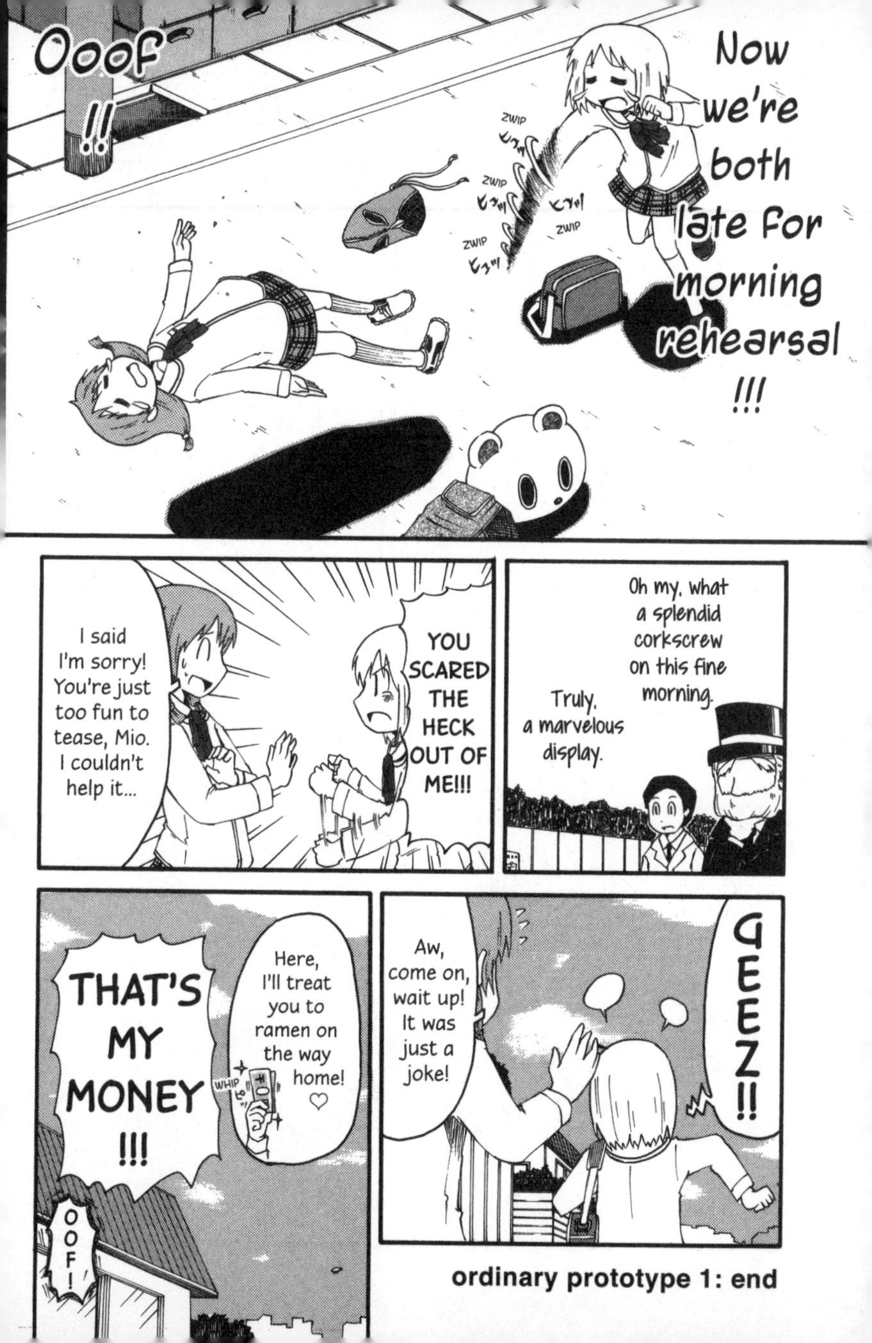
Now we're both late for morning rehearsal!!!
ZWIP
ZWIP
ZWIP
ZWIP
Ooof-!!
Oh my, what a splendid corkscrew on this fine morning.
Truly, a marvelous display.
YOU SCARED THE HECK OUT OF ME!!!
I said I'm sorry! You're just too fun to tease, Mio. I couldn't help it...
GEEZ!!
Aw, come on, wait up! It was just a joke!
Here, I'll treat you to ramen on the way home! ♡
WHIP
THAT'S MY MONEY!!!
OOF!

ordinary prototype 1: end

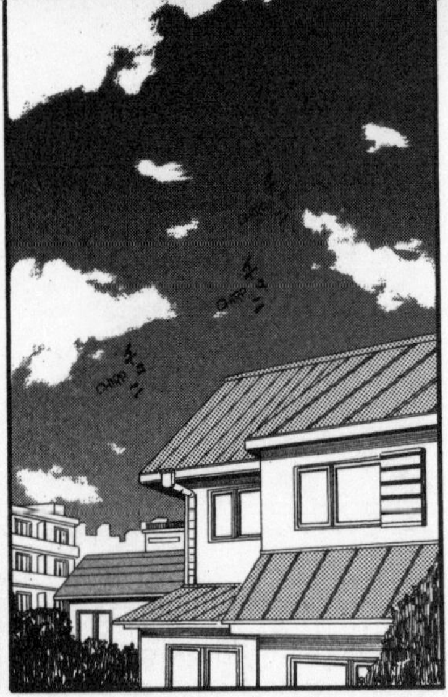

CHIRP
CHIRP
CHIRP

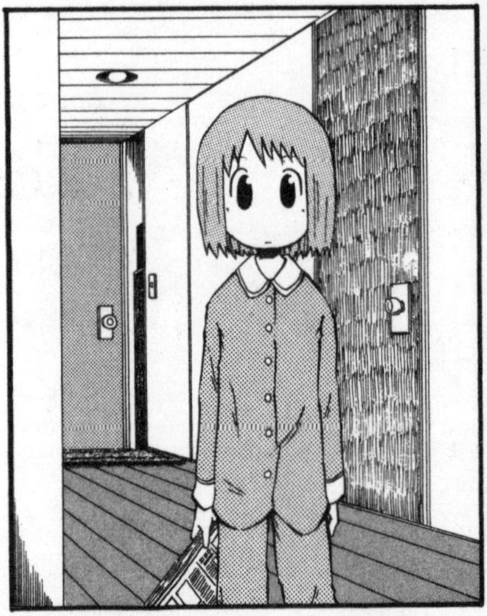

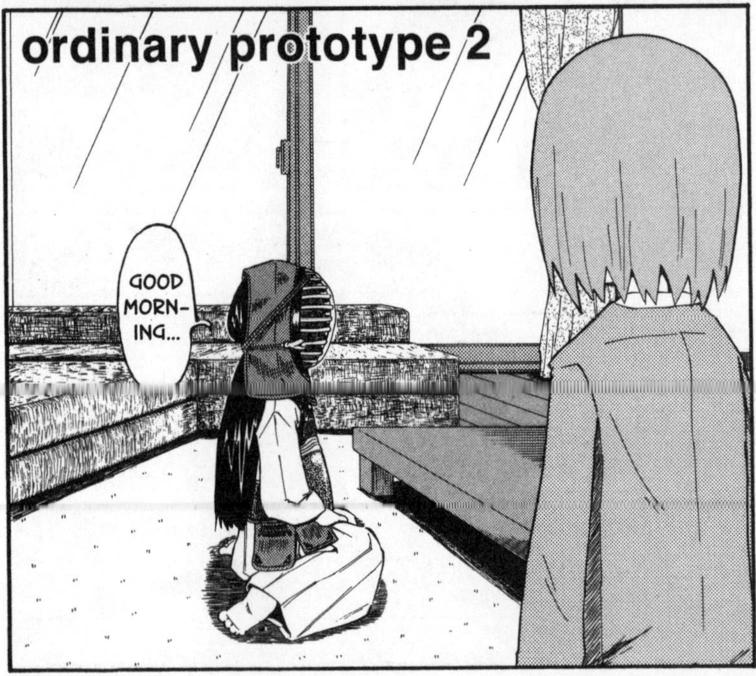

ordinary prototype 2
GOOD MORN-ING...

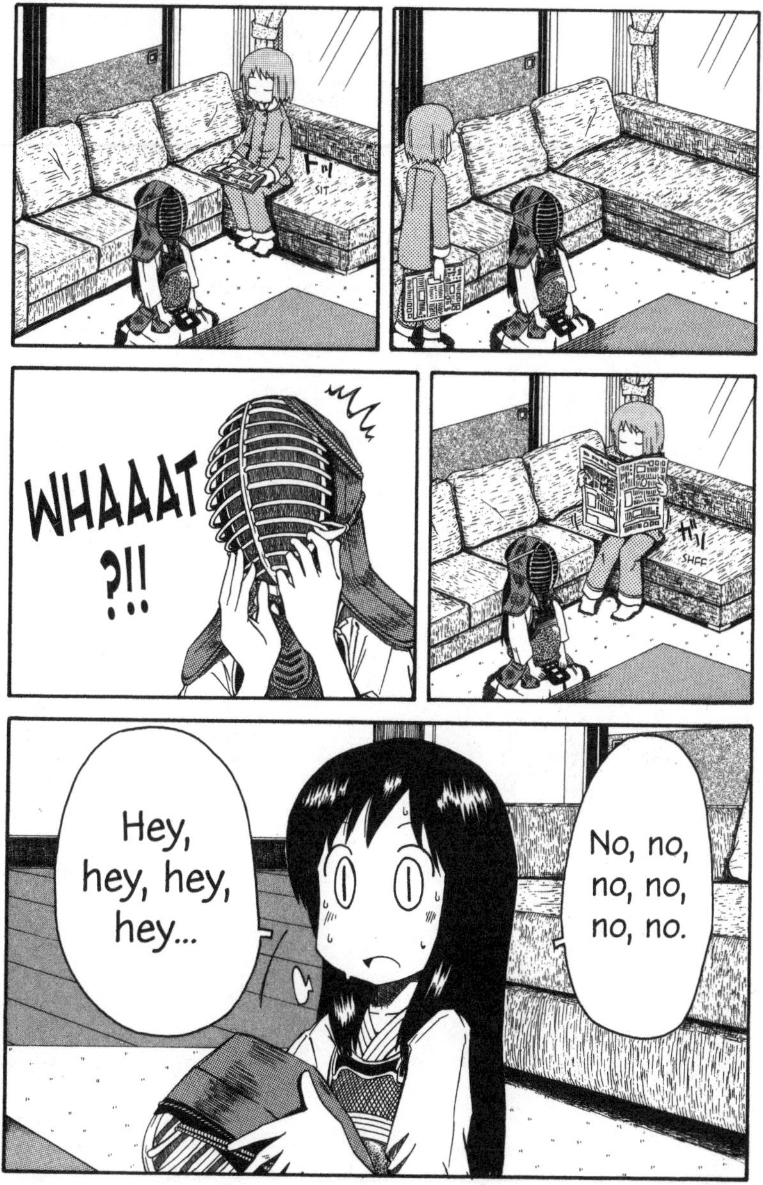
ドッ
SIT
ガリ
SHFF
WHAAAT ?!!
No, no, no, no, no, no.
Hey, hey, hey, hey...

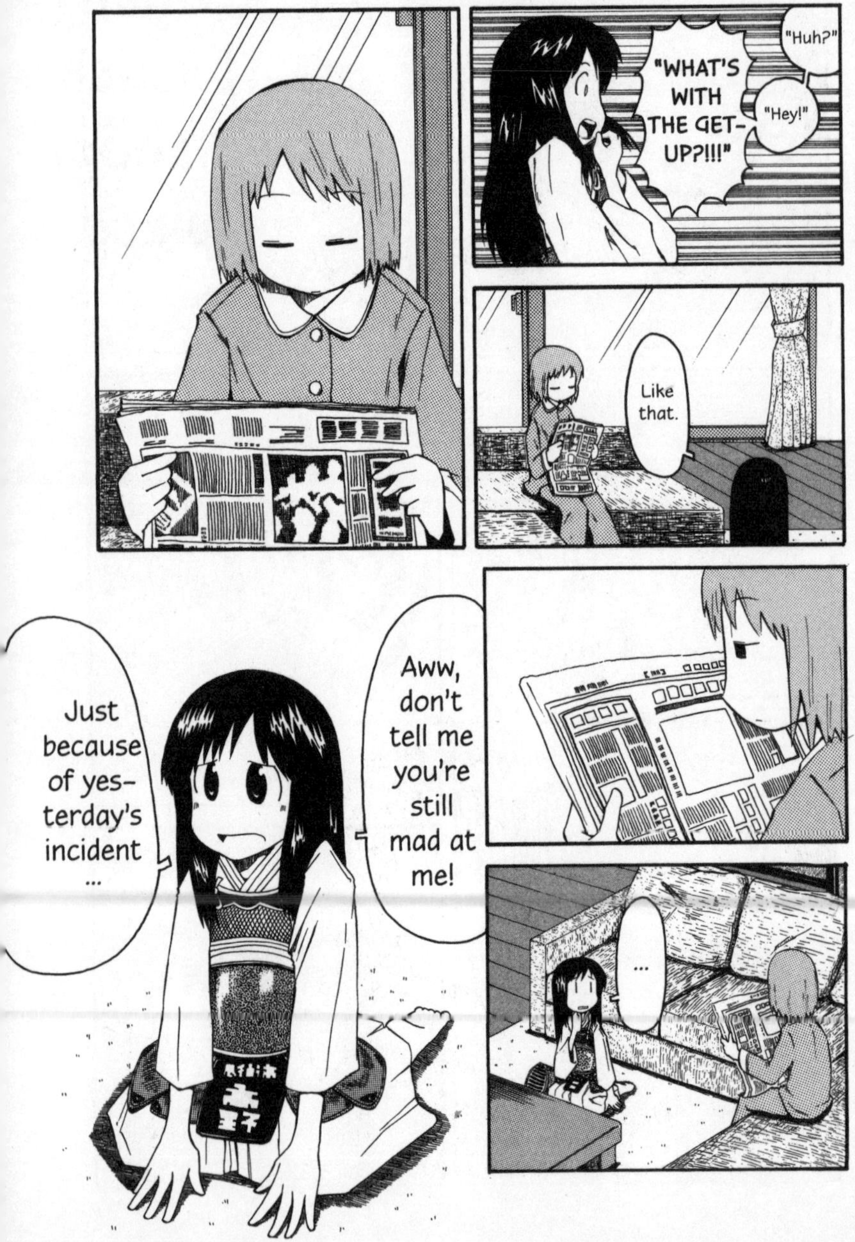
"Huh?"
"Hey!"
"WHAT'S WITH THE GET-UP?!!!"
Like that.
...
Aww, don't tell me you're still mad at me!
Just because of yes-terday's incident ...

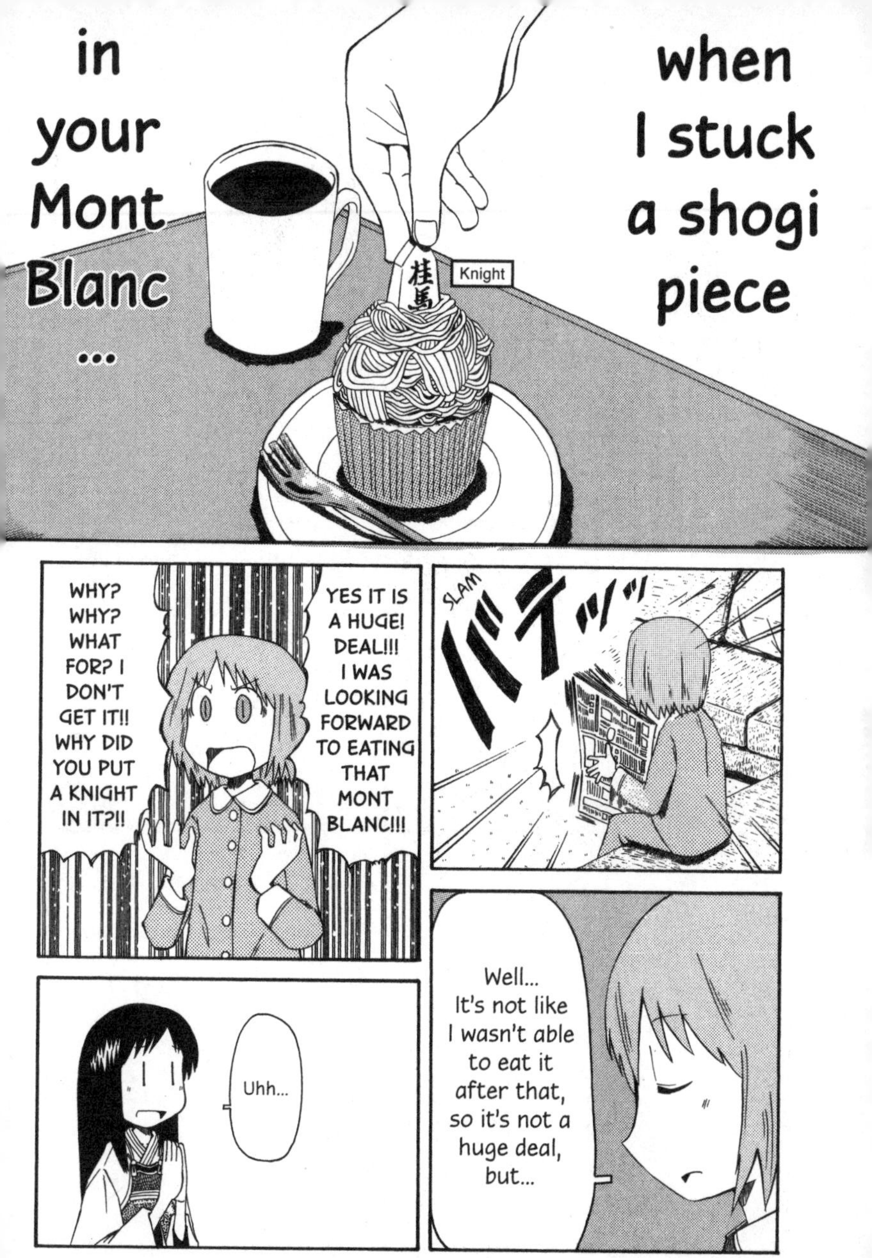
when I stuck a shogi piece
Knight
in your Mont Blanc ...
SLAM
YES IT IS A HUGE! DEAL!!! I WAS LOOKING FORWARD TO EATING THAT MONT BLANC!!!
WHY? WHY? WHAT FOR? I DON'T GET IT!! WHY DID YOU PUT A KNIGHT IN IT?!!
Well... It's not like I wasn't able to eat it after that, so it's not a huge deal, but...
Uhh...

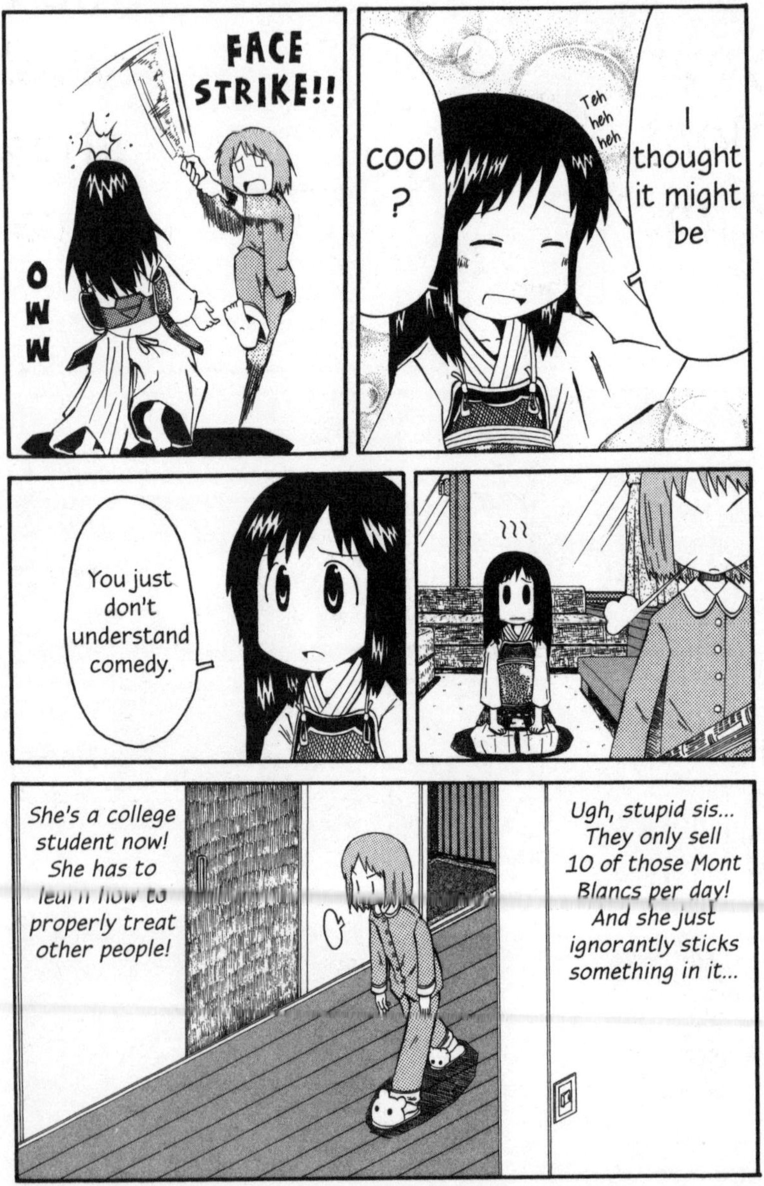
I thought it might be
Teh heh heh
cool ?
FACE STRIKE!!
OWW
You just don't understand comedy.
Ugh, stupid sis... They only sell 10 of those Mont Blancs per day! And she just ignorantly sticks something in it...
She's a college student now! She has to learn how to properly treat other people!

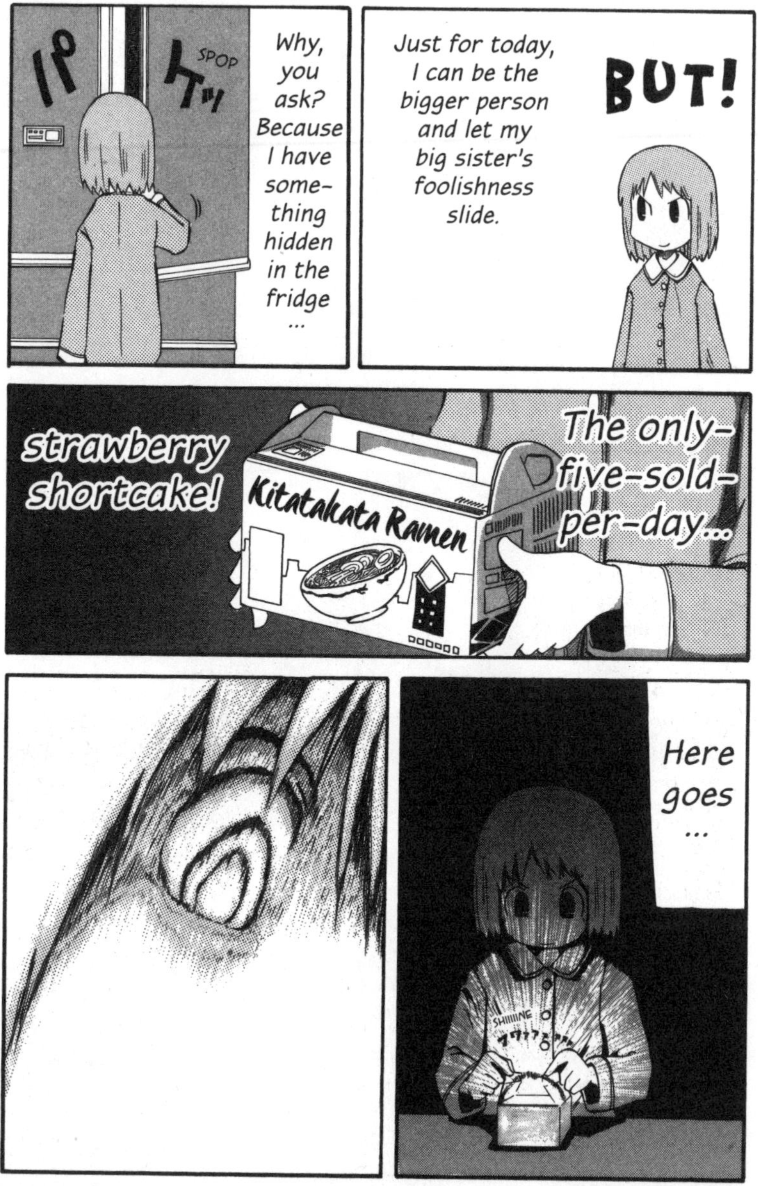
Just for today, I can be the bigger person and let my big sister's foolishness slide.
BUT!
Why, you ask? Because I have something hidden in the fridge ...
SPOP
The only-five-sold-per-day...
strawberry shortcake!
Kitatakata Ramen
Here goes ...
SHIIIIINE

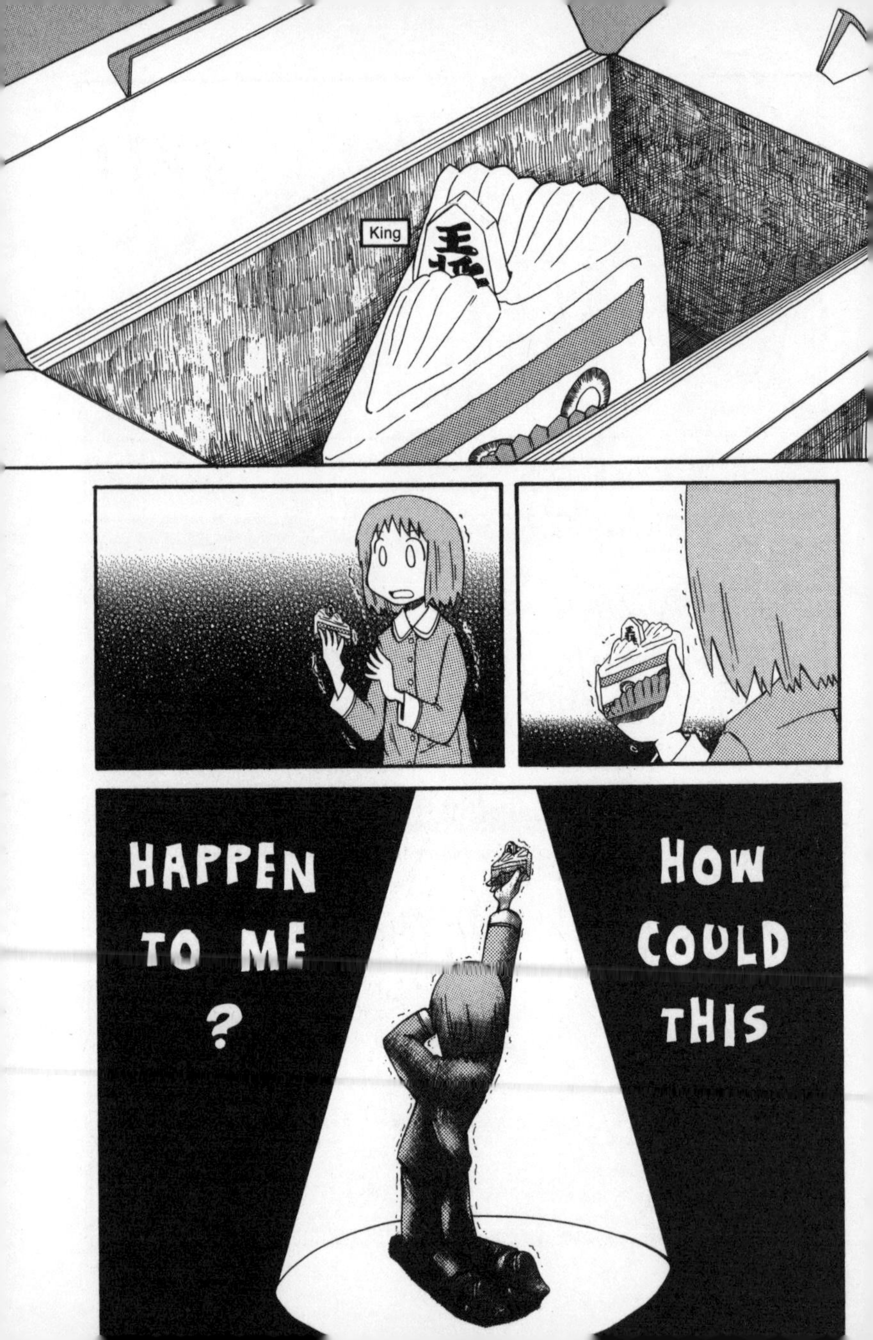
King
HOW COULD THIS
HAPPEN TO ME ?

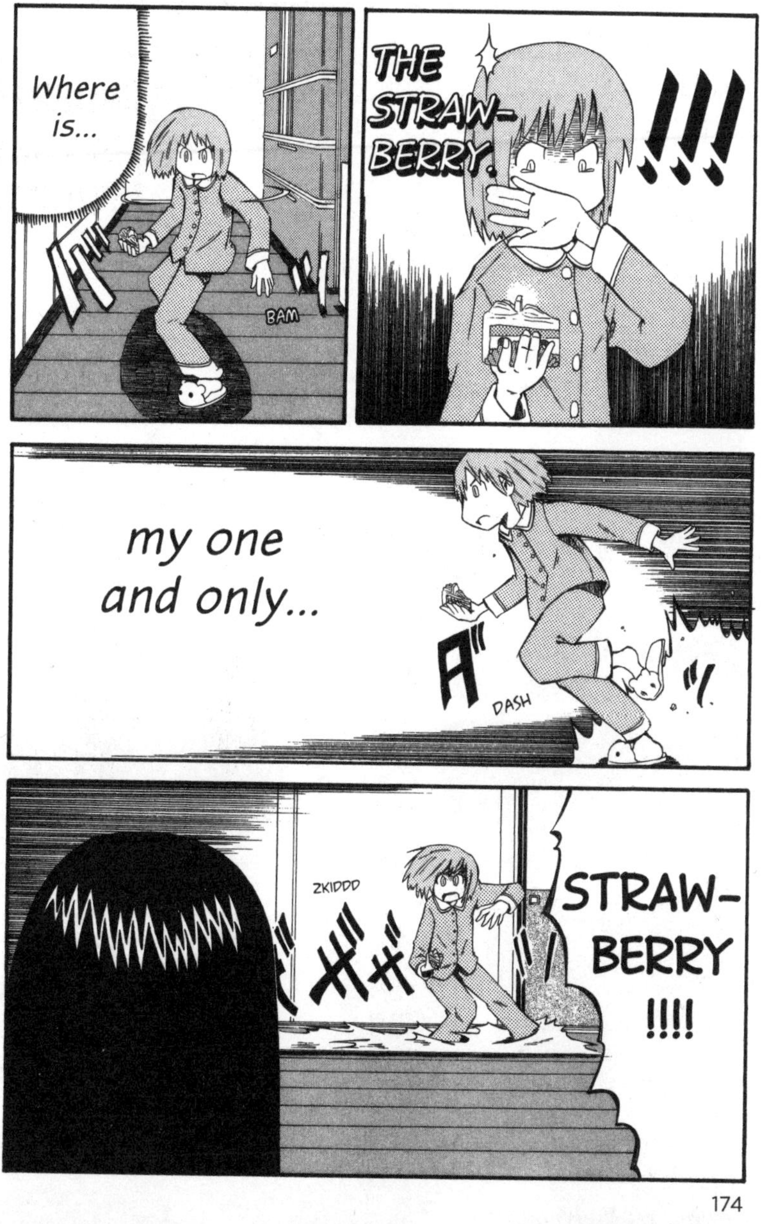
THE STRAW-BERRY...
!!!!
Where is...
BAM
my one and only...
DASH
ZKIDDD
STRAW-BERRY !!!!

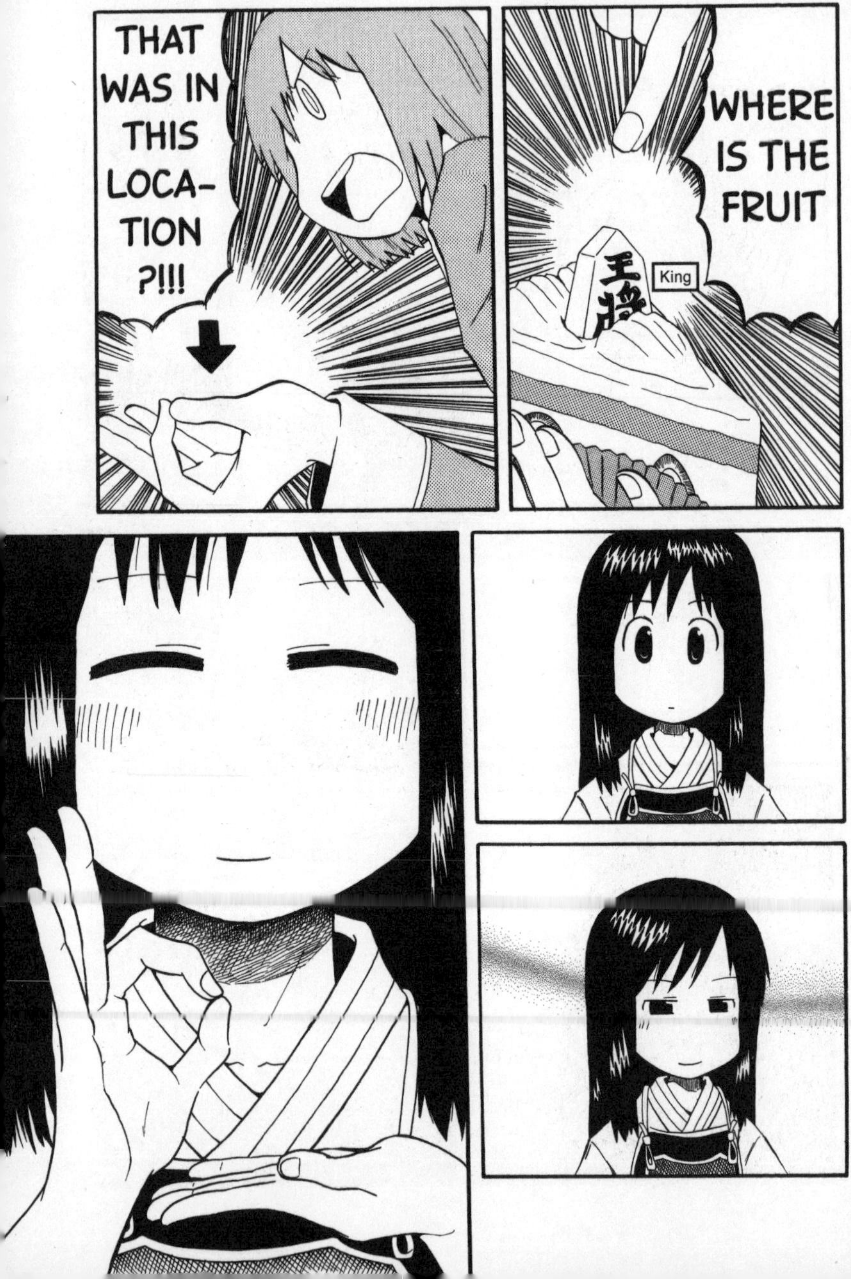
WHERE IS THE FRUIT
王将
King
THAT WAS IN THIS LOCA-TION?!!!

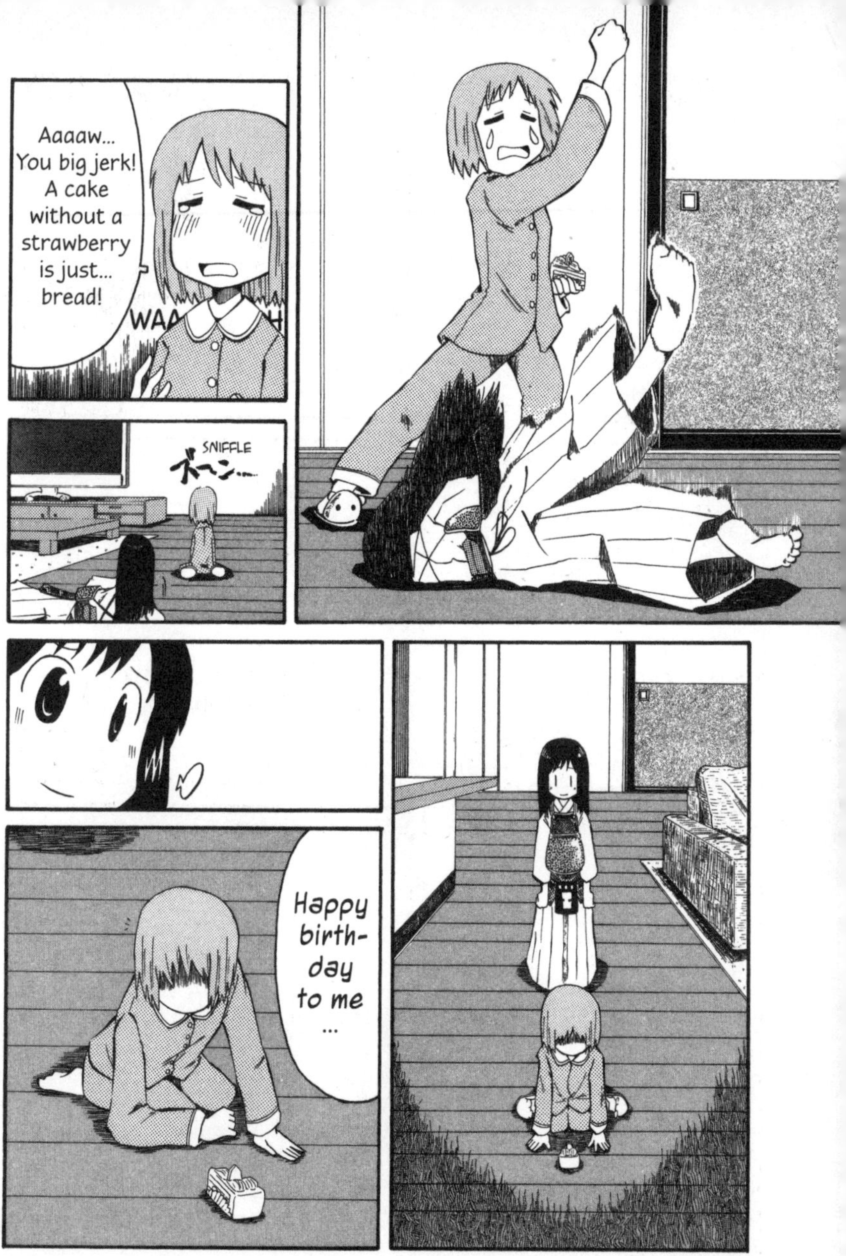
Aaaaw... You big jerk! A cake without a strawberry is just... bread!
SNIFFLE
Happy birth-day to me ...

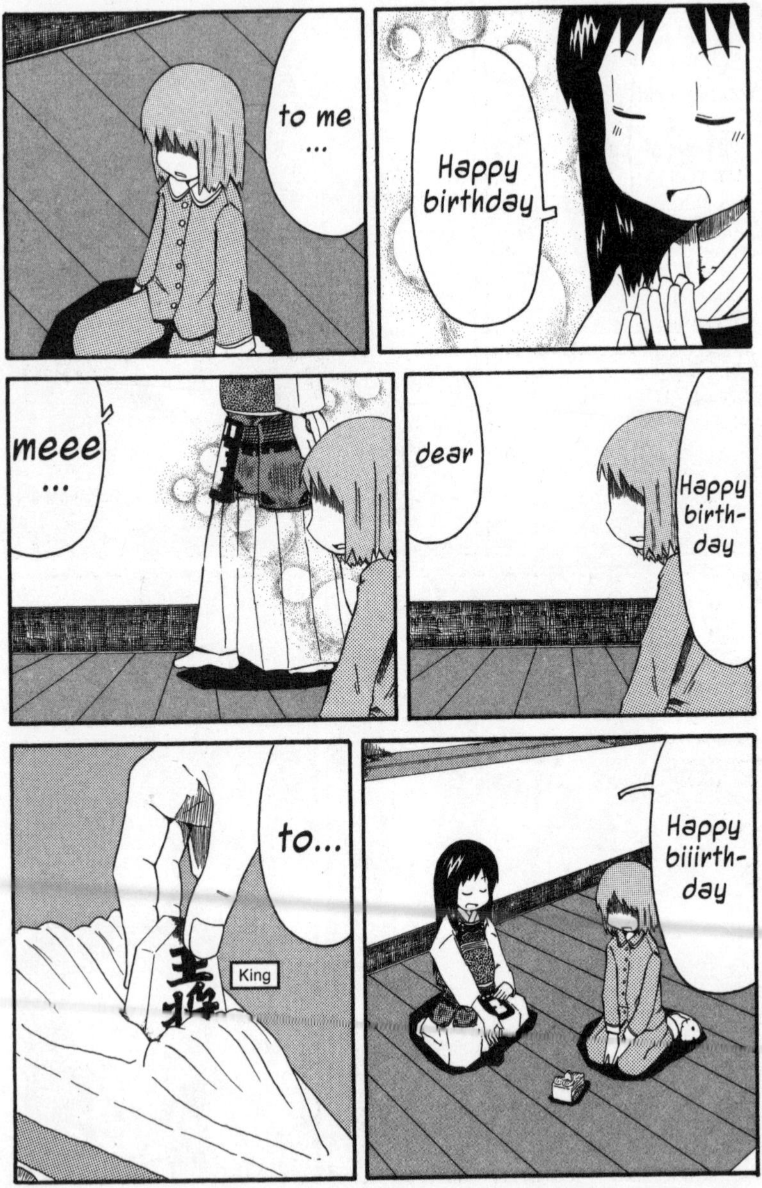
Happy birthday
to me ...
Happy birth-day
dear
meee ...
Happy biiirth-day
to...
King

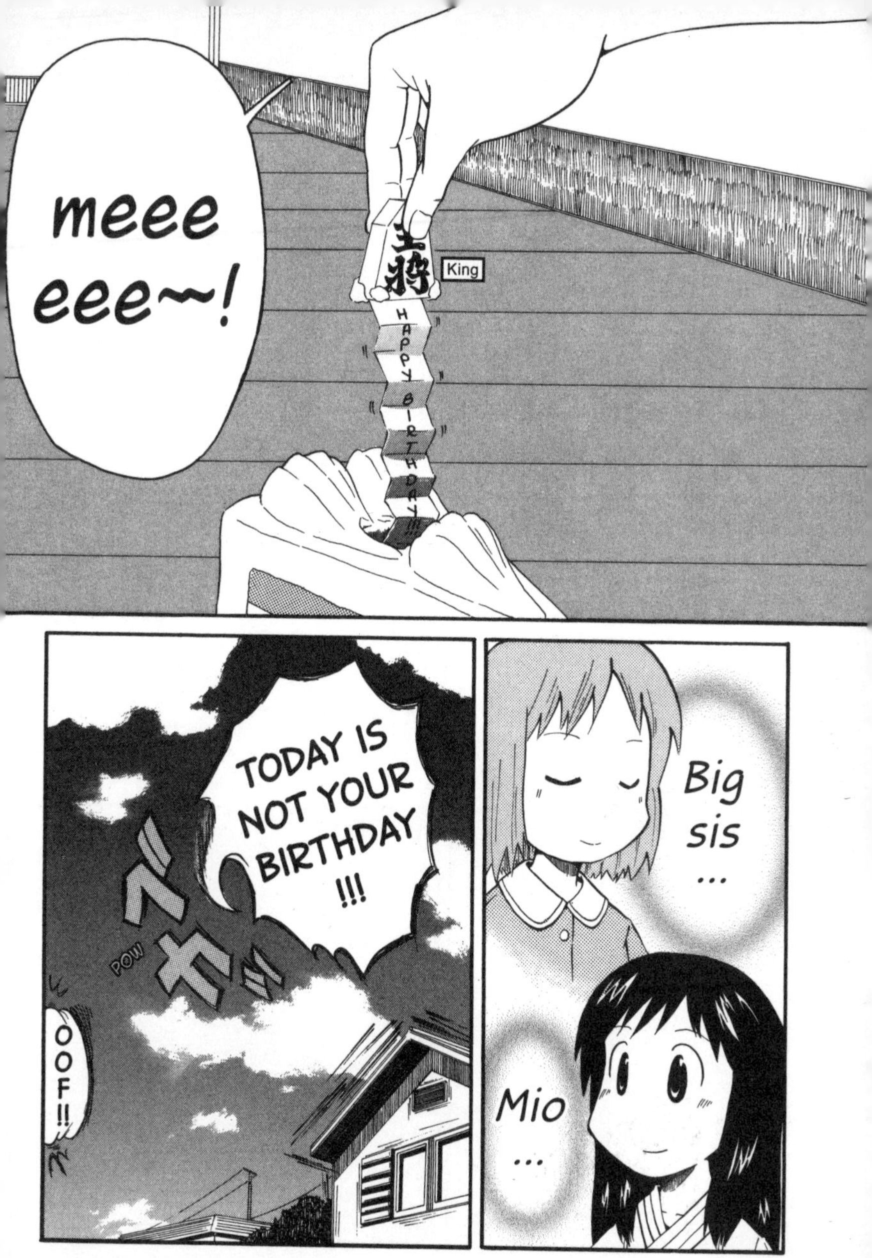
meeee
eee~!
王将
King
HAPPY BIRTHDAY!!!
Big sis ...
Mio ...
TODAY IS NOT YOUR BIRTHDAY !!!
POW
OOF!!

ordinary prototype 2: end

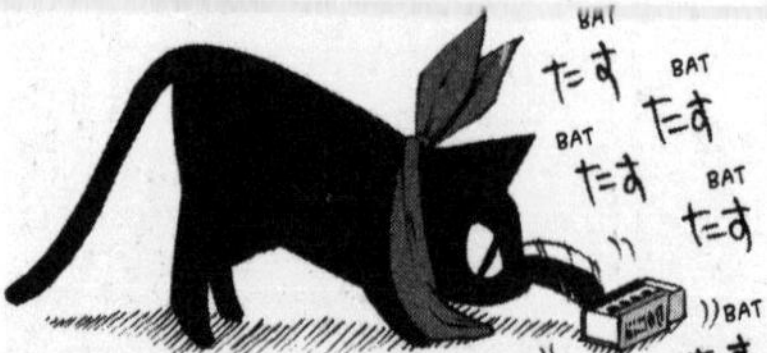
BAT
たす
BAT
たす
BAT
たす
BAT
たす
BAT
たす
たす
BAT
たす
BAT

nichijou 2

my ordinary life

A Vertical Comics Edition

Translation: Jenny McKeon
Production: Grace Lu
          Hiroko Mizuno
          Anthony Quintessenza

First published in Japan in 2007 by KADOKAWA CORPORATION, Tokyo.
English translation rights arranged with KADOKAWA CORPORATION, Tokyo
through TUTTLE-MORI AGENCY, INC., Tokyo.
English language version produced by Vertical Comics,
an imprint of Kodansha USA Publishing, LLC

Translation provided by Vertical Comics, 2016
Published by Kodansha USA Publishing, LLC, New York

Originally published in Japanese as *nichijou 2* by Kadokawa Corporation, 2007
nichijou first serialized in *Monthly Shonen Ace,* Kadokawa Corporation, 2006-2015

This is a work of fiction.

ISBN: 978-1-942993-31-5

Manufactured in Canada

First Edition

Sixth Printing

Kodansha USA Publishing, LLC
451 Park Avenue South
7th Floor
New York, NY 10016
www.readvertical.com

Vertical books are distributed through Penguin-Random House Publisher Services.

nichijou

my ordinary life

(2)

keiichi arawi

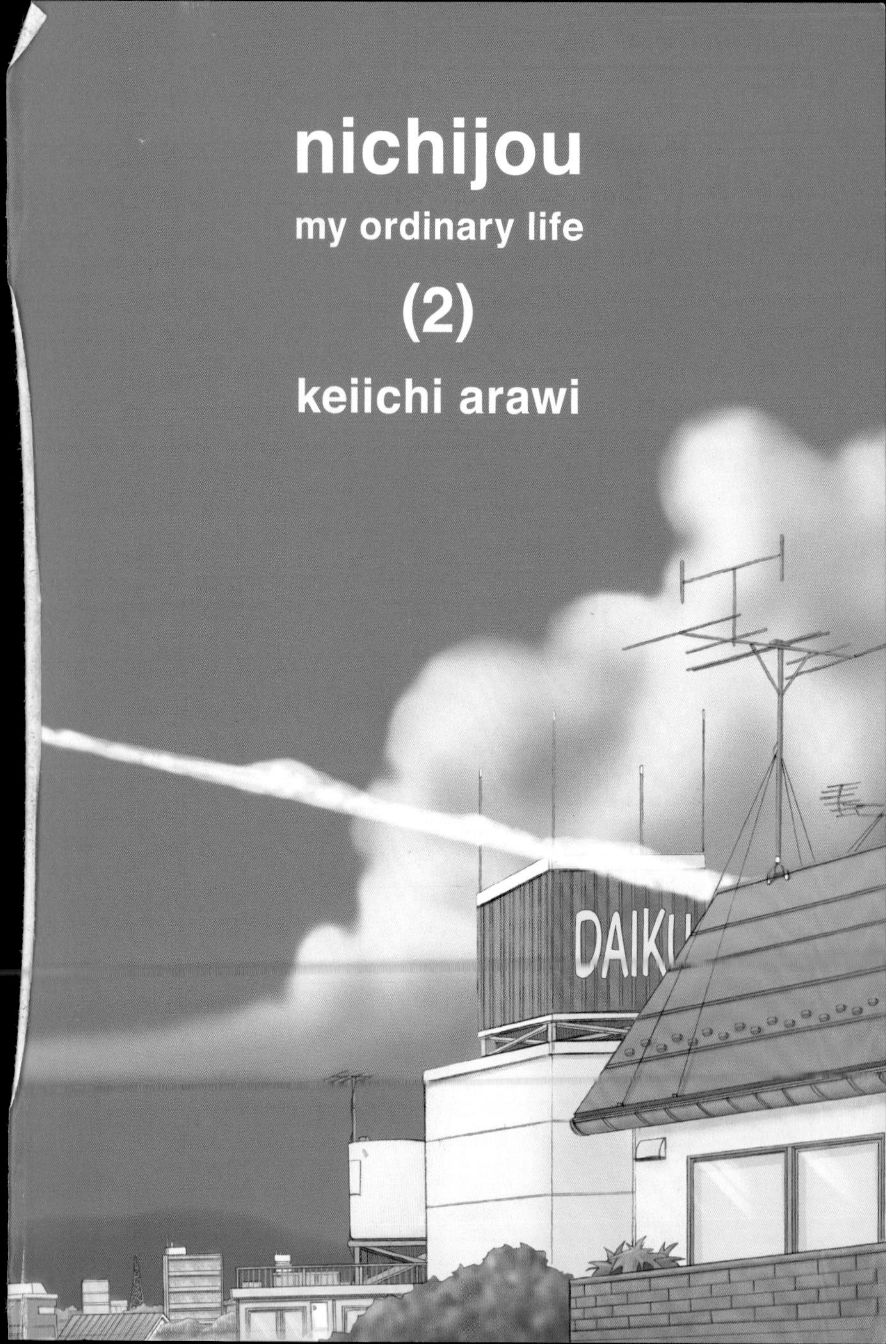

chapter 19

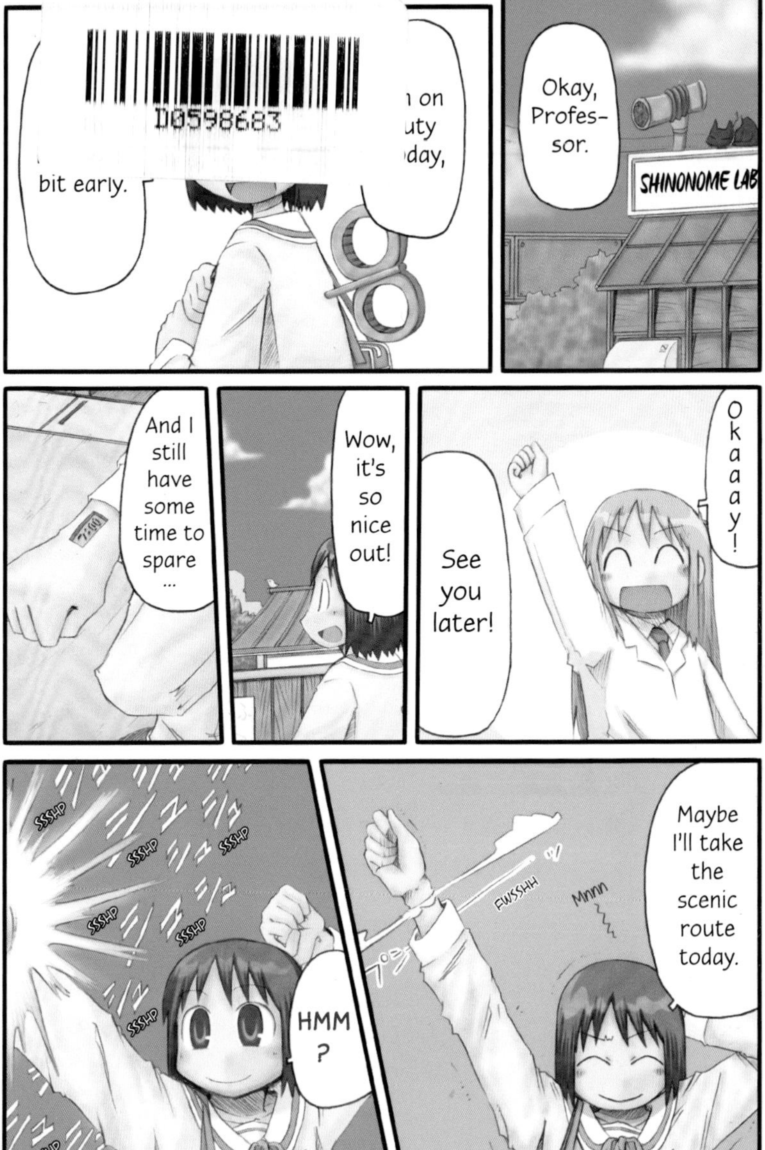

SHINONOME LAB
Okay, Professor.
bit early.
Okaaaay!
See you later!
Wow, it's so nice out!
And I still have some time to spare ...
Maybe I'll take the scenic route today.
Mnnn
FWSSHH
HMM?
SSSHP
SSSHP
SSSHP
SSSHP
SSSHP
SSSHP
SSSHP